TELEVISION COVERAGE
OF INTERNATIONAL AFFAIRS

COMMUNICATION AND INFORMATION SCIENCE

A Series of Monographs, Treatises, and Texts

Edited by
MELVIN J. VOIGT
University of California, San Diego

William C. Adams • Television Coverage of the Middle East
Hewitt D. Crane • The New Social Marketplace: Notes on Effecting Social Change in America's Third Century
Rhonda J. Crane • The Politics of International Standards: France and the Color TV War
Herbert S. Dordick, Helen G. Bradley, and Burt Nanus • The Emerging Network Marketplace
Glen Fisher • American Communication in a Global Society
Edmund Glenn • Man and Mankind: Conflict and Communication Between Cultures
Bradley S. Greenberg • Life on Television: Content Analyses of U.S. TV Drama
John S. Lawrence and Bernard M. Timberg • Fair Use and Free Inquiry: Copyright Law and the New Media
Robert G. Meadow • Politics as Communication
William H. Melody, Liora R. Salter, and Paul Heyer • Culture, Communication, and Dependency: The Tradition of H.A. Innis
Vincent Mosco • Broadcasting in the United States: Innovative Challenge and Organizational Control
Kaarle Nordenstreng and Herbert I. Schiller • National Sovereignty and International Communication: A Reader
Dallas W. Smythe • Dependency Road: Communications, Capitalism, Consciousness and Canada
Herbert I. Schiller • Who Knows: Information in the Age of the Fortune 500

In Preparation:
William C. Adams • Television Coverage of the 1980 Presidential Campaign
Mary B. Cassata and Thomas Skill • Life on Daytime Television
Ithiel de Sola Pool • Forecasting The Telephone: A Retrospective Technology Assessment
Oscar H. Gandy, Jr. • Beyond Agenda Setting: Information Subsidies and Public Policy
Bradley S. Greenberg • Mexican Americans and the Mass Media
Cees J. Hamelink • Finance and Information: A Study of Converging Interests
Robert M. Landau, James H. Bair, and Jean Siegman • Emerging Office Systems
Vincent Mosco • Pushbutton Fantasies
Kaarle Nordenstreng • The Mass Media Declaration of UNESCO
Dan Schiller • Telematics and Government
Jorge A. Schnitman • Dependency and Development in the Latin American Film Industries
Indu B. Singh • Telecommunications in the Year 2000: National and International Perspectives
Jennifer D. Slack • Communication Technologies and Society: Conceptions of Causality and the Politics of Technological Intervention
Janet Wasko • Movies and Money: Financing the American Film Industry
Osmo Wiio • Information and Communication Systems

TELEVISION COVERAGE
OF INTERNATIONAL AFFAIRS

Edited by
William C. Adams
George Washington University

ABLEX Publishing Corporation
Norwood, New Jersey 07648

Printed in the United States of America.

Library of Congress Cataloging in Publication Data
Main entry under title:

Television Coverage of International Affairs.

   (Communication and information science)
   Includes indexes.
   1. Television broadcasting of news—United States.
2. Foreign news—United States. I. Adams, William C. II. Series.
PN4888.T4T44   070.1'9   81-15054
ISBN 0-89391-103-8   AACR2

ABLEX Publishing Corporation
355 Chestnut Street
Norwood, New Jersey 07648

CONTENTS

PREFACE

Americans have come to see the world through the video eye of network television news, and the networks have come to devote a large share of their coverage to international affairs. That coverage has been under increasing fire from Third World leaders and from various domestic interests; it has also been under increasing scrutiny from political communication researchers who want a better understanding of the versions of world news offered by the networks to their massive constituencies.

Thirteen studies of television coverage of international affairs, examining a wide range of issues and events, have been assembled for this volume. In the first chapter, the editor surveys some of the problems and issues in international affairs coverage on television and notes some of the previously published content analyses. The second chapter, by James Larson, shows how much television has focused on international affairs and which countries and regions have been given the most attention. To provide further context for the remainder of the volume, the last chapter is a study by Haluk Sahin, Dennis Davis, and John Robinson of the extent to which viewers acquired information from an international news story on television.

Chapters 3, 4, and 5 are about different aspects of Third World coverage. Peter Dahlgren proposes three dominant motifs as structuring much of the coverage of the Third World. Robert Lichter contrasts the elite broadcast and print journalists with the business elite in their opinions toward US foreign policy and the Third World; and Waltraud Q. Morales reviews Latin American coverage, with special consideration to the treatment of Allende's Chile and the Sandinistas in Nicaragua.

Chapters 6 through 9 all concern aspects of coverage of developed countries or US foreign policy. William Spragens assesses coverage of the 1978 Camp David Summit. Laurence Barton compares ABC, CBS, and NBC coverage of the debate over the US boycott of the 1980 Moscow Olympics. David Paletz and his associates examine the depiction of terrorism in Italy, Northern Ireland, and the United States, and Myles Breen analyzes network news about Australia.

Chapters 10 through 12 are about coverage of Southeast Asia. Robert Entman and David Paletz summarize some previous Vietnam studies and suggest four phases of televised coverage. Peter Rollins contrasts the television images of the battle of Khe Sanh with other evidence and alternative microcosms. William Adams and Michael Joblove discuss the networks' disregard of the 1975–78 Cambodian holocaust.

Eleven of these chapters have not been published previously in any form. Two chapters are substantially revised from their initial appearance in journals. Chapter 11 is drawn from an article in Vol. 4 (Spring 1981) of the *Journal of American Culture*, published at Bowling Green University, and is used here with the journal's permission. Chapter 12 is based on an article published in Vol. 11 (Winter 1980) of *Policy Review* and is used with permission of the Heritage Foundation.

The contributors to this volume have brought a wide range of experience, perspectives, and methods to the study of television news and international affairs. Their chapters represent the culmination of many hours of careful content analysis and study. Their enthusiasm for this book and their cooperation in its creation is deeply appreciated.

Colleagues at George Washington University have also been very supportive of this effort, especially Michael Harmon, David Brown, and Astrid Merget of the Public Administration Department, Dean Burton Sapin of the School of Public and International Affairs, and Dean Norma Maine Loeser of the School of Government and Business Administration. Other George Washington friends and associates who helped in a variety of ways include Karen Bland, Bellen Joyner, Diane Hollyfield, Vanessa Barnes, Karen Arrington, Margaret Sheehan, Linda Trageser, and Rod French. William Vantine, Mary Gillespie, Jim Steadman, Martin Kirkwood, and Brad Bryen are thanked for their research assistance. At Ablex Publishing, Barbara Bernstein, Karen Siletti, and Peter J. Petrizzo were very helpful to work with. Thanks also go to Lyle C. Brown, Shirley Lithgow, Nancy Davis, Martha Glass, Susan Finsen, Michael Robinson, Kathy Reed, Charles Reed, Kelly Reed, Lindsey Reed, and Wilma Adams. This book is dedicated to Professor Robert Darcy of Oklahoma State University, an outstanding and imaginative scholar and teacher.

William Adams
November 1, 1981

CONTRIBUTORS

WILLIAM C. ADAMS is associate professor of public administration at George Washington University, co-editor of *Television Network News: Issues in Content Research*, and editor of *Television Coverage of the Middle East* and *Television Coverage of the 1980 Presidential Campaign*. He is co-author of *An Assessment of Telephone Survey Methods* and his political communications studies have appeared in such journals as *Journalism Quarterly, Journal of Communication, Public Opinion Quarterly, Journal of Broadcasting, Journal of Politics, Policy Studies Journal*, and *Experimental Study of Politics*.

JOHN Z. AYANIAN is a senior history and political science major at Duke University.

LAURENCE BARTON is adjunct assistant professor of journalism at Boston College. He is a doctoral candidate in international communications at Boston University and holds an M.A.L.D. from the Fletcher School of Law and Diplomacy. He has written extensively on global relations for the *New York Times, Boston Globe*, and various magazines and journals. He taught news writing at Tufts University and has worked as a reporter with WCVB-TV in Boston.

MYLES P. BREEN is professor of communication studies at Northern Illinois University in DeKalb. His research has been published in journals such as *Journalism Quarterly, International Journal of Communication Research, Journal of Broadcasting, Central States Speech Journal*, and *Journal of Communication*. He is currently conducting research on the international dispersion of American cultural myths. In 1963 and 1964, Professor Breen worked with the Australian Broadcasting Commission.

SUMITRA CHAKRAPANI holds an M.A. in media studies from Queens College and is a doctoral student in sociology at the City University of New York. Her interests focus on the role of the media in developing countries.

PETER DAHLGREN teaches media and social theory at Stockholm University's School of Journalism. Prior to teaching in Sweden, he had been on the faculties of Queens College and Fordham University. Dr. Dahlgren's research interests include the interplay among media language, power relations, and everyday talk, and how the form of TV news relates to cultural perceptions of "objective" information.

DENNIS K. DAVIS is associate professor of communication at Cleveland State University. He has been a Fulbright lecturer at the University of Amsterdam and the University of Louvain. He is co-author of *The Effects of Mass Communication on Political Behavior* and *Mass Communication and Everyday Life*. He has written many conference papers and articles on international communication, mass communication theory, and political communication. His current research interests include the study of televised presidential campaign debates.

ROBERT M. ENTMAN is assistant professor of public policy studies at Duke University and a member of the Duke Center for the Study of Communications Policy. He holds a Ph.D. in political science from Yale University and has written extensively on politics and the media, telecommunications policy, and environmental policy; he is author of "The Imperial Media" in *Politics and the Oval Office* and co-author of *Media Power Politics*.

PETER A. FOZZARD is a pre-law undergraduate at Duke University.

MICHAEL JOBLOVE holds a B.A. in political science from George Washington University and attended law school at the University of Florida. His communications articles have appeared in the *University of Florida Law Review* and *Cable-Vision* magazine.

JAMES F. LARSON is assistant professor in the College of Communication at the University of Texas, Austin. During the early 1970s, he worked as an editor in the Worldwide English Division of the Voice of America. Later he completed a Ph.D. in communication at Stanford University, where he began a continuing study of international affairs coverage by US television networks. His other research interests include the study of international advertising and the role of mass media during disasters.

S. ROBERT LICHTER is assistant professor of political science at George Washington University and Senior Fellow at the Research Institute on International Change at Columbia University. He is co-author of *Roots of Radicalism*, numerous articles on political activism, and a forthcoming volume on elite journalists.

WALTRAUD QUEISER MORALES is assistant professor of comparative and international studies at the University of Central Florida in Orlando. She traveled widely in Latin America during the years 1973 through 1975; her doctorate is from the Graduate School of International Studies at the University of Denver. Her publications and research center on Latin American affairs, Bolivia, and comparative revolution.

DAVID L. PALETZ is professor of political science at Duke University and president of the Southern Association for Public Opinion Research. Professor Paletz was a Fulbright Scholar at Odense University in Denmark during 1978–79. He has written numerous articles on the impact of news media on American politics, including recent articles in *Public Opinion Quarterly*, *Political Science Quarterly*,

Journal of Politics, Columbia Journalism Review, and *Journal of Broadcasting.* His latest book is *Media Power Politics* (with Robert Entman).

JOHN P. ROBINSON is professor of sociology and director of the Survey Research Center at the University of Maryland. Among Professor Robinson's books and monographs are *Polls Apart: Divergences and Convergences in Public Opinion Polls on Foreign Policy, How Americans Use Time: A Social-Psychological Analysis of Everyday Behavior,* and *The American Public Looks at Foreign Policy.*

PETER C. ROLLINS is associate professor of English at Oklahoma State University. A specialist in American Studies, he has written on American documentary and persuasive films for *Films and History, Journal of Popular Film and Television,* and *American Quarterly.* He has made two historical films—*Will Rogers' 1920s: A Cowboy's Guide to the Times* (Churchill Films, 1976), and a two-hour documentary, *Television's Vietnam: The Impact of Visual Images* (Humanitas Films, 1981).

HALUK SAHIN is associate professor of journalism at the University of Maryland. He has directed program planning and research for Turkish television and worked as a newspaper editor for *Politika* in Istanbul. Dr. Sahin's research interests include ideologies and international communications, media production, and television news; his studies have appeared in such journals as *Media, Culture and Society, Journalism Quarterly, Irish Broadcasting Review,* and *Journal of Communication Inquiry.*

WILLIAM C. SPRAGENS, associate professor of political science at Bowling Green State University, is co-author of *Crisis and Conflict in American Politics* and *From Spokesman to Press Secretary: White House Media Operations,* and author of *Options and Oversight: Programs, Planning, Process and Performance.* His current research deals with media-government relations and the First Amendment, and with popular images of American Presidents.

CAROLE ANN TERWOOD, a graduate of Bowling Green State University, is a data base analyst with Texas Instruments.

TELEVISION COVERAGE
OF INTERNATIONAL AFFAIRS

PART

I

GLOBAL
COVERAGE

1

COVERING THE WORLD IN TEN MINUTES: NETWORK NEWS AND INTERNATIONAL AFFAIRS

WILLIAM C. ADAMS

> Leading television newsmen often remind us that each day they face a task so enormous as to be essentially impossible and quixotic. The affairs of four billion people, in two hundred nations, speaking thousands of languages, are each day distilled into twenty-three minutes of words and images. The elimination is so drastic that it inevitably distorts, even if done with the greatest integrity and goodwill. The very process of selection. . .is bound to confer on a few items a huge importance and to relegate other matters, people, places, and problems to a secondary level of reality, and perhaps oblivion.
>
> Eric Barnouw (1978)

The newscasters' task is even more herculean than Barnouw allows. Over half of the typical broadcast is devoted to domestic American news. All foreign and international stories receive an average of 10 minutes of nightly news time—10 minutes to cover the news of the world. As James Larson shows in the second chapter of this volume, news about international affairs added up to 10.006 minutes on the average weeknight network newscast during the years 1977 through 1979.

With so few minutes of news time, half-hour television news cannot match daily newspapers in absolute quantity of international news—at least not as measured in number of words (visual information is another matter). However, network news actually emphasizes international affairs *proportionately more* than do even large circulation newspapers. Nearly 45 percent of TV news time goes to stories involving other countries. Excluding sports, fashion, advice columns, comics, and so forth, the content studies of the American Newspaper Publishers Association found that small, medium, and large-circulation dailies devoted less than one-quarter of the column inches of general interest items to international news, even including all defense as well as foreign and diplomatic stories (cited in Sterling & Haight, 1978).

Using a very narrow definition of foreign affairs news, Graber still found that nightly network news had proportionately more foreign coverage than did the *Chicago Tribune, Daily News,* and *Sun Times* (1980, pp. 66–67). Larson's data even show television substantially exceeding the proportion of foreign news that Gerbner and Marvanyi (1977) found in the *New York Times.*

CONTROVERSIES OF COVERAGE

The 10-minute average allotment of news time to international news —not to mention surpassing large newspapers in emphasizing international news—is not what most media analysts have supposed. US television has been incorrectly described as overwhelmingly dominated by purely domestic news. The 45 percent focus on international news stories shatters that generalization. (At least one fourth of the news about international affairs is set at the State Department, but it is no less "international" because the locale is Washington, D.C.) Larson's findings clearly show that international news has garnered a major segment of nightly network newscasts.[1]

This 10-minute average, while much greater than expected, still affords an awesomely miniscule window on the world. Brevity is a central problem for television's coverage of international affairs. Obviously, television news cannot begin to provide a running account of the domestic and foreign affairs of nearly 200 countries. A media critic can dissect TV coverage of any foreign country and show it to be incomplete, uneven, and shallow, and to have ignored key developments. These are not unimportant findings, and the extent to which they characterize TV news coverage is worth understanding—nonetheless, such findings are not too surprising. Even hour-long newscasts (presumably doubling international news to around 20 minutes) would only marginally affect the time dilemma.

Granting this serious limitation of time, what are the networks squeezing into these 10 minutes? How is international news being presented to the American people? Most of the content questions surrounding international news coverage can be sorted into one of four clusters of issues: (1) thoroughness vs. superficiality; (2) United States vs. global vantage; (3) left vs. right; and (4) Hobbesian vs. Panglossian perspectives.

---

[1] For research on local television news attention to local and national-international stories, see Adams (1978b and 1980).

Thoroughness vs. Superficiality.   Several key questions concern the extent to which the networks provide reasonably comprehensive accounts of stories or wildly incomplete versions, given the constraints of time. Is international news a high or low priority? Are international stories likely to be long lead items or short studio stories? Are stories covered in a simplistic or complex fashion? Is the news sensationalized or dry? Are crisis highlights stressed, while long-term trends and background stories are overlooked? Do a handful of countries (elite and crisis countries) dominate international news, or is international coverage more thorough and broad-based?

US vs. Global Vantage.   Another set of questions involves the degree to which the perspective and priorities of TV news derive from cultural, geographical, and communications proximity to the United States. To what extent is the news weighted to foreign stories that are most accessible to the telecommunication channels used by the networks? To what extent are "inconvenient" foreign stories neglected? How much do ethnocentric or cosmopolitan worldviews influence the selection and shaping of stories? In what respects might cultural proximity make New Zealand, for example, more newsworthy than New Guinea? How powerfully does direct US involvement increase a story's apparent news value?

Left vs. Right.   A third group of issues identifies more explicitly the ideological dimensions of coverage. Is coverage more sympathetic toward left-wing or right-wing regimes? Are stories pro-pacifistic or pro-military in their orientation? Do they reflect a hardline anti-Soviet stance or a softline benign view of the Soviet Union? Does reporting tend to support more laissez-faire or more statist solutions to foreign economic problems? Are the assumptions of reporters those of US isolationism and non-intervention or those of US internationalism and pro-intervention? Is the coverage jingoistic, presuming the righteousness of the US government's position? Or, is reporting patriaphobic, fearful of acting as an apologist for the government, and inclined to presume US culpability?

This is meant to be a suggestive rather than an exhaustive list, but it captures some of the more controversial questions. Perhaps the most important factor omitted from this last cluster is that of "pro-Arab" vs. "pro-Israeli," which cuts across conventional left-right lines.

These questions of perspective are particularly important when considering international news because foreign stories can be told in starker terms than can domestic stories. The rules of the Fairness Doctrine for American political issues do not apply. As one reporter told Batscha (1975, p. 156):

> In the foreign affairs television story, we can make an interpretative point much easier because there is less sensitivity to the subject than

there is to a domestic subject. In the United States you have to be concerned not to offend the Democrats or the Republicans, for example.

Or, as William S. Paley was quoted as telling CBS news executives (MacNeil, 1968, p. 75): "In this country play it down the middle. Overseas you can be tough."

Hobbesian vs. Panglossian.   There is another set of variables that relate to attitudes about how the world works; that is, about the processes and dynamics characterizing international life. Is the world depicted as a dangerous and treacherous place? Are "unfortunate" foreign events presented as "menacing" to the viewers? Does coverage seem to grant the good will or the sinister motives of most international actors? Are nation-states pictured as able to operate on the basis of reason, negotiation, and restraint, or as almost invariably using power and coercion and acting irrationally? Are individuals molding events or are they powerless against history's juggernaut? Is some sort of international "progress" being made, or is the state of affairs regressing, or holding a shakey status quo?

What "ought" newscasts to resemble on these various issues of thoroughness vs. superficiality, United States vs. global vantage, left vs. right, and Hobbesian vs. Panglossian? Using the conventional notion of objectivity and "journalism review standards," the prevailing norms might be described as follows:

> Television news should try to cover international news as thoroughly as possible in its limited time frame; should give in-depth coverage and not rely on stereotypes and "good pictures"; should disperse its attention throughout the regions of the world, rather than featuring only a few spots; should periodically present stories about every-day political and social life in various countries, rather than only running crisis stories; should try to identify crucial trends and crises before they erupt, instead of focusing on conflicts and violence out of context; should take a critical view of US policies, and not echo the State Department's interpretation of events; should distinguish facts from opinions, and provide objective, non-ideological news.

Assessing the news with these sorts of ostensibly nonpartisan prescriptions is not the only purpose of content analysis. Media analysts are interested in newscast content quite apart from offering critiques of network performances. Conducted properly, television news research should help us better understand the dynamics of politics and society. Nevertheless, the classic liberal model of ideal, unbiased, civic international news[2] seems to lurk in the background of most content analyses, even in those that purport to analyze and describe, rather than to criticize.

The liberal model is under renewed fire both from scholars who maintain that the facade of objectivity masks subservience to the status

---

[2] On the emergence of the "ideology of objectivity" in US journalism, see Schudson (1978).

quo and from those who contend it masks "new class" leftist views. These demythologizers—in explaining the breach of the objectivity model—rarely advocate news relativism; instead, they suggest alternative portrayals that reflect their own notions of an even purer sort of "objectivity" (typically either anti-capitalist or anti-leftist). Although holding different visions of desirable coverage, they join other students of the media in an interest in the nature of global coverage.

CONTENT ANALYSIS

Scholars have begun to analyze systematically television news content, in order to answer the sorts of questions posed above and outlined in Chart 1.1. The debate over a "New World Information Order" has added to the stakes of academic inquiries. Nevertheless, there remains a dearth of formal content analyses of international news on US television.

Some studies that have sought to provide an overview of network attention to foreign countries include those by Warner (1968), Almaney (1970), Larson and Hardy (1977), Hester (1978), and Larson (1979). Larson's chapter in this volume is a definitive update to these earlier studies, and indicates both a shift in the late 1970's toward increased coverage of international affairs overall and toward increased coverage of the Middle East, Africa, and Latin America especially.

Southeast Asia.   The two specific subject areas that have received the most attention from content analysts have been Southeast Asia and the Middle East. Bailey (1976a) measured Vietnam's rank on the network agenda and categorized the topics of Vietnam news stories during the years 1965 through 1970. Bailey (1976b) also studied the nature of interpretative reporting by anchormen. The extent of pro- or anti-Administration bias was calculated by Russo (1971–72) and by Lefever (1974, ch. 5) for Vietnam coverage, and by Pride and Wamsley (1972) for the Laos incursion. Frank (1973) studied the priority of Vietnam in 1972, and Herz (1980) scrutinized elite press and broadcast coverage of the 1972 "Christmas bombings."

Bailey and Lichty (1972) explored the decision to broadcast the film of General Loan's street execution and the images shown in the film. Culbert (1978) has also assessed the visual content of the street execution scenes. Peter Braestrup (1977) authored an extensive account of broadcast and press coverage of the 1968 Tet Offensive and its aftermath. Michael Arlen discussed television coverage of the war in two collections of essays (1969; 1976), and the treatment of the domestic protest movement was reviewed by Pride and Richards (1974), and by Gitlin (1980). McNulty (1975) looked at network "specials" on the Vietnam war, and Lichty (1975) analyzed the final coverage of the "end of the Indo-China war."

Chart 1.1
**Selected Issues in TV Coverage
of International Affairs**

Thorough vs. superficial:
1. Low vs. high priority for international news
2. Simplistic vs. complex presentation of international stories
3. Crises vs. background and trend stories
4. Sensationalized vs. dry coverage

US vs. global vantage:
5. Convenient vs. inconvenient choices of international stories
6. US involvement vs. non-US-involved stories
7. Ethnocentrism and cultural proximity vs. cosmopolitanism
8. Reliance on US government sources vs. skepticism and limited use

Left vs. right:
9. Hardline anti-Soviet stance vs. softline
10. Pro-right-wing regimes vs. pro-left-wing regimes
11. Pro-laissez-faire vs. pro-statist
12. Pro-military vs. pro-pacifistic
13. Isolationist/non-interventionist vs. internationalist/pro-interventionist
14. Jingoist vs. patriaphobic
15. Pro-religious/pro-sectarian vs. pro-secular
16. Pro-Israeli vs. pro-Arab

Hobbesian vs. Panglossian:
17. Dangerous/menacing vs. benign/unthreatening world
18. Irrationality/power vs. rationality/negotiations
19. Sinister motives vs. good will of others
20. Regression vs. progression

Three chapters in this volume add to the literature on TV coverage of Southeast Asia. Robert Entman and David Paletz synthesize much of this previous research and argue that coverage of the war went through several distinct phases. Peter Rollins contrasts the networks' version of the battle of Khe Sanh with alternative perspectives on the battle. William Adams and Michael Joblove explain how attention to the region ended abruptly with the fall of Saigon, and examine the subsequent failure to cover the incalculable loss of life in Cambodia under Pol Pot.

Middle East.   The Middle East replaced Southeast Asia as the major focus of international coverage. The first published content analysis of television's treatment of this region appears to be Gordon's study (1975) of the 1973 war. Aside from Mishra's (1979) brief note, little else in the way of content analysis had been published prior to the publication of *Television Coverage of the Middle East* (Adams, 1981).

William Adams and Phillip Heyl (1981) analyzed Middle East coverage from 1972 through 1980 with special attention to coverage of Afghanistan and Iran, and to correlations with public opinion trends. Magda Bagnied and Steven Schneider (1981) evaluated network coverage of Egyptian President Anwar Sadat's trip to Jerusalem, and Itzhak Roeh (1981) examined the structure of newscast language in reporting Israeli activities in southern Lebanon. Morad Asi (1981) presented the results of a time-series analysis of pro-Israeli and pro-Arab content. Jack Shaheen (1981) appraised several network documentaries about the Palestinians and the Saudis. Montague Kern (1981) explored the use of official sources in covering domestic and foreign elements of the Afghan invasion story. David Altheide (1981) studied coverage of the first six months of the hostage crisis in Iran.

In Chapter 6 of this volume, William Spragens contributes to this growing body of research on Middle East coverage with his study of how the networks approached the 1978 Camp David Summit of President Carter, Israeli Prime Minister Menachem Begin, and Anwar Sadat, one of the key international stories of the decade.

Third World. Apart from Southeast Asia and the Middle East, coverage of the rest of the Third World has received little attention from researchers. Among the few published studies are Sambe's (1980) work on broadcast reporting of the Biafran rebellion against Nigeria, and Harney and Stone's (1969) analysis of coverage given the 1965 Dominican Republic crisis. Otherwise, coverage of Latin America, Africa, and central Asia has been the object of conjecture more than content analysis.

Three provocative chapters in this book concern Third World coverage. Robert Lichter describes the attitudes of elite journalists toward US foreign policy and the Third World (an extension of his earlier 1981 study of their attitudes toward Israel). Peter Dahlgren suggests three primary motifs—social disorder, flawed development, and primitivism—as pervading Third World coverage. Waltraud Q. Morales reviews coverage of all Latin America, and assesses in detail coverage of Chile under Allende and the Sandinista revolution in Nicaragua.

Developed Nations. Remarkably, little that can be called content analysis has been published about coverage of Europe, the Soviet Union, Canada, or Australia, or about US foreign policy (other than in Southeast Asia). Lefever's (1974) book on CBS coverage of national defense issues during 1972–73 is a notable and controversial exception. Also, LeDuc (1980) analyzed five years of network coverage of NATO.

Three chapters in this book add to research in these general areas. Laurence Barton explains the presentation of the US boycott of the 1980

Moscow Olympics. David Paletz, John Ayanian, and Peter Fozzard examine how television reported terrorism in Italy, Northern Ireland, and the United States; and, Myles Breen reviews network inattention to Australia, a study that serves as a useful baseline and comparison for Third World coverage.

Research diversity. As reviewed above, the thirteen studies in this book represent a large expansion of the published scholarly literature on television and certain aspects of international news. These studies illuminate a wide range of issues about the character of that coverage. As will be obvious, they take different methodological approaches and are written from different perspectives. This diversity is useful. By avoiding a procrustean format, the variety of methods and views made for a richer selection of original studies and offers a series of valuably contrasting chapters.

Notwithstanding the significant contributions of the chapters in this volume, certainly more research is needed. Additional content analyses and multi-method replications are needed, and it seems decidedly premature to write a "conclusion" to the subject of US television coverage of international affairs.

THE AUDIENCE

What difference does it make if, as some of the contributors to this volume conclude, the networks did the following: represented the battle of Khe Sanh as another Dien Bien Phu, ignored the holocaust in Cambodia, parroted the government line in mid-1960's news from Vietnam, treated the Sandinistas sympathetically, lionized Anwar Sadat, presented the Olympic boycott as a fitting response to the Soviet move in Afghanistan, sometimes call Australia "Austria," patronize the Third World, and depict terrorism as a madness with neither roots nor origin?

Most viewers are not in a position to second guess the networks about Nicaragua, Egypt, or Cambodia. Viewers can compare TV news with first-hand information about inflation, crime, race-relations, transportation, schools, and other domestic matters, but they cannot test most foreign stories. On subjects that are difficult to question, television sketches for viewers the heroes and villains on the world stage, or screen, outlines the plots and subplots, indicates the role of the United States, and describes the ongoing drama. (For discussions of television's impact on the general public and on political elites, see Comstock et al. 1978; Adams, 1978; Graber, 1980; and Paletz and Entman, 1981.)

When Americans are asked about their favorite news source, national television consistently tops the list, almost no matter how the question is phrased. People even say they prefer television for complex issues. One national survey asked (Sussman, 1981): "If there is a situation in the news that is hard to understand or controversial, which part of the major news media would you trust the most to help you understand?" "National television" said 46 percent of those polled. Only 17 percent replied "major newspapers," and 25 percent said "national news magazines." On other questions, the television response is usually even higher, with around two-thirds of the respondents saying television is their main source of national and international news.

In this context, the chapter by Sahin, Davis, and Robinson (Chapter 13) is a particularly effective corrective to the natural tendency of the content analyst to think that typical viewers watch as carefully as researchers. Their findings reveal that most viewers missed the key point of a relatively simple international story. Of course, regular viewers may still, over time, acquire from TV news a store of information about world affairs, and they may be influenced to some degree in their attitudes toward various countries and leaders, in their orientation toward the US role, and in their opinions about the way the world works. Be that as it may, the shock of the Sahin, Dennis, and Robinson chapter helps the reader resist supposing that viewers absorbed totally the content which the other chapters ascribe to various television news stories.

REFERENCES

Adams, William C., ed. 1981. *Television Coverage of the Middle East.* Norwood, N.J.: Ablex.

———. 1978. Network News Research in Perspective: A Bibliographic Essay. In William C. Adams and Fay Schreibman, eds., *Television Network News: Issues in Content Research.* Washington, D.C.: School of Public and International Affairs, George Washington University, 11–46.

———. 1978b. Local Public Affairs Content of TV News. *Journalism Quarterly* 55 (Winter 1978): 690–695.

———. 1980. Local Television News Coverage and the Central City. *Journal of Broadcasting* 24 (Spring 1980): 253–265.

——— and Phillip Heyl. 1981. From Cairo to Kabul with the Networks, 1972–1980. In William C. Adams, ed., *Television Coverage of the Middle East.* Norwood, N.J.: Ablex, 1–39.

Almaney, Adnan. 1970. International and Foreign Affairs on Network Television. *Journal of Broadcasting* 14 (Fall 1970): 499–509.

Altheide, David. 1981. Iran vs. US TV News: The Hostage Story Out of Context. In William C. Adams, ed., *Television Coverage of the Middle East.* Norwood, N.J.: Ablex, 128–157.

Arlen, Michael J. 1969. *Living-Room War.* New York: Viking.

———. 1976. *The View from Highway 1.* New York: Farrar, Straus and Giroux.

Asi, Morad. 1981. Arabs, Israelis, and TV News: A Time-Series, Content Analysis. In William C. Adams. ed., *Television Coverage of the Middle East.* Norwood, N.J.: Ablex, 67–75.

Bagnied, Magda and Steven Schneider. 1981. Sadat Goes to Jerusalem: Televised Images, Themes, and Agenda. In William C. Adams, ed., *Television Coverage of the Middle East.* Norwood, N.J.: Ablex, 53–66.

Bailey, George, 1976a. Television War: Trends in Network Coverage of Vietnam, 1965–1970. *Journal of Broadcasting* 20 (Spring 1976): 147–158.

———. 1976b. Interpretive Reporting of the Vietnam War by Anchormen. *Journalism Quarterly* 53 (Summer 1976): 319–324.

——— and Lawrence W. Lichty. 1972. Rough Justice on a Saigon Street: A Gatekeeper Study of NBC's Tet Execution Film. *Journalism Quarterly* 49 (Summer 1972): 221–29, 238.

Barnouw, Erik. 1978. Foreword. In William C. Adams and Fay Schreibman, eds., *Television Coverage of the Middle East.* Washington, D.C.: School of Public and International Affairs, George Washington University.

Batscha, Robert M. 1975. *Foreign Affairs News and the Broadcast Journalist.* New York: Praeger.

Braestrup, Peter. 1977. *Big Story.* Boulder, Colo.: Westview Press.

Comstock. George; Steven Chaffee; Natan Katzman; Maxwell McCombs; Donald Roberts. 1978. *Television and Human Behavior.* New York: Columbia University Press.

Culbert, David. 1978. Historians and the Visual Analysis of Television News. In William C. Adams and Fay Schreibman, eds., *Television Network News: Issues in Content Research.* Washington, D.C.: School of Public and International Affairs, George Washington University, 139–154.

Frank, Robert S. 1973. *Message Dimensions of Television News.* Lexington, Mass.: Lexington Books.

Gerbner, George and George Marvanyi. 1977. The Many Worlds of the World's Press. *Journal of Communication* 27 (Winter 1977): 55–60.

Gitlin, Todd. 1980. *The Whole World is Watching.* Berkeley, Calif.: University of California Press.

Gordon, Avishag H. 1975. The Middle East October 1973 War as Reported by the American Networks. *International Problems* 14 (Fall 1975): 76–85.

Graber, Doris. 1980. *Mass Media and American Politics.* Washington, D.C.: Congressional Quarterly Press.

Harney, Russell F. and Vernon A. Stone. 1969. Television and Newspaper Front Page Coverage of a Major News Story. *Journal of Broadcasting* 13 (Spring 1969): 181–188.

Herz, Martin. 1980. *The Prestige Press and the Christmas Bombing, 1972.* Washington, D.C.: Ethics and Public Policy Center.

Hester, Al. 1978. Five Years of Foreign News on US Television Evening Newscasts. *Gazette* 14 (1978).

Kern, Montague. 1981. The Invasion of Afghanistan: Domestic vs. Foreign Stories. In William C. Adams, ed., *Television Coverage of the Middle East.* Norwood, N.J.: Ablex, 106–127.

Larson, James. 1979. International Affairs Coverage on US Network Television. *Journal of Communication* 29 (Spring 1979): 136–147.

——— and Andy Hardy. 1977. International Affairs Coverage on Network Television News: A Study of News Flow. *Gazette* 23 (1977).

LeDuc, Don R. 1980. Television Coverage of NATO Affairs. *Journal of Broadcasting.* 24 (Fall 1980): 449–465.

Lefever, Ernest. 1974. *TV and National Defense: An Analysis of CBS News, 1972–73.* Boston, Va.: Institute for American Strategy.

Lichter, S. Robert. 1981. Media Support for Israel: A Survey of Leading Journalists. In William C. Adams, ed., *Television Coverage of the Middle East.* Norwood, N.J.: Ablex, 40–52.

Lichty, Lawrence W. 1975. The Night at the End of the Tunnel: How TV Reported the End of the Indo-China War. *Film Comment* 11 (July–August 1975): 32–35.

MacNeil, Robert. 1968. *The People Machine.* New York: Harper and Row.

McNulty, Thomas M. 1975. Vietnam Specials: Policy and Content. *Journal of Communication* 25 (Autumn 1975): 173–180.

Mishra, V. M. 1979. News from the Middle East in Five U.S. Media. *Journalism Quarterly* 56 (Summer 1979): 374–378.

Paletz, David L. and Robert M. Entman. 1981. *Media Power Politics.* New York: Free Press.

Pride, Richard A. and Barbara Richards. 1974. Denigration of Authority? Television News Coverage of the Student Movement. *Journal of Politics* 36 (August 1974): 637–660.

———— and Gary L. Wamsley. 1972. Symbol Analysis of Network Coverage of Laos Incursion. *Journalism Quarterly* 49 (Winter 1972): 635–640.

Roeh, Itzhak. 1981. Israel in Lebanon: Language and Images of Storytelling. In William C. Adams, ed., *Television Coverage of the Middle East*. Norwood, N.J.: Ablex, 76–88.

Russo, Frank D. 1971–72. A Study of Bias in TV Coverage of the Vietnam War: 1969 and 1970. *Public Opinion Quarterly* 35 (Winter 1971–72): 539–543.

Sambe, John A. 1980. Network Coverage of the Civil War in Nigeria. *Journal of Broadcasting* 24 (Winter 1980): 61–67.

Schudson, Michael. 1978. *Discovering the News: A Social History of American Newspapers*. New York: Basic Books.

Shaheen, Jack. 1981. Images of Saudis and Palestinians: A Review of Major Documentaries. In William C. Adams, ed., *Television Coverage of the Middle East*. Norwood, N.J.: Ablex, 89–105.

Sterling, Christopher H. and Timothy R. Haight. 1978. *The Mass Media: Aspen Institute Guide to Communication Industry Trends*. New York: Praeger.

Sussman, Barry. 1981. Public Has Sharp Complaints About News Media, Poll Says. *Washington Post*, August 16, 1–2.

Warner, Malcolm. 1968. TV Coverage of International Affairs. *Television Quarterly* 7 (Spring 1968): 60–75.

2

INTERNATIONAL AFFAIRS COVERAGE ON US
EVENING NETWORK NEWS, 1972–1979

JAMES F. LARSON

During the 1970's, network television news expanded its role as an important "window on the world" for the American public. The purpose of this chapter is to describe international affairs coverage on the early evening news broadcasts of the ABC, CBS, and NBC television networks during the eight-year period from 1972 through 1979. Although the immediate focus of the chapter is on the content of network television news, content alone is not the entire concern of the inquiry. Also of interest are factors that shape the picture of the world presented by television, as well as the impact of that picture in different spheres of human activity. Taken together, these interests establish the context for content research and encompass a broad range of questions concerning the role of television as an international news medium.

THE CONTEXT OF INTERNATIONAL NEWS COVERAGE

Newsgathering technology improved greatly in the 1970's, and the proportion of Americans who relied primarily on television for news about world affairs continued to grow. At the end of 1978, more than two-thirds of the population cited television as their principal source of news, an increase from 60 percent who mentioned television in 1971 (Roper, 1979).

Also during the past decade, all Western news media came under increased international scrutiny as part of the debate over a "New World

15

Communication Order."[1] That debate has important ramifications for all news media, including network television in the United States.

Of the many questions about television news and its impact, three areas are particularly important to this chapter on international news and will be summarized before presenting the analysis of content. The first set of questions relates to the role of new technology, especially satellites and electronic newsgathering (ENG), in television's growth as an international news medium. The second group of questions concerns the political impact of foreign news coverage in the United States. Finally, a third set of questions revolves around the debate over the flow of news and its implications for coverage of foreign affairs by US television networks.

Newsgathering Technology

Technological developments greatly facilitated the recent growth of television as an international news medium. Two technologies in particular—satellite communication and electronic newsgathering (ENG) equipment—have drastically altered the manner in which network television gathers foreign news.

The potential applications of satellite technology in the gathering and dissemination of international news have long been recognized by communication practitioners, scholars, and government officials. In the late 1960's, a large group of governmental experts on space communications met under UNESCO auspices in Paris to consider the implications of satellite communication for a number of fields. One of their recommendations was that future communication satellites should be designed to help balance the flow of visual news in the world (*Broadcasting from Space*, 1970). Earlier, Wilbur Schramm (1968, p. 14) had expressed the view that "satellites can potentially make a real difference in news availability throughout the world."

Most of the technology on which these earlier hopes were based is now available. The Intelsat Global Satellite System expanded rapidly during the 1970's. At the start of the decade, only 24 nations possessed earth stations, a number that had more than quadrupled by decade's end (*COMSAT Report*, 1980). Such growth greatly expands the potential number of locations from which visual news may be transmitted on a timely and virtually instantaneous basis. If past experience is a guide, however, the simple availability of satellite channels will not automatically alter prevailing patterns of news flow.

---

[1] The new order in the field of global communication has been variously referred to as the "New World Information Order," "New International Information Order," and "New International Information and Communication Order." This chapter uses the terminology suggested by the International Commission for the Study of Communication Problems (*Many Voices*, 1980).

Based on the early years of operation of the INTELSAT System, Hulten (1973) observed that satellites had simply increased the news flow between news centers of the world, and had not appreciably influenced flows from peripheral areas to these centers or flows between minor areas. He concluded, "While satellites make possible television news from countries previously inaccessible, the new technology would not appear to alter underlying news interests and news evaluation patterns" (Hulten, 1973, p. 36).

In addition to the prevailing news selection criteria as an influence on the flow of news, it is a political reality that the use of satellite facilities requires the consent of the country from which the pictures are being transmitted. For example, during the hostage crisis in Iran, that country's government made an early decision to allow foreign news coverage by US network television. Later in the crisis, first CBS, then the other two networks, were denied access to the satellite facilities for broadcasting reports that offended the government of Iran (Quint, 1980).

In addition to expanded use of satellite transmissions, during the 1970's all of the networks made the transition from the use of film to the use of videotape. This change was made possible by improvements in electronic newsgathering technology, consisting of small, lightweight cameras and videotape editing equipment.

By eliminating the need for film processing, electronic newsgathering greatly decreased the time required to prepare a visual report and transmit it to New York via satellite. Increased speed, together with more portable cameras and editing equipment, has helped to change the manner in which foreign correspondents gather the news. Today, many correspondents travel from one news event to another, often over a wide geographical area, and are only loosely tied, if at all, to a home base or bureau.

TV News and Foreign Policy

The central question concerning the political impact of television's international news coverage is the one addressed for the print media in Cohen's (1963) classic study *The Press and Foreign Policy:* What are the consequences for the foreign policy-making environment of the way that the press (here, network news) defines and performs its job, and of the way that its output is assimilated by the participants in the policy process (Cohen, 1963, p. 4)? Cohen chose to focus on print media, partly for practical reasons. (In the absence of television news archives, the products of the newspaper press were less ephemeral than those of television or radio.) However, the questions he posed about newspapers are appropriate for network television today. As with newspapers, television plays three major roles in the foreign policy field.

The first role of television news is that of *observer*. In this role, it functions as a newsgathering organization selecting certain aspects of international affairs to be presented to the American public. The role as an observer of foreign affairs encompasses a number of specific concerns. One issue is the changing role of the foreign correspondent, mentioned earlier in connection with new technology for newsgathering. Current practices of globetrotting foreign correspondents raise concern over their lack of linguistic, cultural, or political knowledge about the nations on which they report.

Another issue is the relationship between government officials and network television news. Viewers have come to expect that the President and the Secretary of State will receive continuing coverage while they are in this country and particularly when they are on overseas trips. Along with government officials at other levels, they exert great influence on the international news that comes to the attention of the American public.

A second role of television news is that of *participant* in the foreign policy process. In recent years, television news has assumed an increasingly active role in public diplomacy. It is now relatively common, for example, to see network news correspondents interviewing heads of state or other senior officials of foreign governments. During the hostage crisis in Iran, network news organizations found themselves participating more directly than ever before in a diplomatic process. This new role for television news raises a host of questions about the conduct of foreign policy.

Finally, a third role of television news in relation to foreign policy is that of *catalyst*. In this role, television news is thought to influence opinion elites and hence the process of foreign policy formation. Cohen (1963) observed that such elites depended more heavily on newspapers than on radio and television for foreign affairs news and comment. Cohen's view must now be modified by the increased role of television news as a participant in public diplomacy, together with its increased capabilities provided by the new technology. Today, network television news fills a more important role as a catalyst in the foreign policy process than it did prior to 1963.

The "New World Communication Order" Debate

A fundamental premise of this chapter is that televised coverage of international news in the United States, or any country for that matter, cannot be considered apart from the international debate on communication issues. The following summary of that debate on the shape of a "New World Communication Order" highlights issues that relate more directly to televised coverage of international news in the United States.

The "New World Communication Order" is a broad rubric and involves issues which began to be discussed in the 1960's. Around 1970, communication policy makers, researchers, and other professionals began to work for a consensus on some of the major issues. Included were such topics as new communication technologies, transborder data flow, ownership and control of communication industries, rights and responsibilities of journalists, and the cultural impact of different forms of communication.

The flow of news has been at the crux of the international debate from its inception and remains one of the most politically controversial issues. Major arguments center on imbalances in the quantity of news flowing among nations of the world and in its "quality" or content. A special concern of many developing nations is the flow between their capitals and the world news centers in developed nations. Also of interest is the flow of news among Third World countries themselves, the flow between countries with different political and economic systems, and the flow between large and small nations.

The major world news agencies—Associated Press, United Press International, Reuters, and Agence France-Presse—have been singled out for special attention in the debate concerning the international flow of news. Third World nations are particularly concerned because of their widespread dependence on these Western news agencies for most international news.

This international debate over the flow of news and the activities of news organizations suggests additional reasons why the performance of the US television networks is of interest outside as well as within the United States. Other nations may find reason to examine the US networks in the central thesis of Tunstall's book, *The Media Are American* (1977). He argues that, because the United States has consistently led in the development of new media, it has had an enormous influence over the subsequent development of new media in most other countries. Katz and Wedell (1978) examined the same thesis from a different perspective, based on case studies of the development of broadcasting systems in 11 nations. To the extent that Tunstall's (1977) thesis is true of television news, a better understanding of the US network news organizations may shed light on television news in other parts of the world. While the evidence concerning US influence is not conclusive, available information does justify special scrutiny of the American networks.

The freedom of news organizations to cover international affairs can be affected by the international debate over the flow of news. At the 1976 general conference of UNESCO in Nairobi, a draft declaration on fundamental principles governing the use of mass media was put to a vote. Article 12 of the draft declaration sparked intense political debate. It stipulated: "States are responsible for the activities in the international sphere of all mass media under their jurisdiction" (UNESCO General Conference, 1976). The draft declaration was postponed and was never adopted in that form. However, the debate led to the formation of the MacBride Commission and served to underscore the issue of the relationship between governments and media organizations. In the years since the Nairobi General Conference of UNESCO, many nations have begun to formulate national communication policies. This trend toward the establishment of national communication policies, particularly in the Third World, is of major concern to television news organizations, whose ability to gather and disseminate news will be directly shaped by such policies.

A related issue that should concern US television news organizations is the international discussion concerning the Western concept of news. Many journalists, researchers, and politicians from developing countries argue that the traditional Western notion of news should be broadened to include not only "events" but also "processes." "For instance, hunger is a process while a hunger strike is an event; a flood is an event, a struggle to control floods is a process" (*Many Voices*, 1980, p. 157). Television journalism may bear the brunt of Third World criticism on this point because it is thought the medium itself is ill-suited for portraying gradual, long-term, and often non-visual processes.

METHODOLOGY

The remainder of this chapter is devoted to a description of international affairs coverage on network television's early evening news broadcasts during the eight-year period from 1972 through 1979. The description is based on quantitative measures from Vanderbilt University's *Television News Index and Abstracts*. It is longitudinal in nature, allowing a differentiation of stable, long-term patterns in network news coverage from short-term or brief episodes in such coverage (Frank, 1973, p. 22; Schramm, 1964, p. 58; Patterson, 1978, pp. 179–180). Because the methodology was an extension of two earlier research efforts (Larson & Hardy, 1977; Larson, 1978), an abbreviated description of procedures is presented here.

The initial content analysis of the *Television News Index and Abstracts* was conducted only after a test to determine its reliability as a source of data about international news coverage (Larson & Hardy, 1977). That test revealed a very high degree of reliability for the *Index and Abstracts*.

The research adopts a broad but practical definition of international news: Any news story that mentions a country other than the United States, regardless of its thematic content or dateline, is considered an international story. Such a conceptualization of international news has several advantages. It is easily operationalized and can be coded with a high degree of reliability. While it may appear excessively broad or inclusive at first glance, in practice it results in only slight inflation of the total amount of international news when compared to other definitions found in the communications literature. Finally, the definition captures the central dimension of international news because nations are the principal actors in international affairs.

Data presented in this chapter are based on a random sample of weeknight network news programs, stratified by year. The total sample includes an average of three weeknight newscasts per month for each network over the 1972–79 period; in other words, over 13 percent of all weeknight broadcasts over the eight years were sampled for the content analysis. The total sample contains 286 newscasts for NBC, and 288 for both ABC and CBS. The total number of international news stories found in these sample programs ranges from 1,789 on ABC to 1,884 on CBS. In the initial study, sampling error was computed for mentions of countries and territories. It was acceptably small for the entire sample and for yearly breakdowns (Larson, 1978).

The content dimensions of television news contained in this chapter are all based on a detailed delineation of story units and coding categories for use with the *Television News Index and Abstracts*. Intercoder reliability was .89 or higher for all content categories used in the study (see also Larson, 1978).

The basic unit of analysis for this examination of televised coverage of international news is the individual news story. With this as the basic analytical building block, the description of the nature of international news coverage uses three "levels": story level, newscast level, and the level of nations involved in news reports.

Story Level. The first level describes the format of sampled stories over the eight-year period. International news stories take one of three major forms. First is the *anchor report,* read from a New York, Washington, London, or other studio by the anchor and often accompanied by a still picture, map, diagram, or artist's sketch. Although such reports may originate from a variety of sources, they come primarily from the major international news agencies.

A second form is the *domestic video report,* originating live or taped in Washington, New York, or another US location. Sometimes called "foreign news at home" (Elliott & Golding, 1974), the vast majority of this category are correspondents' reports from the White House, State Department, Pentagon, Congress, or United Nations (Batscha, 1975).

The third form of the international news story is the *foreign video report,* originating outside the United States and either taped, filmed, or live. Most such reports are prepared by network correspondents in the field and transmitted to New York via satellite.

Newscast Level. The newscast forms a second descriptive level for analysis of television news. Content data gathered at the story level can be aggregated to describe overall characteristics of the news conveyed during entire newscasts. Newscast level description is important because it represents the basic package in which news is delivered by the networks and in which news is consumed by the public.

Nation Level. A third descriptive level deals with the nations involved in international news. This level has been described as *news geography,* and it concentrates on the "who" and the "where" of network television news; that is, the types of actors and the locations in which activities are reported (Harris, 1976).

This chapter's account of eight years of international news coverage by the three US networks begins at the story level and follows with descriptions of newscast content and the geography of TV news.

INTERNATIONAL NEWS ON THE NETWORK AGENDA

Format of International Stories

Over the 1972–79 period, 45 percent of all the international news stories aired by the networks came in the form of anchor reports. For these reports, the networks are heavily dependent on the major news agencies. According to one estimate (Batscha, 1975), 70 to 80 percent of the stories read on camera by an anchor correspondent are gleaned from the wire services. As indicated in Table 2.1, the proportion of foreign news reported by anchor correspondents decreased noticeably during the eight-year period. From 1972 through 1974, at least half of all foreign news stories consisted of anchor reports, but this decreased to a low of 38 percent by 1979.

Domestic video reports accounted for 25 percent of all international news broadcasts by the three networks during 1972–79. The proportion of such reports increased slightly, mainly during the last three years of the period. All three networks showed a decrease in the amount of international news conveyed through domestic video reports during 1974. The most plausible explanation for this decrease is the emphasis on Watergate; Washington correspondents may have spent less time at the State Department and more time near Judge Sirica's courtroom. This shift illustrates the interdependence of news judgments concerning domestic and international affairs.

Foreign video reports made up the remaining 30 percent of international news coverage by the three networks. The proportion of such reports was fairly stable over the eight-year period, although the fluctuations appear slightly greater if individual networks are examined.

Table 2.1

Three Major Story Types as Percentages of All International News Stories on ABC, CBS, and NBC, 1972–79

Year	Anchor Report				Domestic Video Report				Foreign Video Report			
	ABC	CBS	NBC	All Networks	ABC	CBS	NBC	All Networks	ABC	CBS	NBC	All Networks
	(%)	(%)	(%)	(%)	(%)	(%)	(%)	(%)	(%)	(%)	(%)	(%)
1972	44	55	51	50	28	25	19	24	28	20	30	26
1973	51	48	53	51	22	23	18	21	28	29	29	29
1974	56	55	50	54	16	15	16	16	28	29	34	30
1975	49	42	48	46	23	21	20	21	28	37	32	32
1976	45	46	44	45	24	20	22	22	32	34	34	33
1977	36	38	44	39	32	33	32	32	32	28	24	28
1978	37	37	46	40	30	36	27	31	33	27	27	29
1979	40	40	33	38	27	33	28	29	33	27	39	33
Average 1972–79	44	45	46	45	26	26	23	25	30	29	31	30
N = (stories)	789	842	831	2462	460	494	411	1365	540	548	563	1651

Note: Some row percentages may not add to 100% because of rounding.

Number of International Stories

On the average, nightly news broadcasts during the 1972–79 period contained a total of 17 news stories dealing with domestic and international news. In the weeknights sampled, the total ranged from a low of nine to a high of 26 stories in one night.

The mean level of international news coverage for all networks was 6.3 stories, or 37 percent of the stories in a typical network news broadcast. This coverage was comprised, on the average, of 2.8 anchor reports, 1.9 foreign video reports, and 1.6 domestic video reports. Although there were some small differences across networks, all three used these formats in about the same proportions.

As shown in Table 2.2, clear changes in international news coverage occurred over time. The number of stories devoted to international news was highest at the start and at the end of the period. The higher than average number of international stories in 1972 focused on Indochina, and in 1979 on the Middle East. (See Adams & Heyl, 1981.) Stories devoted to international affairs dropped noticeably in 1974, presumably due to network preoccupation with Watergate and domestic politics.

Time Devoted to International Stories

The amount of time devoted to international news is an alternative measure of emphasis that corresponds very closely to the count of the number of international stories.

The mean length of an international news story on network television for the period under study was 1 minute 28 seconds. As shown in Table 2.3, anchor reports were typically the shortest, averaging 31 seconds in length. The average length of both domestic and foreign video reports was 2 minutes 8 seconds. The length of individual international stories in the sample ranged from 7 seconds to 6 minutes 30 seconds. Approximately one third of the sampled news items were 30 seconds or shorter in length, while about one-quarter of the stories were longer than 2 minutes.

After accounting for station breaks and commercials, each network has about 22 or 23 minutes of air time remaining for news. During the four years from 1976 through 1979, the networks devoted an average of 9 minutes 22 seconds of that time to international news. As Table 2.4 indicates, there was an increase in the amount of time devoted to international news during each of the four years. The same trend appears for each network, corresponding to the pattern shown earlier in Table 2.2 which was based on the number of international stories.

Table 2.4 shows differences in the relative emphasis given international news by the three networks. CBS consistently gave more time to international affairs during the 1976–79 period, averaging over one and one half more minutes per newscast than NBC, which devoted the least amount of time to international news.

Table 2.2
Number of Stories Per Newscast on ABC, CBS and NBC, 1972–79

			International News Stories				
						All Three Types	
Year	Network	Total Stories	Anchor Report	Foreign Video Report	Domestic Video Report	Number	% of Total Stories
1972	CBS	17.7	3.7	1.4	1.7	6.9	39
	ABC	15.2	3.4	2.2	2.1	7.7	50
	NBC	16.6	3.8	2.2	1.4	7.4	45
1973	CBS	15.6	2.7	1.6	1.3	5.6	36
	ABC	14.8	2.9	1.6	1.3	5.8	39
	NBC	17.2	3.1	1.7	1.1	6.0	35
1974	CBS	20.2	3.0	1.6	0.8	5.4	27
	ABC	16.1	2.7	1.3	0.8	4.7	29
	NBC	18.4	2.8	1.9	0.9	5.6	30
1975	CBS	19.5	3.1	2.7	1.5	7.3	37
	ABC	18.3	3.4	1.9	1.6	6.9	37
	NBC	18.4	3.3	2.2	1.4	6.8	37
1976	CBS	17.5	3.1	2.3	1.3	6.7	38
	ABC	17.1	2.6	1.8	1.4	5.8	34
	NBC	16.9	2.2	1.7	1.1	5.1	30
1977	CBS	17.2	2.5	1.8	2.2	6.5	38
	ABC	15.8	2.2	2.0	2.0	6.2	39
	NBC	16.1	2.4	1.3	1.7	5.4	34
1978	CBS	15.6	2.4	1.8	2.4	6.6	42
	ABC	16.8	2.3	2.0	1.9	6.2	37
	NBC	16.9	3.3	1.9	1.9	7.1	42
1979	CBS	17.3	2.9	2.0	2.4	7.4	43
	ABC	17.1	2.6	2.1	1.7	6.4	37
	NBC	15.5	2.4	2.8	2.0	7.3	47
1972–79 Averages	CBS	17.6	2.9	1.9	1.7	6.5	37
	ABC	16.4	2.7	1.9	1.6	6.2	38
	NBC	17.0	2.9	2.0	1.4	6.3	37
All Networks		17.0	2.8	1.9	1.6	6.3	37

N = (newscasts) ABC CBS NBC
288 288 286

Table 2.3
Mean Length of International News Stories in Seconds, 1976–79

Year	Anchor Report				Domestic Video Report				Foreign Video Report			
	ABC	CBS	NBC	All Networks	ABC	CBS	NBC	All Networks	ABC	CBS	NBC	All Networks
1976	29	28	24	27	120	132	128	127	102	106	113	107
1977	33	27	32	31	120	132	106	119	113	137	139	136
1978	38	33	22	31	124	138	131	131	129	146	134	136
1979	45	30	25	33	136	141	121	133	131	133	134	133
Average 1976–79	36	30	26	31	125	136	122	128	119	131	130	128
N = (stories)	357	398	371	1126	259	304	244	807	294	288	280	862

Table 2.4
Mean Length of Time Per Newscast for International News
on Weeknight TV News, 1976–79
(in minutes and seconds)

Year	ABC	CBS	NBC	All Networks
1976	7:20	8:22	6:37	7:26
1977	8:56	10:03	7:17	8:45
1978	9:39	11:12	9:42	10:11
1979	10:27	11:27	11:21	11:05
1976–79	9:07	10:16	8:44	9:22
(n)	(147)	(146)	(144)	

Rank of International Stories

As a whole, the international news stories sampled during the 1976–79 period are distributed very evenly throughout the news broadcasts. The frequency distribution of ranks one through 16 is very flat for all three networks. However, an examination of ranks by story formats provides a better picture of the structure of international news presentation on network television. To simplify the analysis, stories in the sample were divided according to whether they were in the first or second half of the newscast.

As shown in Table 2.5, all networks place a higher priority on video reports, both domestic and foreign, than on anchor reports. Domestic video reports receive the highest priority, with an average of 67 percent of such reports appearing during the first half of the newscast. Foreign video reports receive nearly as much emphasis. For all networks, almost 62 percent of such reports appear during the first half of the newscast. Anchor reports of international news are more likely to come later in the program. About 65 percent of these reports come during the second half of the newscast.

The data on story ranks provide corroboration for the frequent observation that network television places a high priority on visual action. Equally important, however, is the weight given by the networks to Washington and New York correspondents, whose reports generally contain less visual action than those of the foreign correspondents.

THE NEWS GEOGRAPHY OF NETWORK TELEVISION

Study of the news geography (Harris, 1976) of network television concentrates on the types of actors in the news and the locations in which activities are reported. Without question, nations are the most important actors in international affairs, although not the only ones. Other categories of actors would include, for example, international organizations, multinational corporations, and prominent individuals.

Table 2.5
Percentage of International News Appearing in First and Second Half
of Newscast by Major Story Types, 1976–79

Half	Network	Story Type			
		Anchor Report	Domestic Video Report	Foreign Video Report	All Types
First Half	ABC	37.4	68.0	59.0	53.1
	CBS	37.8	64.5	64.2	53.7
	NBC	29.3	68.0	61.4	49.9
	All Networks	34.8	66.8	61.5	52.2
Second Half	ABC	62.6	32.0	41.0	46.9
	CBS	62.2	35.5	35.8	46.3
	NBC	70.7	32.0	38.6	50.1
	All Networks	65.2	33.2	38.5	47.8
N = (stories)	ABC	910			
	CBS	989			
	NBC	896			

The following description of news geography is based on an analysis of the countries mentioned in international news stories and, for foreign video reports, those nations from which the stories originate. Content data were gathered for both countries and territories. Unless otherwise specified, references to nations or countries also include territories. Two territories that were coded separately were Northern Ireland and Hong Kong.

Nations Mentioned on Network TV News

The nations mentioned in a news story provide a useful and convenient indicator of the international character of the news item. During the 1972–79 period, more than three-quarters of all international news stories broadcast by the US networks mentioned two or more nations. However, in 61 percent of those stories, one of the nations mentioned was the United States, a strong confirmation that international news is usually defined in terms of the interests of the nation where it is broadcast or published. When mentions of the United States are ignored, 44 percent of all stories broadcast by the networks mentioned two or more foreign nations.

The total number of foreign nations mentioned in international news stories ranged from one to a high of 15, but fewer than 10 percent of the stories mentioned four or more foreign countries. At the same time, an entire newscast typically covered stories involving around eight or nine foreign countries. The number of different foreign nations dealt with in a single night's newscast ranged from one to 22. What countries were being covered?

Table 2.6 shows the coverage given to the 50 nations most frequently mentioned on each of the three networks. Each nation is ranked according to the extent of coverage on each network. (The entire table is ordered according to the extent of coverage given nations by ABC news.) Taken as a whole, the table provides one description of network television's news geography for the eight-year period, 1972–79. Several aspects of the pattern deserve mention.

Table 2.6
Coverage of 50 Most Frequently Mentioned Nations, 1972–79,
Expressed as a Percentage of Sampled International Stories

	ABC		CBS		NBC	
Nation	Rank	% of Stories	Rank	% of Stories	Rank	% of Stories
USSR	1	16.3	1	16.5	1	15.1
Israel	2	15.2	2	13.2	2	13.9
South Vietnam	3	12.0	3	11.0	3	11.3
North Vietnam[a]	4	9.3	4	8.4	4	9.4
Great Britain[b]	5	8.3	7	7.6	7	7.0
Egypt	6	8.1	5	8.0	5	8.3
France	7	6.9	6	7.9	6	7.2
China, People's Republic	8	6.0	9	5.1	8	5.2
Lebanon	9	4.6	11	4.2	13	3.4
Japan	10	4.4	14	3.5	15	3.0
Iran	11	4.2	8	5.2	9	4.5
West Germany	12	3.9	10	4.7	10	4.2
Syria	13	3.8	12	3.9	12	3.6
Cambodia	14	3.7	13	3.7	11	3.7
Cuba	15	3.1	17	2.8	16	2.8
Italy	16	3.0	19	2.6	14	3.1
Rhodesia	17	2.4	20	2.6	24	1.6
South Africa	17	2.4	15	3.1	20	2.0
Saudi Arabia	18	2.3	18	2.8	17	2.8
Jordan	19	2.0	23	2.1	25	1.5
Northern Ireland	20	2.0	26	1.5	27	1.4
Turkey	21	1.9	25	1.7	26	1.4
Canada	21	1.9	21	2.4	19	2.3
Switzerland	22	1.7	16	3.0	22	1.7
South Korea	23	1.6	22	2.3	18	2.3
Cyprus	24	1.5	28	1.3	29	1.2
Mexico	25	1.4	25	1.7	23	1.7
Spain	26	1.3	24	1.6	24	1.8
India	26	1.3	31	1.1	29	1.2
Greece	27	1.3	26	1.5	25	1.5
Thailand	27	1.3	29	1.2	21	1.8
Laos	28	1.2	37	0.7	28	1.2
The Philippines	28	1.2	31	1.1	31	1.0
Uganda	28	1.2	32	1.0	30	1.1
Panama	29	1.2	27	1.4	35	0.8

Table 2.6 (Continued)

Nation	ABC		CBS		NBC	
	Rank	% of Stories	Rank	% of Stories	Rank	% of Stories
Portugal	30	1.1	27	1.4	29	1.2
Angola	30	1.1	30	1.1	31	1.0
The Netherlands	31	1.0	34	0.9	32	0.9
Argentina	31	1.0	34	0.9	36	0.7
Austria	32	0.8	38	0.6	38	0.6
Ireland	33	0.8	36	0.7	35	0.8
Sweden	33	0.8	34	0.9	35	0.8
Chile	33	0.8	30	1.1	32	0.9
Iraq	34	0.7	33	1.0	36	0.7
Pakistan	34	0.7	41	0.4	38	0.6
Norway	35	0.7	40	0.5	41	0.4
Poland	35	0.7	34	0.9	30	1.1
The Vatican	35	0.7	38	0.6	34	0.8
Libya	35	0.7	33	1.0	37	0.7
Nicaragua	35	0.7	36	0.7	35	0.8
Zaire	35	0.7	34	0.9	36	0.7
N = (stories)		1789		1884		1805

[a] After the year 1976, all references to Vietnam were coded as North Vietnam.
[b] Excludes Northern Ireland.
Note: Rankings are based on the absolute number of stories in which each nation was mentioned. Due to rounding, nations with different ranks may appear to be mentioned in the same percentage of sampled stories. Because more than one nation may be mentioned in each story, percentages sum to more than 100 percent.

First, only about 20 of the nations in the world are mentioned in more than two percent of the international news stories on each network. Relatively speaking, a nation that appears in more than two percent of the international news broadcast by a network receives "extensive coverage."

Second, the approximately 20 nations that appear frequently on the network news include a number of countries that were involved in wars or major conflicts during the time period studied. Notably, they include all of the combatants in the Vietnam War and the 1973 War in the Middle East.

Third, most of the other frequently-mentioned nations are world powers, politically or economically, such as the USSR, Great Britain, France, the People's Republic of China, West Germany, and Japan. Conversely, developing nations are less likely to appear on the network news unless they are involved in conflict.

Tables 2.7 and 2.8 break down the sample into two equal time periods, 1972–75 and 1976–79, presenting data for 20 nations most frequently mentioned during each period. They portray several rather dramatic shifts in the attention pattern of network television news.

The first major change in coverage across the two time periods involves nations that participated in the Indochina War. During the 1972–75 period, North and South Vietnam, Cambodia, and Laos received extensive coverage on all networks. (See Chapter 10 by Entman and Paletz.) In the ensuing four-year period, all but North Vietnam dropped out of the network news picture. This shift in coverage was major, both in the sense that it involved several nations from the same geographical region and also because nearly all of those nations dropped from relatively extensive levels of coverage to hardly measurable amounts of coverage.

In a second major shift of attention, the US television networks devoted increased time to several nations from the Middle East. As shown in Tables 2.7 and 2.8, Israel, Egypt, Lebanon, Syria, and Saudi Arabia all received a greater amount of coverage during the second four years than during the first. Because each of these nations had been ranked among the top 20 for the initial four years of the sample, this shift in coverage may be

Table 2.7
Coverage of 20 Most Frequently Mentioned Nations, 1972–75[a]

	ABC		CBS		NBC	
Nation	Rank	% of Stories	Rank	% of Stories	Rank	% of Stories
South Vietnam[b]	1	23.0	1	22.0	1	21.3
USSR	2	14.6	2	15.9	2	14.3
Israel	3	14.5	4	11.1	4	12.2
North Vietnam	4	13.9	3	11.9	3	13.6
France	5	7.1	5	9.0	5	8.7
Great Britain[c]	6	6.8	6	8.9	6	7.6
Egypt	7	6.6	8	4.9	7	7.0
China, People's Republic	8	6.4	8	4.9	9	4.8
Cambodia	9	5.9	7	6.5	8	6.2
Syria	10	4.9	11	3.7	10	4.7
Japan	11	4.2	10	3.8	11	4.0
Lebanon	12	3.3	12	2.7	13	3.0
West Germany	13	2.9	9	4.4	12	3.6
Northern Ireland	14	2.7	14	2.0	14	2.6
Turkey	15	2.6	15	1.9	18	1.8
Cyprus	16	2.4	15	1.9	18	1.8
Laos	17	2.2	21	1.1	16	2.0
Greece	18	1.9	16	1.8	15	2.1
Portugal	19	1.7	13	2.2	18	1.8
Saudi Arabia	20	1.6	18	1.6	15	2.1
N = (stories)		878		893		909

[a] Rankings are based on the number of sampled stories in which each nation was mentioned; percentages sum to more than 100 percent. Since rankings differ slightly across networks, this table is based on 20 nations most frequently mentioned on ABC.

[b] After 1976, all references to Vietnam were coded as North Vietnam.

[c] Excludes Northern Ireland.

Table 2.8
Coverage of 20 Most Frequently Mentioned Nations, 1976-79[a]

Nation	ABC		CBS		NBC	
	Rank	% of Stories	Rank	% of Stories	Rank	% of Stories
USSR	1	17.9	1	17.1	1	15.9
Israel	2	15.9	2	15.1	2	15.5
Great Britain[b]	3	9.7	6	6.5	5	6.4
Egypt	4	9.6	3	10.7	3	9.5
Iran	5	7.6	4	8.6	4	8.2
France	6	6.7	5	7.0	6	5.6
Lebanon	7	5.9	7	5.6	11	3.8
China, People's Republic	8	5.6	9	5.3	6	5.6
Cuba	9	5.2	14	3.9	10	3.9
North Vietnam[c]	10	4.8	8	5.4	7	5.0
Rhodesia	11	4.7	11	4.7	14	3.1
South Africa	12	4.6	9	5.3	10	3.9
Japan	12	4.6	17	3.2	18	2.0
Italy	13	4.5	17	3.2	9	4.2
Saudi Arabia	14	3.0	15	3.8	12	3.5
Syria	15	2.7	12	4.1	17	2.5
Jordan	16	2.6	19	2.6	21	1.6
Switzerland	17	2.5	13	4.0	19	1.9
Canada	18	2.3	16	3.3	15	3.0
Panama	19	2.2	20	2.5	21	1.6
N = (stories)		911		991		896

[a] Rankings are based on the number of sampled stories in which each nation was mentioned; percentages sum to more than 100 percent. The table is based on 20 nations most frequently mentioned on ABC.

[b] Excludes Northern Ireland.

[c] After 1976, all references to Vietnam were coded as North Vietnam.

characterized as a major intensification of existing coverage by the networks. (See Adams & Heyl, 1981.) However, for another Middle Eastern nation, Iran, the shift of coverage was much more dramatic. That country, which had received relatively little coverage in 1972–75, was among the five most extensively covered nations in the world in 1976–79, largely because of an extremely high level of attention during 1979. (See also Altheide, 1981.)

A third change in the pattern of network news coverage involved the African nations of Rhodesia and South Africa. Both ranked high in the amount of coverage received during 1976–79, but do not appear among the top 20 nations for the preceding four-year period.

Tables 2.7 and 2.8 show a fourth shift involving Turkey, Cyprus, and Greece. Each of those nations ranked among the top 20 in the 1972–75 period because of their involvement in the conflict on Cyprus in 1974. None was similarly ranked during the 1976–79 period.

Several other changes in the attention pattern of network news relate to individual nations. Cuba, Italy, Switzerland, Canada, and Panama all received increased coverage during the 1976–79 period, while coverage of West Germany, Northern Ireland, and Portugal declined.

Regional Coverage

Network coverage of major geographical regions during the 1972–79 period shows some long-term, and consistent patterns, along with some significant trends. Here it will be possible to note the pattern of attention given to each region over the eight-year period and some probable reasons for that attention.

Table 2.9 presents data on the extent of network television coverage given to the following geographical divisions:

1. Eastern Europe and USSR
2. Western Europe
3. Middle East
4. Africa (Sub-Sahara)
5. South Asia
6. Southeast Asia and Pacific
7. East Asia
8. Latin America
9. Canada

In the case of the Middle East, which includes the tier of Arab states above the Sahara, and Eastern Europe, which includes the USSR, groupings are based on geopolitical as well as geographic considerations.[2]

Table 2.10 reports the regional distribution of all sampled international stories. Because nations from more than one region may be mentioned in a single news story, the percentages for all regions sum to more than 100 percent.

Western Europe received more coverage than any other region and received it consistently over the eight-year period. As already noted, Great Britain and Northern Ireland, France, West Germany, and Italy are all

---

[2] "Latin America" was used to refer to all countries and territories in the Western Hemisphere south of the United States. "Africa" encompassed all of the continent except the Mediterranean Arab states which were put in the "Middle East" grouping. In addition, the "Middle East" included those countries south of Turkey and on the Arabian peninsula, along with Iran. Afghanistan was grouped with "South Asia," along with Bangladesh, Bhutan, Sikkim, Pakistan, Nepal, India, Sri Lanka, and the Indian Ocean states. "East Asia" included China, Japan, Taiwan, Mongolia, North and South Korea, and Hong Kong. "Southeast Asia and the Pacific" consisted of Vietnam, Thailand, Laos, Cambodia, Malaysia, Philippines, Singapore, Indonesia, Australia, New Zealand, and other states and territories of the Pacific. "Eastern Europe and the USSR" was composed of Albania, Bulgaria, Czechoslovakia, East Germany, Hungary, Poland, Romania, the USSR, and Yugoslavia. The remainder of Europe was labeled "Western Europe."

Table 2.9
Coverage of Major Geographical Regions, 1972–79[a]

Region	Network	1972	1973	1974	1975	1976	1977	1978	1979	1972–79
		%	%	%	%	%	%	%	%	%
Eastern Europe	ABC	14.9	10.1	22.4	17.4	19.6	17.0	27.4	15.6	17.9
and U.S.S.R.	CBS	18.3	12.8	21.0	17.1	16.7	15.0	30.1	15.1	18.3
	NBC	15.4	12.0	21.3	14.6	14.0	17.1	22.6	16.1	16.7
Western Europe	ABC	29.1	20.8	34.0	27.9	23.4	39.1	33.8	25.2	29.1
	CBS	31.7	28.2	46.7	30.4	30.8	38.8	31.4	22.8	32.2
	NBC	30.9	25.4	37.6	31.4	30.2	38.2	30.7	18.4	30.0
Middle East	ABC	10.8	26.1	24.4	24.7	21.5	23.5	26.9	48.3	25.7
	CBS	7.1	22.1	24.6	19.8	22.9	23.8	23.4	47.1	24.2
	NBC	8.1	23.4	29.7	21.3	21.8	20.6	26.9	46.4	25.0
Africa	ABC	1.5	0.5	1.9	4.9	17.2	20.9	10.7	8.8	8.4
(Sub-Sahara)	CBS	1.3	0	3.1	6.5	18.3	17.1	13.8	9.2	9.0
	NBC	1.5	0.5	1.5	3.4	16.2	13.6	10.5	6.9	6.5
South Asia	ABC	2.6	1.0	1.9	2.0	1.0	4.4	1.3	3.4	2.2
	CBS	2.5	0	1.5	1.9	1.3	1.3	3.4	1.8	1.8
	NBC	3.9	0.5	0.5	1.7	0	2.5	2.3	2.7	1.9
Southeast Asia	ABC	53.0	40.6	10.9	26.3	9.6	9.1	6.0	11.8	21.9
and Pacific	CBS	54.2	40.5	7.2	28.9	7.1	9.6	7.1	11.0	20.5
	NBC	56.0	44.0	5.0	25.9	7.8	9.6	7.4	11.9	21.7

Table 2.9 (Continued)

Region	Network	1972	1973	1974	1975	1976	1977	1978	1979	1972–79
		%	%	%	%	%	%	%	%	%
East Asia	ABC	16.4	10.6	7.1	6.5	13.4	11.3	8.6	14.3	11.2
	CBS	13.3	7.7	7.7	8.0	12.1	10.8	10.0	12.5	10.4
	NBC	13.1	7.7	8.9	7.1	12.3	9.1	9.7	13.8	10.3
Latin America	ABC	2.6	5.8	10.9	7.3	15.8	13.0	14.1	18.1	10.8
	CBS	5.8	8.2	7.2	8.4	10.4	14.6	14.2	15.1	10.7
	NBC	4.6	3.8	9.4	8.0	11.2	14.1	14.0	13.4	9.8
Canada	ABC	0.4	1.9	3.2	1.2	3.8	3.0	2.6	0	1.9
	CBS	1.7	1.0	2.1	1.1	3.3	3.8	3.8	2.6	2.4
	NBC	1.2	1.9	1.5	1.7	3.4	3.5	3.1	2.3	2.3
N = (stories)	ABC	268	207	156	247	209	230	234	238	1789
	CBS	240	195	195	263	240	240	239	272	1884
	NBC	259	209	202	239	179	199	257	261	1805

a Measured by the percentage of sampled international stories in which one or more nations from the region are mentioned.

quite extensively covered by the networks. Because of the close political and economic ties between Western Europe and the United States, its coverage on network television remains relatively stable and at a high level from year to year.

The second most extensively covered region of the world was the Middle East, where the United States also has strong political and economic interests. Coverage of this region increased sharply with the October 1973 war and continued at a high level over the eight years, especially after Sadat's trip to Jerusalem (Bagnied & Schneider, 1981) and the Camp David Summit of 1978 (Spragens, Chapter 6). Coverage of the area increased further in 1979 with the start of the crisis in Iran that would lead to the seizure of American hostages near the year's end.

Southeast Asia and the Pacific received a great amount of attention during the 1972–79 period. Much of that coverage is accounted for by the Vietnam War, which dominated the news in 1972 and 1973, and again received extensive coverage in 1975, the year of US withdrawal from Vietnam. While the networks devoted some attention to the refugee problem in Southeast Asia in 1979, the massive loss of life in Cambodia under the Pol Pot regime between 1975 and 1978 was largely ignored (see Adams and Joblove's chapter in this volume).

Network television devotes more attention to the USSR than to any other single nation in the world (other than the United States). This attention almost totally explains the relatively consistent pattern of coverage for Eastern Europe and the USSR. East Germany, Yugoslavia, and Poland did receive some coverage during 1972–79, although coverage of other Eastern European nations was almost nonexistent.

The relatively stable pattern of coverage given to East Asia and the Pacific corresponds with US political and economic ties to that region. China and Japan (and to a lesser extent the two Koreas) each receive some significant attention. News appearances of East Asian nations are especially likely to be linked to an official state visit or some other major political occurrence.

Latin American coverage by the networks showed a gradual increase over the 1972–79 period. With the exception of Mexico, coverage of most Latin American nations came in response to crises. (See Chapter 5 by Morales in this volume.)

Sub-Saharan Africa received very little coverage during the first half of the 1972–79 period. Then, in response to crises such as those in Angola and Rhodesia, its coverage increased sharply in 1976 through 1978. Over the long term, the networks devote scant attention to Africa; but in response to major conflict or unrest, they commit some resources to the Sub-Saharan part of the continent.

The nations of South Asia rarely appeared on the network early evening news broadcasts during the eight-year period sampled. This region of the world received the lowest level of attention of any area. Although not a comparable "region," Canada was also given relatively little coverage.

The patterns discussed above show up clearly in Table 2.10, which divides the sample of news broadcasts into two equal, four-year time periods. It shows the increased coverage of the Middle East, Africa, and Latin America, as well as the dramatic decrease in coverage of Southeast Asia and the Pacific.

Table 2.10
Coverage of Major Geographical Regions,
1972–75 and 1976–79, for All Networks[a]

Region	1972–75	1976–79
	%	%
Eastern Europe and USSR	16.3	18.9
Western Europe	30.1	30.0
Middle East	19.5	30.1
Africa (Sub-Sahara)	2.3	13.3
South Asia	1.8	2.2
Southeast Asia and Pacific	34.2	9.1
East Asia	9.7	11.5
Latin America	6.6	14.1
Canada	1.6	3.5
N = (stories)	2680	2798

[a] Measured by the percentage of sampled stories in which one or more nations from the region are mentioned, percentages sum to more than 100 percent.

TELEVISION'S WORLDVIEW

The findings of this study of over 5,400 international news stories over an eight-year period both refute and confirm some of the conventional claims about network coverage of global affairs. Gans (1979) and others who say that US television news is heavily domestic are exaggerating. However much such a characterization might have been true in the late 1960s (the period from which Gans draws most of his observations), it is no longer accurate.

Rather than being relegated to a minor segment of the newscasts, international stories have assumed a prominent place on the network agenda. Over the 1976–79 period, all three networks gave an average of 40 percent of their news time to international affairs—a substantial figure that reflects consistent nightly coverage, and not infrequent, isolated stories. International news coverage increased steadily on all networks during the 1970's. By 1978, half of all the news time on CBS weeknight newscasts was devoted to international news.

To characterize broadly the entire period, the typical newscast was found to include about two foreign video reports (with each usually over two minutes in length) along with two domestic video stories about international affairs (with each also running over two minutes long). Later in the typical newscast, the anchor was likely to read about three studio reports on international news, averaging just over half a minute each. This again adds up to a sizeable share of nightly news attention. While obviously on some nights the amount of world news was less, on other nights the proportion would be even greater.

To characterize further the flavor of typical international news, the data suggest which countries and regions were likely to have been mentioned in the late 1970's. This average composite newscast would have been likely to have one or two stories involving the Soviet Union, two stories about the Middle East (probably in reference to Israel, Egypt, Lebanon, and/or Iran), two stories involving Western European countries (most likely Great Britain, France, or Italy), one briefer story mentioning Latin America (Cuba being most commonly included), another briefer story related to Sub-Saharan Africa (perhaps about Rhodesia or South Africa), and possibly a story including East Asia (usually China or Japan). (Regions and countries will, of course, overlap into some of the same stories.)

By contrast, in the early 1970's, the newscast would have been likely to carry two or three stories from Southeast Asia. Then, it would have been much less likely to include news about countries in Africa or Latin America, and more likely to include one story (rather than two stories) about the Middle East.

Again, the findings of this study indicate that a reconsideration of some past opinion about television news is in order. While TV news was still a long way from providing "extensive" coverage of much of the Third World, there was a clear trend toward increased coverage of several regions. By the late 1970's, television's "neglect" of certain regions was not as great as many people still believed. Over the time span analyzed, there was a definite trend toward increased attention to Africa, the Middle East, and Latin America, although coverage of Southeast Asia decreased and attention to South Asia remained low.

A substantial part of these shifts reflected coverage of crises in some, but not all, of the nations within a region. Given the nature of Latin American and African crisis coverage during the late 1970's, those regions could again fall to lower levels of coverage, barring a concerted effort by the networks to offer broad and sustained coverage. On the other hand,

Western Europe and the Soviet Union received relatively high, "steady-state" levels of coverage during the 1970's. These areas, along with the Middle East, would seem unlikely to slip to lower amounts of coverage because of direct US involvement and interests, and because of established newsgathering practices; their coverage would be subject to still further increases in times of crisis.

Despite its crisis-orientation, television's increased attention to previously overlooked parts of the Third World was an important development. If the patterns of the 1980's reflect the tendencies of the 1970's, US network television news may increasingly broadcast more broad-based and worldwide coverage, as well as more total international coverage overall.

REFERENCES

Adams, William C. and Phil Heyl. 1981. From Cairo to Kabul with the Networks, 1972–1980. In William C. Adams, ed., *Television Coverage of the Middle East*. Norwood, N.J.: Ablex, 1–39.

Altheide, David L. 1981. Iran vs. US TV News: The Hostage Story Out of Context. In William C. Adams, ed., *Television Coverage of the Middle East*. Norwood, N.J.: Ablex, 128–157.

―――― and Robert P. Snow. 1979. *Media Logic*. Beverly Hills, Calif.: Sage.

Bagnied, Magda and Steven Schneider. 1981. Sadat Goes to Jerusalem: Televised Images, Themes, and Agenda. In William C. Adams, ed., *Television Coverage of the Middle East*. Norwood, N.J.: Ablex, 53–66.

Batscha, Robert M. 1975. *Foreign Affairs News and the Broadcast Journalist*. New York: Praeger.

Broadcasting from Space. 1970. UNESCO Reports and Papers on Mass Communication, No. 60. Paris: UNESCO.

Cohen, Bernard. 1963. *The Press and Foreign Policy*. Princeton, N.J.: Princeton University Press.

COMSAT Seventeenth Annual Report to the President and the Congress. 1980. Washington, D.C.: Communications Satellite Corporation.

Elliott, Philip and Peter Golding. 1974. Mass Communication and Social Change: The Imagery of Development and the Development of Imagery. In Emanuel de Kadt and Gavin Williams, eds., *Sociology and Development*. London: Tavistock.

Epstein, Edward J. 1973. *News From Nowhere*. New York: Random House.

Frank, Robert S. 1973. *Message Dimensions of Television News*. Lexington, Mass.: D.C. Heath.

Gans, Herbert J. 1979. *Deciding What's News*. New York: Pantheon.

Harris, Phil. 1976. Selective Images: An Analysis of the West African Wire Service of an International News Agency. Paper presented at a conference of the International Association for Mass Communication Research, University of Leicester.

Hulten, O. 1973. The INTELSAT System: Some Notes on Television Utilization of Satellite Technology. *Gazette* 19 (1): 29–37.

Katz, Elihu and George Wedell. 1978. *Broadcasting in the Third World*. Cambridge, Mass.: Harvard University Press.

Larson, James F. 1978. America's Window on the World: US Network Television Coverage of International Affairs, 1972–1976. Ph.D. dissertation, Stanford University.

―――― and Andy Hardy. 1977. International Affairs Coverage on Network Television News: A Study of News Flow. *Gazette* 23 (4).

Many Voices, One World: Report by the International Commission for the Study of Communication Problems. 1980. Paris: UNESCO.

Patterson, Thomas E. 1978. Assessing Television Networks: Future Directions in Content Research. In William C. Adams and Fay Schreibman, eds., *Television Network News: Issues in Content Research*. Washington, D.C.: School of Public and International Affairs, George Washington University, 177–187.

Quint, Bert. 1980. Dateline Tehran: There Was a Touch of Fear. *TV Guide* (April 5): 6–12.

Roper, Burns W. 1979. *Public Perceptions of Television and Other Mass Media*. New York: Television Information Office.

Schramm, Wilbur. 1964. *Mass Media and National Development*. Stanford, Calif.; Stanford University Press.

———. 1968. *Communication Satellites for Education, Science, and Culture*. UNESCO Reports and Papers on Mass Communication, no. 53. Paris: UNESCO.

Tuchman, Gaye. 1978. *Making News*. New York: Free Press.

Tunstall, Jeremy. 1977. *The Media are American*. New York: Columbia University Press.

UNESCO General Conference Nineteenth Session Records, Nairobi. 1976. 19C/91, Annex I, 3, 4.

PART

THIRD
WORLD

3

THE THIRD WORLD ON TV NEWS: WESTERN WAYS OF SEEING THE "OTHER"

PETER DAHLGREN
WITH
SUMITRA CHAKRAPANI

The professed purpose of network television news is journalistic—to inform viewers of the day's events. Most viewers, however, are really not left with "information" in the usual sense of the term. A variety of research suggests that the majority of viewers recall at best only isolated fragments of a program they have just watched (Robinson, 1980; Neuman, 1976; Katz et al., 1977). This is not to say they are left with nothing. On the contrary, the significance of TV news far exceeds that of a daily dispenser of discrete informative messages. As several recent studies have suggested, what TV news conveys to its audience is sets of images, impressions, and stereotypes (e.g., Sahin et al., Chapter 13 in this book; Gans, 1979; Aronowitz & Haik, 1980). Treated cumulatively, the programs give rise to a particular symbolic universe, a relatively stable and recognizable "world of TV news," that is self-contained, coherent, and proceeds according to its own internal logic and dynamics.

This world of TV news tends to frame social reality in specific ways. The homogeneous structure of formats and the recurring narrative features are derived from and reinforce certain culturally assumed notions of "news." The topics selected and excluded, the points of view accorded and denied legitimacy, and indeed the implicit concept of what is to be included in the realm of "politics"—all are definitive features of the world of TV news. The upshot of this is that over time—again the cumulative phenomenon is significant—TV news promotes certain "ways of seeing" the world,[1] and thus, of necessity, excludes other ways.

---

[1] The phrase comes from John Berger—*Ways of Seeing* (1973).

The standard journalistic criteria of objectivity and impartiality are of course important but less relevant to our purpose. Rather, our concern with the worldview of TV news is to treat it as an agency of citizen socialization, and less as a source of information. Ways of seeing are a reflection of existing social practices and commitments, and they serve as a force for the promotion of those commitments.

In analyzing TV news programs as continual promoters of specific ways of seeing—as contributors to the construction of a particular social reality—we look to features of programs that are consistent and patterned. The social importance of TV news is found in those elements that define it as a cultural genre or, phrased differently, constitute the essential components of the world of TV news. From this perspective, TV news is treated as a daily recurring cultural artifact that not only defines our concept of news but also reveals in part who we are as a society and how we think. In turn, it contributes to the reproduction of these traits. This "cultural revelation" becomes all the more marked when the world of TV news shows us societies other than our own.

As recent studies have confirmed, television news coverage of the Third World is at best sparse. Reporting on Middle East conflicts is one of the few major exceptions (Adams, 1981). Hester (1978) concluded from his research, "Many portions of the globe scarcely existed as far as viewers of US network TV news were concerned. Such areas. . . included Latin America, much of Africa, much of Eastern Europe, and large parts of Asia." James Larson's extensive survey of 1972–79 international news in the second chapter of this volume supports similar conclusions. The sparsity of the coverage is clearly of critical interest, but that is not our prime concern here. Starting with the fact that there is little reporting from most parts of the Third World, our concern shifts to the content of the little coverage that does appear.

In what follows, we report the findings of our examination of the portrayals of the Third World which are characteristic of network TV news. We excluded stories in which the United States was a direct or overt participant, in order to focus on news reports dealing entirely with Third World countries.

Since most of such reports concern political crises, we selected a variety of such major events from 1977 through 1979. Using the *Television News Index and Abstracts* of Vanderbilt University, we were able to compile a list of all network stories broadcast during the time of the selected crisis. In addition, as we surveyed the *Index* listings around the time of the respective crises, we came upon random, isolated news items about other political events in the Third World. While not necessarily related to the larger "crises," such stories also represent reporting about the Third World, and were added to the data base. After examining the abstracts of these stories, we selected 42 news stories of varying length to obtain as diverse a picture as possible. Vanderbilt loaned these stories on audio cassettes and they were transcribed as texts. Although an analysis of the video portion would certainly enhance this research (Adams, 1978), based on our own and others' research, we do not believe it would significantly alter the finding of this study.

Data were drawn from all three networks. Quantitative studies indicated no significant differences in their volume of Third World coverage (Larson, 1978). In terms of journalistic criteria, there may be small differences in their handling of specific stories. On the level of cultural perception, however, we could find no reason for treating them separately. All three networks contribute essentially the same elements that define the world of TV news.

The countries and time periods of the news reports selected were as follows:

Pakistan	March & July 1977
Ethiopia/Eritrea	October 1977, March & June 1978
Philippines	April 1978
Afghanistan	April & May 1978
Peru	May 1978
Guatemala	June 1978
Bolivia	July 1978
Nicaragua	July 1979
El Salvador	October 1979
Central African Republic	September 1979

Given the nature of Third World coverage, as well as our selection process, the number and extent of reports on each country varied. Several countries—Peru, Guatemala, Bolivia, and Central African Republic—were represented by only one or two stories, while a few countries had numerous stories. Reporting on Nicaragua, for instance, was comparatively extensive and included background pieces as well.

As stated, this project examines and provides a reading of this coverage with the intention of probing the ways TV news promotes seeing the Third World. "Ways of seeing" is actually a two-dimensional concept. It refers both to the nature of the world created by the cultural object or text in question as well as the relationship which this "world" fosters between itself and its audience. Thus, the goal is to illuminate the prevailing features of the Third World as shown by the world of TV news and to specify how the audience is situated in relation to it.

Examination of the broadcast material led to the identification of three major themes or motifs in coverage of the Third World; each motif in turn has a number of sub-motifs. Following the methodology of structural anthropology (Levi-Straus, 1959), we can treat each of these motifs as evoking its own bipolar opposite. The meaning of each motif thus resides in the tension between its actual and its implied negation or antithesis. These motifs, together with their implied bipolar opposites, constitute the decisive elements that characterize Third World reporting.

Each major motif and its opposite gives rise to a primary feature that defines the relationship, fostered by the world of TV news, between the audience and the portrayed Third World. These features, which we call dispositional orientations, collectively situate the audience in a particular manner toward the Third World. Any one story may contain more than one motif and may evoke more than one dispositional orientation. The point is that, as a whole, the reporting makes available a particular matrix of vision through which to see the Third World. These categories may be summarized as follows:

Table 3.1

Definitive Motifs and Sub-motifs	Implied Bipolar Opposite	Dispositional Orientation
Social Disorder	Order/Stability	Irony
Political violence	Harmony	
Political subversion	Redemption	
Military combat	Peace	
Flawed Development	Successful Development	Skepticism
Governmental corruption	Ethical government	
Human rights abuses	Humanitarianism	
Communism	Capitalism	
Primitivism	Modernism	Fascination
Exoticism	Familiar	
Barbarism	Civilized	

We will discuss each of these motifs and provide examples from the broadcasts. As we shall see, the implied bipolar opposite of each motif is not just an abstract construction which provides a logical resolution to a theoretical tension. These bipolarities capture some specific touchstones within the Western culture's perception of itself and its relation to the Third World. The dispositional orientations evoked by the motifs reveal modes of consciousness which are historically very well grounded.

VIOLENCE

Disorder looms eternal in the Third World, according to the cumulative imagery that emerges from network news reports. The disorder motif, with sub-motifs of violence/unrest, subversion, and combat, is the most pervasive of the three major motifs. Indeed, the other two major motifs, flawed development and primitivism, often appear almost ancillary to disorder. Let us examine a few examples of the presentation of disorder in the Third World to establish its significance before turning to its implied bipolar opposite, stability, and to a discussion of the accompanying dispositional orientation of irony. In several ways, the following story is typical:

> Seventeen military police guards were killed and six others were wounded last night in Guatemala City, when a land mine hanging from a tree was exploded as their truck passed. The men had been on guard duty, at factories. A leftist group called the Guatemala Workers Party claimed responsibility, presumably in partial retaliation for the reported killing last week by the army of more than 100 Indians squatting on farmlands (ABC, 6/15/78).

This story was not part of an ongoing crisis coverage of Guatemala; there were no other stories on Guatemala for weeks before or after this report. Although the story ostensibly appears without a history, it is quite comprehensible. Like so many TV news stories, it requires virtually no prior knowledge to be readily assimilated.

The viewer has little difficulty making sense of the story because the narration is comprised of familiar elements. They signal that this is a routine story of political violence in Latin America. Elements of the narrative require no reflective analysis; rather, they merely ask the viewer to retrieve a few standard images and stereotypes from his or her existing bank of stock perceptions. "Military police guards" are killed and wounded by a bomb planted by "a leftist group." As a dramatic narrative, the axis of conflict lies simply with the manifestation of political violence, signaling social disorder. The story reconfirms impressions of life in Latin America, and succeeds in terms of the general logic and dictates of television: it is easily understood, demands little of the viewer, and follows a narrative structure.

Important elements in the story contribute to the motif of social disorder. Interplay between foreground and background in the story is a key feature. The act of violence, the most extreme version of social disorder, is in the foreground and is the central point of the story. The act has a dramatic quality by virtue of the element of surprise: it intrudes here on everyday life in a manner which is seemingly both random and routine. We gather this from the background sketched in the course of the narrative. This background, which the viewer is invited to take for granted, helps situate the act and give it meaning. Through the act, we understand and accept the background; but, we are not given the means to understand the act or the setting in any context *beyond* themselves.

The background indicates that "the men had been on guard duty at factories." Factories apparently require military police to guard them in the unstable countries of Latin America. The guarding of factories is in itself not of any interest in the context of the story, but merely confirms instability. Who committed the act? "A leftist group called the Guatemala Worker's Party." Like military police guards, the "leftists" are but vague stock characters lurking in the background. They plant bombs to kill the military police, who appear to be defenders of the social order. Viewers may well surmise that it is as a result of these trouble-makers that the factories needed guarding in the first place. The ongoing conflict between "leftists" and "military police guards" is a standard conflict which is part of the context for the violent action highlighted in the foreground.

Another part of the background emerges in the reference to the presumed motivation for the bombing, namely the alleged slaughter of more than 100 Indians squatting on farmlands. (This attribution of a motive is a bit unusual because such acts are often treated as "irrational" and "senseless.") This piece of information on the one hand adds to our understanding of why the bomb was placed. On the other hand, it leaves a curious distinction between the narrative's focus of attention on the violence in the foreground and all that it takes for granted in the background.

In the report, the background—the guarding of factories, the Guatemala Worker's Party, the land question, the Indians and the alleged massacre—is left unexplained. Viewer attention to these topics is surpressed in favor of the dramatic pivot of the action and immediacy of the violence itself. Using violence as a frame for the violent act becomes a tautology. The explanatory process is circular: A violent act occurs because the situation is unstable. It is unstable because there are violent acts. Foreground explains background, which in turn explains foreground. To break this chain and leave the viewer with a new understanding, the narrative would have to offer *political* explanations of the background elements, as well as the bombing itself. The guards, the leftists, the land question, and the Indians would have to be located in such contexts as Guatemalan politics and economy, class conflict, and militarism.

As the story stands, a random act of violence is outlined. It disrupted the flow of everyday life. According to the statistics provided, the act was serious, but not catastrophic. It had a quirky element or two (e.g., a land mine hanging from a tree). Yet, in the context of the background, this random act of violence becomes routine, because of the sense of general instability. The event then is not of any real importance as "news." It tells us nothing new, but instead serves to remind the viewer that all is "normal" in this country in Latin America; nothing has changed. Social disorder and political violence continue.

This brief news story shows not only avoidance of politics and history as means of understanding events, but also a reification of violence. Violence, in the context of this narrative, becomes an actor in an ongoing drama. Violence embodies itself and acts through the characters of news stories. Almost as if the characters are possessed by a demon, they act out the intentions of this demonic spirit rather than acting as independent historical subjects.

This treatment of violence imposes a coherence of sorts on events and rapidly becomes a unifying motif for many reports on the Third World. Consider these examples:

> Violence marred Pakistan's general election today. Eight persons were killed, 150 others injured during the clashes between opposing political groups... (CBS, 3/7/77)
>
> A communist-called national strike began in Peru today, and there was violence. Demonstrators, protesting government-ordered price increases for food, fuel and transportation, blocked roads and hurled rocks at traffic... (CBS, 5/22/78)

In both cases, violence is the focus of brief news stories. Each narrative positions the violence in the foreground, while the social and political factors which it expresses recede to the background. Viewer interest is situated with the fact of the occurrence of the violence. The immediate motives offered by the story, as with the first example, provide explanation only within the terms of the story. In one case, violence is said to result from "clashes between opposing political groups," and in the other, because of "a communist-called national strike." Again, these are formula background explanations. While they are adequate to make some sense of the event, they do not help to understand the social context giving rise to such events in the first place. Each story only further confirms the existence of social disorder in the Third World without adding any insight.

Interest in violence is frequently expressed in terms of a quantitative rendering of its effect. The measure of violence becomes a barometer of the extent of the disorder which prevails:

> That successful Afghanistan coup last week by pro-communist army officers apparently was bloodier than first reported. Western newsmen finally reaching the capital say as many as three to ten thousand persons died in the fighting. (CBS, 5/2/70)

In answering the question, "How bloody was the fighting?," this story underscores the image of a furious, unleashed Nature acting on society; people become its agents. Once again, we have a routine background—a "coup" by "pro-communist army officers." This aids in understanding the immediate cause of the violence in the story, but does not help in understanding why such events occur.

The stories cited above were all very short news items. No doubt their brevity accentuates the imagery of violence as a force beyond human intentions. Linguistically, such formulations as "violence marred..." locate "violence" as the active subject of a sentence. At issue is not just a question of newspeople's habituation to certain patterns of phrasing, but rather the way TV news refracts social reality. This prevailing view of violence is present even in the longer, more detailed stories. A two-minute story on the situation in Nicaragua, describing the advance of the Sandinista guerrillas, dwells on the details of disruption. Near the beginning of the report, the newsman describes the effect of the conflict:

> ...This is all there is left at one of Managua's supermarkets. Everything has been looted.... Because of situations like this, the food shortage has reached crisis proportions.... At the few places with food to sell...there are virtual mob scenes, and the guards have to push hard on the gates to keep out the crowds... (CBS, 7/3/79)

This account displays the severity of the situation. An empty, looted supermarket is a perfect indicator of the traumatic dislocation of everyday life. And the cause? Clearly this is a consequence of the revolution, but *why* is there such a conflict? The report concludes:

> ...And in the shattered barrios of Managua, almost everyone agrees that the worst may not be over. People believe that the Sandinista guerrillas may have withdrawn for now, but they'll be back for another round of war.

Once again, a circular explanation is presented: There was violence because violence was sought. Our primary concern is not this failure of formal logic; it is rather the implicit way of seeing that emerges in this manner of framing events. Violent events occur because these societies are unstable and plagued by violence. Violence comes to supercede human motive and volition as the subject; it is "violence," not people, acting in many of the stories.

This violence is a very particular kind. It is overt, blatant, and often irrational. That the Sandinista guerrillas will be "back for another round of war" suggests that they enjoy fighting, an indication of their lack of reason. The portrayal of violence has an immediate ideological dimension (see Chomsky & Herman, 1979). Violence is generally perpetrated upon the defenders of the status quo. The systematic coercion and terror that many of these governments use to maintain their power is usually not termed "violence." A whole vocabulary of euphemisms has been substituted.

Beyond the implicit commitment to one side or another that may dwell within the news reports, attributing instability and disorder as inherent traits of these societies (with violence as an active agent shaping the flow of events) results in a virtual ontology of the Third World. Devoid of social, political, and historical causation, the manifestations of disorder and violence take on the quality of eternal essences which define the nature of these countries. "That's just the way they are."

Much of the meaning of the social disorder theme can be understood using the concept of bipolar opposites, which structural anthropology has developed as a paradigm for analyzing myth. The bipolar opposite of the motif of social disorder is, of course, social order, or stability. The sub-motif of violence is contrasted with harmony and the resolution of conflict by "civilized" means.

What develops is a case of "them" and "us" which has long historical roots. Namely, "they," the people and societies of the Third World, appear as unstable and prone to violence. Incessant glimpses of disorder and violence serve as a reminder that these societies continue to act out their essential character; they are virtually driven by violence. "We," on the other hand, the industrialized West, are typified by order and stability, a higher form of civilization.

It must be underscored here that this way of seeing the Third World and the West does not function on an analytic level, but rather on a mythic one. The perspective is more unconscious than conscious; it hovers in cultural space, ready to be appropriated in thinking about developing nations. This bipolarity does not suggest that the West is devoid of disorder and violence; TV news itself makes that a difficult illusion to maintain. Instead, this mythic rendering serves as a prism through which to view disorder and violence. In the Third World, it expresses a basic essence. In the West, it signals imperfection, deviance, a lapse of the West's genuine tradition and destiny.

The West stands for rationality: science over magic, purpose over activity, Man over Nature. Against this idealization looms the arationality of the primitive: magic, activity without purpose, Nature dominant over Man. Moreover, the "primitive" is exemplified by forms of human association traditionally held to be threatening to the smooth functioning of societies predicated upon market logic: loyalties of tribe and region, collective and spontaneous action, prioritizing labor's meaningfulness rather than its market value, and so on.

The origins of such perceptions can be traced back to the colonial and imperial legacy which Europe and America imposed on these societies. For centuries, "the native" has been seen as sorely deficient in civilization, particularly when his behavior was at odds with Western economic interests. In transforming Third World societies, often by force, into instruments to serve their will, Westerners reassured themselves of their cultural superiority.

News, as a form of social knowledge, is inevitably ahistorical in its orientation; it is not to be expected to remind the audience that the instability of the Third World is at least in part due to the West's role over several centuries. TV news merely draws upon and contributes to a convenient cultural amnesia that it did not create. Before returning to the role of TV at the end of this chapter, let us briefly look at the other two sub-motifs of social disorder: political subversion and military combat.

SUBVERSION AND COMBAT

Political subversion functions to cast the Third World country in question in a slightly different light. While still "primitive," perhaps, the axis of the dramatic movement shifts to imply that the country is making some progress toward development and modernism (i.e., becoming more like "us"), but is threatened by a pollution of external origin. The obvious ideological effect, similar to that of the portrayal of violence, is to invite the viewer to sympathize with those groups that stand for stability and order (officialdom, the military, etc.) against those who would upset it (leftists, guerrillas, revolutionaries, etc.). But again, the way of seeing goes deeper than partisanship for the status quo. In the context of the dramas, the natives are cast as victims, with the implication that they need Western help. In this sub-motif, social disorder is not so much their fault (except that, being "primitive," they are vulnerable) but is to be blamed on conspiratorial communist strategies. In the drama, communism does not represent primitivism; it expresses instrumental rationality (goal-oriented), albeit evil. The helpless, naive natives need deliverance from communism, much as they previously needed the salvation of Christianity.

The bipolar opposite of this subversion becomes redemption, and America and the West are the redeemers. In a long analytical piece, unusual for TV news in attempting to trace the history of a specific crisis, the anchorman clarifies the United States' concern with Nicaragua:

> ...Some American officials are now predicting the ouster of President Anastasio Somosa and his replacement with a rebel junta with a strong Marxist coloration. Why is the United States worried about a country the size of Wisconsin with a couple of million people? Well... mainly because the rebels have received some help from Cuba. It is possible that Nicaragua may soon be in the communist camp. How did all this come about? Richard Vilariani has all the answers... (NBC, 7/6/79)

The child is in danger of being duped by evil outsiders, and thus cannot really be held accountable. It could be said that such coverage contains a tension or split. On one side, disorder and violence emanate from the essential character of their societies; on the other side, it is a product of external agents. But this is not really problematic. Ways of seeing are not constructed in accordance with logical coherence, but emerge out of cultural perception. Such perception can both express and conceal contradiction. This dual vision articulates both the West's need to see itself as superior to Third World societies, and to see Western intervention in these societies as beneficial for them.

Historical references did find their way into this report, however. In the long news analysis of Nicaragua which was quoted in part above, the reporter comments:

> U.S. marines landed periodically in Nicaragua. . . to put down political disorders and to make the country safe for American investment. . . the dynastic rule is the product of the U.S. occupation. . .

Such revelations of historical accountability on TV news are new and still rare, but do suggest that ways of seeing cannot exist totally independent of changes in the world they encounter and attempt to grasp.

Military combat, the final sub-motif of social disorder, is not so specifically anchored in the historical relations between the West and the Third World. Portrayals of combat strengthen the imagery of disorder—from "unstable" to "war-torn." But reports of combat tend to diffuse the cultural references of "us and them," and instead become a more generalized polarity between "here and there." Viewers are provided a self-contained spectacle, often fixing their attention on details of the action:

> Cuban soldiers are backing Ethiopian forces, but so far they apparently have not been fighting the Eritrean rebels. . . . Despite the difficulty at keeping their men supplied, the Eritreans are still holding the Ethiopians three weeks after the offensive began. The Cubans. . . remain inside Asmara, uncertain whether the guerrillas they once trained can now be defeated. . . (ABC, 6/15/78)

The "play by play" aura is like a sports report, and interest resides within the boundaries of the competition. The participants are not necessarily lacking in rationality; they utilize instrumental reason to achieve the goal of winning.

While the West can identify with this trait, and while war is not unique to the Third World, the net effect remains one of enhancing the primary motif of societies in disorder.

IRONY AS REASSURANCE

We have already referred to the historical roots of the West's superiority complex over the Third World. The next step is to understand how these TV news reports situate the viewer in a dispositional orientation of irony toward the Third World. The concept of "irony" is used here in the sense that Northrop Frye (1957) and other rhetorical critics (Chesbro & Hamsher, 1976) utilize the term. It refers to a relationship between the audience of a drama and the main protagonist in that drama, where the audience is situated in a position of superior knowledge, competence or insight vis á vis the protagonist. While it may take comic expression (in the recognition that we know something he does not know), the hallmark is not comedy but the audience's awareness of the protagonist's relative inferiority in regard to some specific criteria or dramatic circumstance.

Each of the implied bipolar opposites addresses the West's understanding of itself as contrasted with the image of the Third World. Their political violence is unfortunate; Westerners may feel sorry about it, deplore it, but such events typify the Third World. Reports of political subversion underscore their victimization at the hands of diabolical agents, but also emphasize their helplessness and need for Western support. The spectacle of combat, similarly, further illustrates their disorder, and our stability.

Psychoanalytic theory holds that individuals may project onto others qualities that they despise but subconsciously fear is lurking within themselves. The effect may be one of catharsis: to attribute to the "other" such qualities may offer a purging relief. This does not mean that such qualities are not indeed present in the Other, but only that to choose to define the Other as embodying these traits is to some extent an expression of subjective need, not objective appraisal.

So it may well be with the collective psyche of the West, still struggling to come to terms with Freud's basic insights. The notion of "rational man" is a Western cultural construct, one which is becoming more difficult to maintain as evidence suggests that its usefulness is approaching a twilight. The idealization of primitive natives can be seen not only as an ideological corollary of imperialism, but as a psychocultural projection. In this projection, Western man attributes to the native his fears about the potentially irrational nature raging within himself. The "native" represents Western man's own repressed demonic alter ego. Projecting such qualities on the native serves as a form of cultural reassurance.

While irony may prevail as the major pillar of the dispositional orientation, it is not the only one. Skepticism and fascination are also elements of the ways of seeing the Third World. But let us first turn to their respective motifs.

FLAWED DEVELOPMENT

A dispositional orientation of irony need not by any means exclude sympathy. Sympathy is present in the understanding that many of these societies are truly making efforts to develop along the models offered by the West. In the news reports, several key terms recur regularly to symbolize this march toward westernization, in particular, "reforms" and "elections." These words often take on a purely evocative rhetorical function. Reference to their occurrence in a Third World country signals a positive step. Reports may sometimes reify events, even when the social reality ultimately belies the ostensible aims of the formalities.

News stories usually make it clear that the road to development along Western models is a difficult one. Chief among the obstacles which may flaw this march of progress is, aside from the disorder we have discussed, the corruption of local officials. Human rights abuses and communism also feature as impediments.

> National Assembly elections were held in the Philippines today, and were supposed to be the first step from martial law to democracy. . . . It was a most unusual election. Leading the government party ticket was Imelda Marcos, who just happens to be the wife of the President. And the party's campaign manager was none other than President Marcos himself, who automatically becomes Prime Minister in the new Parliament.

The tone is sarcastic, which is not really representative. Rather, the most recognizable element here is that the story reminds us that the epic road to Western-style democracy is hindered by corruption in these societies.

At times, corruption serves as an explanatory device for the familiar social disorder. This explanation was circular in that corruption then becomes an instance of the same general instability. For example:

> Unofficial reports from Pakistan say at least 7 people were killed in widespread violence during a general strike yesterday. The strike was called to protest alleged rigging of the recent elections won by the government of Prime Minister Bhutto. (CBS, 3/27/77)

In the West, governmental corruption tends to have a person-specific aura to it; the focus is on the individuals who commit the deeds. Removal of these individuals, by implication, restores the integrity of the system. Corruption in the Third World takes on more of a systemic quality, for two reasons. First, the reporting is much less person-oriented. The actors in the stories tend to be faceless abstractions or collectivities; the dramas are less "hero-centered" than political reports about our own societies (Smith, 1979). Secondly, there is the ready association of "corruption" with the well established qualities of instability and underdevelopment. Third World leaders are seen as not being sufficiently sophisticated to resist such temptations, which stand in the way of orderly government.

Nobody would deny that corruption is indeed rampant in many of these countries. The issue is not factuality but ways of seeing. Corruption, as it takes on an ontological quality, again becomes associated with the essence of these people. Once a reasonable level of order is attained, further development is blocked for reasons having to do with innate character. The dispositional orientation which is evoked is skepticism: Will they, and can they, ever really be like us? Projection again comes into play. The bipolar opposite, ethical government, is what the American audience identifies with. US lapses are sporadic, theirs are systematic.

A similar treatment characterizes human rights violations, a submotif that is of more recent origin, specifically in President Carter's initiatives to put this on the media agenda. It remains a concept highly linked to Third World societies. The term is not applied, for example, to legal or paralegal actions taken by any Western government, such as England's handling of some IRA prisoners.

This subject of "human rights violations" is also a case of changing perceptions in the light of historical developments. Past reporting rarely called attention to gross atrocities commited by many governments of the "free world," but silence on these matters becomes increasingly embarrassing and untenable. The paradox is that while such reports cause problems for US allies, they tend to reinforce the notion that it is perhaps the very nature of these societies which contributes to a flawed development:

> . . . Somoza's position was further undermined by an embarrassing loss of support from the Carter Administration which had criticized him for human rights abuses and cut off military aid. (NBC, 7/6/79)
>
> . . . Ferdinand Marcos, leader of this former American colony, wishes he had never heard of Jimmy Carter's human rights campaign. Amid American complaints that has curbed democracy in the Philippines, President Marcos has called Congressional elections, but on his own terms. . . (NBC, 4/16/78)

The ultimate obstacle to Western development remains, of course, communism. If the political violence and instability, as well as military combat, result in a Marxist or socialist oriented government, the disposition of skepticism edges toward dismissing the country altogether.

It is as if once a country is launched on this direction, US interest in it ceases:

> Afghanistan's radio reported today that the Military Revolutionary Council that took power in a coup has named a civilian as President and Prime Minister. Diplomats in India say he is general secretary of Afghanistan's Communist Party. The Soviet news agency TASS described him as an outstanding National revolutionary. (CBS, 4/30/78)

The associations that this evokes are so clear: the country is now in the Soviet orbit, and thus no longer pertinent to US concerns. With an air of finality, the viewer is virtually invited to strike this country from his or her mental map of developing countries. Its flaws become total.

PRIMITIVISM

Idealization of the primitive is implicit in much of the reporting, becoming relatively explicit only occasionally. When reports highlight overt manifestions of primitivism, they can be grouped under one of two sub-motifs, exoticism and barbarism.

If the bipolar opposite of "primitivism" can go under the rubric of "modernism," the corresponding term for "exotic" is "familiar." The exotic is unfamiliar, strange, and curious in relation to everyday reality. Mores, costume, artifact, and locale are among the indices with which the observer can record exoticism, and in so doing expropriates the native, the Other, as a source of impulses through which the observer can better define himself. The observer can also create an idealized domain for projecting fantasies that provide the completion of elements experienced as lacking in the observer's own reality.

It makes sense that historically Bohemia was essentially a product of the bourgeoisie's need for "something else." Bohemia came to symbolize those elements which the more imaginative members of the bourgeoisie found wanting in their own world: "freedom," "commitment," "creativity," "passion," and so on. In short, Bohemia was an appealing romantic "Other" to bourgeois society.

From the beginning of the colonial era, Westerners developed a similar view of the natives encountered in the colonies. This vision in the Western imagination was dualistic: it was at once attractive (such as the appeal of the natives' "naturalness," authenticity) and somewhat threatening (such as images of savagery and later of "swarming masses" unbounded by rationality). If Bohemia was at all perceived as a threat, it was at best a mild, titillating one. So long as Bohemia did not take on political overtones, it remained domesticated and safe. The primitive, on the other hand, was a more unknown quantity, but no less fascinating. In passing, it can be recalled that the basic concept of *Tarzan* expressed the Western mind's desire to resolve, in fantasy, this dualism: the character of Tarzan was a European gentleman who adopted the ways of the jungle.

Television news often shows the attractive, exotic side in reporting, which evokes *National Geographic* travelogs:

> . . . It is 200 miles, across the lowlands of Eritrea, before the terrain begins to buckle and roll into the rock strewn mountains around the province's capital of Asmara, and once within reach of the front line

around the city, the journey can only be completed on foot... (ABC, 6/15/78)

Another example from an NBC "Special Segment" on El Salvador:

...Travel books call it the jewel of the Americas, colorful markets, friendly natives, peaceful streets, and its true, until the shooting starts... (NBC, 9/20/79)

Within primitivism's dualism, the pole opposite the exotic is the barbaric, the classic image of savages living beyond the constraints of civilization:

The Associated Press reports from the central African nation of Chad that rioting gangs murdered more than 800 persons, most of them Moslems, over the weekend. The incident, 300 miles south of the capital city was described as one of Africa's bloodiest massacres in recent years... (CBS, 3/6/79)

In this story, violence itself does not evoke the aura of savagery as much as the link to the "primitive" forms of tribal wars and religious fanaticism. Savagery is violence grounded in unreason. Another example shows barbarism personified in a single character:

The Central African Empire was declared a republic today, its emperor overthrown in a bloodless coup last night. Emperor John Bedell Bokassa I: he seized the government 14 years ago and he became a spectacular and cruel dictator.... He forced palace visitors to kneel, often had prisoners beaten to death, and reportedly ordered the massacre of 200 school children because they refused to wear uniforms... (NBC, 9/21/79)

The barbaric side of the primitive is as enthralling as the exotic. This does not mean that it is portrayed as positive, but that the reaction it invites from the viewer is a fascination of the lurid, presupposing that the observer is situated at a safe distance. The voyeur of morbidity can witness primitive savagery because the events are external to his lived world and require no practical response on his part. Tourists who "take in" a spectacle of atrocity are only threatened to the extent that they may recognize this manifestation as a repressed part of their own nature.

The tripartite dispositional orientations of irony, skepticism, and fascination capture the West's historical view of the Third World, and this vision is reproduced as well in the TV news broadcasts. Irony reflects the smugness of the West's perceived position of its superiority. At the same time, fascination taps a different strain—the lure of the Other as symbolic of what the modern world denies: to be part of Nature and not external to it. The West's fascination with the Third World echoes the longing for a Paradise Lost.

HISTORICAL AND MYTHIC WAYS OF SEEING

Reports of the Third World, like the other stories on TV news, offer the viewer a form of truth, the literal truth of facticity, the hallmark of journalistic knowledge. Like all human enterprises, US journalism is sometimes more successful than others in attaining its goals. This analysis of portrayals of the Third World has assumed normal professionalism on the part of the news organizations.

Our findings suggest not criticisms of journalistic competence, but rather a view which emphasizes the historical specificity of the symbolic world of TV news, and its relation to social interests. We would be foolish to suggest that TV news should or could be at odds with the culture to which it belongs. "Objectivity" may well be a necessary fiction for the maintenance of the institution of journalism, but that in itself is not "news," nor is it the main focus of our conclusions.

Ways of seeing the social world carry with them the means for making sense of new events which take place. Thus, TV news provides us with not only reports of occurrences but also culturally-rooted explanations for interpreting them. For simplicity's sake, we may distinguish between two fundamentally different modes of seeing: mythic and historical.

Mythic modes, which prevail on TV news, provide meaning to events and affairs by stressing the eternal and recurring features of the human condition. Their hallmark is a catalog of essences—qualities in people, groups, and societies which are inherent in their biological nature. Mythic ways of seeing explain reality by an appeal to ontological properties, as exemplified by reports on political violence in the Third World.

Such forms of consciousness stand in opposition to historical ways of seeing which seek to explain social reality by analyzing the socio-political and economic factors of the past and present. Moreover, historical approaches usually assume that perceptions, attitudes, opinions, and thought are influenced by the specifics of historical circumstances. And perhaps most importantly, historical modes interpret the present as always in transition. What is now need not be in the future, because history has not come to an end. The future is open.

In most cultures, the mythic mode prevails over the historical. This is hardly surprising. The analytic quality of historical perspectives, including dialectical reflection and thinking about thought itself, situate these perspectives on the margins of society's mental activities. Television news is but one example of the prevalence of mythic consciousness, no doubt an especially strong example due to the ahistorical biases of the television medium (immediacy and action).

Ways of seeing do not express the conscious intentionality of individuals. In the context of a social system, however, ways of seeing cannot be neutral. They tend to be anchored in particular social locations, both in terms of class relations and hierarchies within a society and between societies. The prevalence of the mythic over the historical is not to be blamed on specific individuals or institutions (casting it as a problem to be dealt with by "reforms"), nor can it be dismissed as irrelevant to the social system as a whole. The mythic reactions to the Third World which TV news fosters—irony, skepticism, and fascination—are congruent with the global relations which characterize imperialism. Seen in this light, TV news evidences an implied commitment to a particular form of international order.

Studies in several Western countries over the past few years have shown that the world of TV news, in its depiction of domestic politics and social developments, tends to be hegemonic (see Schlesinger, 1979; Glasgow University Media Group, 1976, 1980; Gitlin, 1979; Dahlgren, 1980). That is to say, the ways of seeing which it offers to the public are decidedly in keeping with the needs and interests of the social classes and groups who command economic and political power. This class bias in favor of the powerful is by no means airtight or total; the contradictions of the social order have a way of manifesting themselves on the screen. We hasten to repeat that TV news' support of the minority who wield power cannot be explained as simply the product of the broadcasters' deliberate choice. However, why TV news looks the way it does, the sociology and political economy of its production, is beyond our concerns here. The question is dealt with in several recent studies (e.g., Fishman, 1980; Golding & Elliott, 1978).

The hegemonic character of TV news is a central feature of its role within Western societies. Although TV news' proximity to the political economic processes of the international arena are more remote compared to the domestic arena, its ways of seeing reveal a hegemonic approach in characterizing social and political realities between countries. The role TV news plays in reproducing those areas of popular consciousness relevant to international political economy is at least as far from being airtight or lock-step as its domestic role. As on the domestic level, however, this "leakiness" does not preclude an ultimate commitment to specific social interests. The concrete "effects" on the audience may or may not be measurable, but the extent of TV news' success as a purveyor of hegemonic ways of seeing is a different research question.

TV news' portrayals of the Third World are a political and cultural phenomenon that can be challenged, not with the expectation of changing TV news, but rather with the goal of altering our perception of it. We must look beyond the standard concepts of TV news, not because this cultural artifact, this agency of citizen socialization, is particularly inadequate in some manner, but because it is so much *more* than it presents itself to be. We need to develop new "ways of seeing" TV news, if we are to resist it.

REFERENCES

Adams, William C. 1978. Visual Analysis of Newscasts: Issues in Social Science Research. In William C. Adams and Fay Schreibman, eds., *Television Network News: Issues in Content Research.* Washington, D.C.: School of Public and International Affairs, George Washington University, 155–173.

———, ed. 1981. *Television Coverage of the Middle East.* Norwood, N.J.: Ablex.

Arnowitz, Stanley and David Haik. 1980. The Impertinence of the Image: The CBS Evening News. Paper presented at the Eastern Sociological Association annual convention, March 1980.

Berger, John. 1973. *Ways of Seeing.* New York: Penguin.

Chesbro, James and Caroline Hamsher. 1976. Communication, Values, and Popular Television Series. In H. Newcomb, ed., *Television: The Critical View.* New York: Oxford University Press.

Chomsky, Noam and Edward S. Herman. 1979. *The Washington Connection and Third World Fascism.* Boston, Mass.: South End Press.

Dahlgren, Peter. 1980. TV News and the Supression of Reflexivity. *Urban Life* 9 (July 1980): 201–16.

Fishman, Mark. 1980. *Manufacturing the News.* Austin, Tex.: University of Texas Press.

Frye, Northrop. 1957. *Anatomy of Criticism.* Princeton, N.J.: Princeton University Press.

Gans, Herbert J. 1979. *Deciding What's News.* New York: Pantheon.

Gitlin, Todd. 1979. News as Ideology and Contested Area: Toward a Theory of Hegemony, Crisis, and Opposition. *Socialist Review* (1979), 9:6.

Glasgow University Media Group. 1976. *Bad News. Vol 1.* London: Routledge and Kegan Paul.

———. 1980. *Bad News, Vol. 2.* London: Routledge and Kegan Paul.

Golding, Peter and Philip Elliott. 1978. *Making the News.* London: Longman.

Hester, Al. 1978. Five Years of Foreign News on US Television Evening Newscasts. *Gazette* 14:1.

Katz, Elihu; Hanni Adoni; and Pnina Parness. 1977. Remembering the News: What the Picture Adds to Recall. *Journalism Quarterly* 54 (Summer 1977): 231–239.

Larson, James. 1978. International Affairs Coverage on U.S. Network Television. *Journal of Communication* 29 (Spring 1979): 136–147.

Levi-Straus, Claude. 1959. *Structural Anthropology.* New York: Anchor.

Neuman, W. Russell. 1976. Patterns of Recall Among Television News Viewers. *Public Opinion Quarterly* 40 (Spring 1976): 115–123.

Robinson, John P.; Dennis K. Davis; Haluk Sahin; and Thomas O'Toole. 1980. Comprehension of Television News: How Alert is the Audience? Paper presented at the Association of Education for Journalism Convention; Boston, Mass; August 1980.

Schlesinger, Philip. 1979. *Putting 'Reality' Together.* London: Sage.

Smith, Robert Rutherford. 1979. Mythic Elements in Television News. *Journal of Communication* 29 (Winter 1979): 75–82.

4

AMERICA AND THE THIRD WORLD: A SURVEY OF LEADING MEDIA AND BUSINESS LEADERS

S. ROBERT LICHTER

Western journalists stand accused of practicing a kind of "informational imperialism" against Third World nations. Their accusers include representatives of nonaligned and Soviet-bloc nations who propose to correct "abuses" of press freedom by empowering UNESCO to regulate the flow of news and information around the world. One apparent aim of this measure would be to legitimize government control over the news.

The rationale for this proposed New World Information Order is the perceived domination of international communications by Western capitalism and its ideological vehicle, the news media. As Paul Lewis wrote (1981a):

> Advocates of a New Order complain that the business of disseminating news and information around the world is dominated by the Western Capitalist countries. These countries are the headquarters of the big news agencies, they produce the most widely circulated magazines and films, and they have the most powerful radio transmitters and the best communications satellites.
>
> As a result, supporters of a New Order say, the rest of the world gets a picture of developing and Communist countries that emphasizes their failures and plays down successes.

More specifically, the Western press is held to serve the interests of capitalism by "presenting developing countries in a bad light and suppressing their authentic voices" (Lewis, 1981b).

There is a certain irony in this criticism of the Western press. It was not so long ago, after all, that the Johnson and Nixon administrations periodically lashed out against major news organizations ranging from the television networks to the *New York Times* for their "negative" or even "anti-American" coverage of the war in Vietnam (see, e.g., Gates, 1978; Halberstam, 1979). Since that time, the Third World coverage by the major US media has been hit by attacks from both ends of the political spectrum. Thus, Gans' charge that "conservative dictators. . . are apt to be treated more kindly than socialist ones" (1978, p. 37) can be counterposed to the Reagan administration's highly publicized assertions of bias in the opposite direction (cf. Lefever, 1974). Indeed, journalists often defend their record by arguing that coverage must be balanced if it offends critics of both the right and left.

The UNESCO challenge, like those of American politicians ranging from Lyndon Johnson to Spiro Agnew, proceeds from a fairly straightforword assumption about news decisions. It is assumed that the news product is directly influenced by journalists' social and political perspectives (see Robinson, 1978). According to this interpretation, favored figures and issues receive favorable coverage, while enemies of the fourth estate can expect either bad press or no press at all. This assumption is by no means accepted without reservation by scholars (Epstein, 1973; Tuchman, 1972, 1973; Hirsch, 1977). Nonetheless, critics like those advocating a New World Information Order clearly seek to combat what they view as Western journalists' cultural and political biases against the less developed non-Western countries.

This paper attempts a partial test of their criticism, by examining the attitudes of leading US journalists toward issues concerning America's relationship toward the Third World. Because advocates of a New World Information Order imply that the American media serve the interests of corporate America, journalists' attitudes will be compared with those of top executives from *Fortune 500*-listed corporations. Thus, it becomes possible to measure both the major media's attitudes toward the Third World and their concordance with the perspective of big business.

RESEARCH PROCEDURES

Our data are drawn from a recent study of leading journalists and broadcasters at national news media outlets. As part of a much broader survey, these subjects were asked their opinions concerning America's past and present relations with the Third World. Before examining their responses, the methods used in this study will be described so that readers can gauge for themselves the significance of the results.[1]

---

[1] This survey was conducted by Response Analysis, a survey research organization, under the direction of the present author and Stanley Rothman of Smith College, the senior investigator. The study was conducted under the auspices of the Research Institute on International Change at Columbia University.

The target group of this research consisted of those individuals who constitute the "national news media elite." The media elite was defined as individuals having substantive input into news and public affairs content at the media outlets most influential in forming opinion within other national elites. The following organizations were sampled: *New York Times, Washington Post, Wall Street Journal, Time, Newsweek, U.S. News and World Report*, the news departments at the three television networks, and the news and public affairs departments of PBS and three major public broadcasting stations—WNET in New York, WGBH in Boston, and WETA in Washington, D.C. (For evidence that these outlets are the most influential see Johnstone et al., 1976; Rivers, 1965, 1971; Weiss, 1974.) Relevant personnel in the print medium were reporters, columnists, department heads, bureau chiefs, editors, and executives with responsibility for news content. In the broadcast medium, we sampled correspondents and anchors, producers, film editors, and news executives.

Selection of respondents was based on a stratified probability sampling strategy, randomizing within organizations. All subjects in the sample first received a letter from the principal investigators asking them to participate in a study of social leadership. This was followed by a telephone call from an interviewer, who arranged an appointment. Most of those contacted agreed to be interviewed and successfully completed the questionnaire. An average session lasted about 90 minutes. Interviews were conducted during the fall and winter of 1979–80.

Of the 340 journalists in the sample, 82 would not consent to be interviewed, a refusal rate of 24 percent. Another 20 could not be contacted during the time allotted for the survey. If these subjects are included as non-respondents, the completion rate drops from 76 to 71 percent of the entire sample. This is a very satisfactory response rate, especially since the interviews required substantial amounts of time and effort from a leadership group not always known for its cooperation with researchers.

As a comparison group, 216 business executives were interviewed. For this study, permission of parent companies to survey their employees was obtained. Otherwise, sampling and interview procedures followed the format used for the media sample, and the interviews were conducted during the same time period. To represent the business elite, a sample was drawn from the top and middle management of seven *Fortune 500* corporations drawn from all major sectors of the economy. The firms included a multinational oil company, a major bank, a public utility with plants in several states, a "fast-growth" company in the computer industry, a nationwide retail chain, a "high-technology" firm involved in the aerospace industry, and a highly diversified multinational corporation with concerns ranging from heavy industry to financial services. From this group, a response rate of 96 percent was obtained. (For an analysis of media and business elites' attitudes on the subject of the US commitment to Israel, see Lichter, 1981.)

MEDIA, BUSINESS, AND THE THIRD WORLD

Five items in the questionnaire were pertinent to Third World criticisms of American policy. Both journalists and businessmen were asked to respond to the following statements:

1. Without the help they have gotten from the West, Third World nations would be even worse off than they are now.
2. American economic exploitation has contributed to Third World poverty.
3. It is immoral for the United States to use so much of the world's resources while so many nations remain impoverished.
4. The main goal of US foreign policy has been to protect US business interests.
5. It is sometimes necessary for the CIA to protect US interests by undermining hostile governments.

Obviously, someone sympathetic to the complaints of the more vocal sectors of the Third World would tend to disagree with the first and last of these five statements and agree with the other three. The actual responses of our media and business leaders are shown in Table 4.1.

On four out of the five statements, a majority of journalists take the Third World position. They reject the notion that the West has helped the Third World by an overwhelming three to one margin. Substantial majorities are willing to criticize their country's consumption of resources as immoral and to indict America as an exploiter of poor nations and a cause of world poverty. A majority also rejects the use of CIA intervention to undermine hostile goverments as an instrument of foreign policy. Of course, such intervention is often aimed at Third World countries and has been a particular focus of criticism from nonaligned nations. Finally, exactly half the media elite see the protection of business interests as the main goal of US foreign policy, a view that also has gained currency in underdeveloped countries. They allege that exploitation of Third World resources by multinational corporations is tacitly or explicitly encouraged by the policies of Western governments, including the United States.

As might be expected, businessmen are considerably less likely to criticize these American policies and practices. A majority rejects every one of these Third World criticisms by margins ranging up to nearly nine to one. There is an overwhelming consensus among businessmen that the Third World would be even worse off without Western assistance. Nearly nine out of ten businessmen (88 percent) subscribe to this notion, as com-

Table 4.1

Attitudes of Media and Business Elites Toward U.S.-Third World Relations

(In Percentages)

Statement*		Strongly Agree	Agree	Disagree	Strongly Disagree	Total	N
1. The West has helped the Third World	Media	6	19	50	25	100%	235
	Business	33	55	10	2	100%	212
2. American exploitation adds to Third World poverty	Media	15	40	24	20	100%	234
	Business	3	19	34	44	100%	211
3. US use of resources is immoral	Media	19	38	27	16	100%	236
	Business	7	41	26	26	100%	212
4. US foreign policy mainly protects business	Media	11	39	28	22	100%	237
	Business	5	27	42	26	100%	212
5. The CIA should undermine hostile governments	Media	26	19	36	19	100%	235
	Business	26	49	15	11	100%	212

Group differences on all items are significant at $p < .001$

* Abbreviated format. Complete renderings appear in text.

pared to only one in four journalists. Conversely, almost four out of five businessmen (78 percent) reject American responsibility for Third World poverty, almost double the proportion of journalists. By a two to one margin, they disagree that the State Department is an extension of the corporate boardroom; and despite the severe criticism aimed at the CIA in recent years, three out of four business leaders would mandate it to uphold US interests by undermining hostile governments. Only one criticism of American practices draws some sympathy from the business community. Almost half agree that the United States' heavy consumption of resources is immoral. Their other responses suggest, however, that this apparent twinge of guilt does not imply a sense of American responsibility for global economic inequality. Nor do they seem willing to place limits on the use of American power to uphold perceived national interests.

The mea culpae thus emanate not from corporate America but from the journalistic community. Far from serving as mouthpieces for American capitalism abroad, broadcast and print journalists were far more likely than business leaders to sympathize with Third World criticisms on all five issues. The two groups' responses differed by magnitudes that reached a startling 63 percent. (That figure represents the difference between the 88 percent of businessmen who feel the West has helped the Third World and the mere 25 percent of journalists who think so.) Even when the two groups come closest to agreement (in affirming that the US use of resources is immoral), majorities fall on opposite sides of the question. Moreover, almost 1 in 5 journalists agree strongly with this criticism, compared to only 1 in 14 businessmen.

In sum, the elite press seems substantially more aligned with Third World concerns than does the corporate business community. But, there is another aspect of these data that deserves attention. The differences between the two groups' responses reflect a division of opinion among the journalists, compared to relative consensus among the businessmen. The business leaders overwhelmingly rejected all five Third World criticisms by margins that averaged almost three to one (72 to 28 percent) and dropped below a two to one ratio only once. By contrast, journalists were much more evenly divided. Only once did their approval of Third World criticisms garner a majority exceeding 57 percent, so that a shift of 8 percent or less on four of the five issues would have shifted the majority to the opposite side of the question.

Therefore, insofar as stories may be influenced by the sympathies of journalists, one would expect to see an assortment of positive and negative reports about US relations with the Third World in major media outlets. Indeed, one would expect to see a mixture of stories that, if anything, would be somewhat sympathetic toward Third World problems, even when this implies criticism of American policies.

ORGANIZATIONAL AND OCCUPATIONAL DIFFERENCES

Is this diversity of opinion also reflected among various organizational and occupational strata within the national news media, or are there significant differences? For example, is the outlook of print journalists different from that of their colleagues in broadcasting? Our media elite sample consists of 10 major news organizations, comprising daily newspapers, weekly magazines, and both commercial networks and public television. Do members of all these organizations hold roughly similar attitudes toward the Third World, or are there differences that might also be reflected in differing editorial policies?

Finally, it is widely assumed that the most liberal members of the media are line reporters, who are reigned in by more conservative editors or other representatives of management. Might such occupational differences structure attitudes toward international as well as domestic issues?

To address these questions, we shall focus on the charge that American economic exploitation causes Third World poverty. Of the five questionnaire items, this allegation best epitomizes the criticisms of those who advocate a New World Information Order. They see themselves as victims of American and European imperialism engaged in a struggle to correct a global imbalance of political and economic power.

Not too surprisingly, four out of five business executives rejected this statement (Table 4.1). Indeed, given the quasi-Marxist overtones of this particular criticism, it is perhaps surprising that even one out of five business leaders would admit to sympathy for it.

The media elite, on the other hand, was much more divided over this issue. A majority (55 percent) of the leading US journalists expressed agreement with the statement that "American economic exploitation has contributed to Third World poverty." However, 45 percent dissented; and those who "strongly disagreed" (20 percent) slightly outnumbered those who "strongly agreed" (15 percent).

This diversity of opinion, as well as the centrality of the issue, makes this item a good test of differing attitudes within the media elite. We first examined differences between those from the print and broadcast media, then fine-tuned the comparisons to take account of job functions and membership in particular media outlets. Results are shown in Tables 4.2 through 4.4.[2]

At first glance, it appears that attitudes are associated with the type of news medium. Table 4.2 shows that TV news personnel are significantly more sympathetic to the charge of American exploitation than their print

---

[2] Because of the small number of cases in several cells of these tables, response categories were collapsed into "agree" and "disagree."

counterparts. In fact, nearly two thirds (64 percent) of television journalists endorse this charge, whereas a slight majority (51 percent) of print journalists are in opposition to it.

Table 4.3 continues to support this general pattern. The alleged conservative leanings of executives and administrators are nowhere in evidence. If anything, the reverse is true, although the overall pattern is not statistically significant. Within the print medium, slight majorities of both reporters and editors reject the contention of American imperialism, while a majority of news executives endorse it.

Among the television sample, all occupational groups are in substantial agreement, with support levels ranging from 56 percent among network production staffs to 82 percent among reporters. Of special interest, however, is the difference between network production personnel and independent producers. Among the latter group, which is almost entirely affiliated with public broadcasting, almost three out of four (73 percent) agree that "American exploitation has contributed to Third World poverty." The difference between network personnel and independents on this issue provides a hint that the apparent distribution of attitudes according to type of medium actually may represent a spurious association.

In fact, the print-versus-broadcast distinction suppresses more interesting differences between news organizations, regardless of medium. This is demonstrated by Table 4.4, which summarizes opinions according to membership in the 10 media outlets sampled.

Table 4.4 shows that most of the print-TV difference was attributable to overwhelming support for this criticism from those in public broadcasting. Fully 83 percent of the PBS sample, five out of every six subjects, is willing to support Third World criticism of American economic exploitation. By contrast, the support level at the three networks ranges from 64 percent at ABC to only 45 percent at CBS. The networks' combined average of a 54 percent agreement is almost indistinguishable from the overall media sample mean of 55 percent.

The variation in attitudes among the networks was less than that observed in the print media, where agreement levels ranged from 61 percent at the *New York Times* and the *Washington Post* to only 35 percent at *Time*, 33 percent at the *Wall Street Journal*, and a mere 28 percent at *U.S. News and World Report*. The conservative and business-oriented editorial policies of *U.S. News* and the *Journal* coincide here with the attitudes of their staffs. Nonetheless, even these journals' personnel are somewhat more receptive to allegations of American imperialism than are the business leaders.

The overall set of differences among news organizations is highly significant ($p = .001$). The key to this association, however, is the high

Table 4.2
Percent Agreement that US Adds to Third World Poverty:
Print vs. Television Journalists

	Agree	Disagree	Total	N
Print	49	51	100%	136
Television	64	36	100%	98

Corrected Chi-square = 4.61, D.F. = 1, p < .03

Table 4.3
Percent Agreement that US Adds to Third World Poverty,
by Media Job Function

	Agree	Disagree	Total	N
Print				
Executive	56	44	100%	18
Editor	46	54	100%	28
Reporter	49	51	100%	90
TV				
Executive	64	36	100%	25
Production (network)	56	44	100%	45
Independent Producer	73	27	100%	11
Reporter	82	18	100%	17

Chi-square = 9.54, D.F. = 6, not significant

Table 4.4
Percent Agreement that US Adds to Third World Poverty,
by News Organization

	Agree	Disagree	Total	N
Print:				
New York Times	61	39	100%	23
Washington Post	61	39	100%	31
Wall Street Journal	33	67	100%	15
Newsweek	56	44	100%	18
Time	35	65	100%	23
US News & World Report	28	72	100%	18
TV:				
ABC	64	36	100%	22
CBS	45	55	100%	29
NBC	57	43	100%	14
PBS	83	17	100%	41

Chi-square = 27.8, D.F. = 9, p < .001

agreement recorded by PBS personnel. When this group is excluded from the comparison, the differences among all other news outlets fail to attain statistical significance.

It is at least arguable that PBS represents a very special case within the media elite. First, we are using "PBS" as an umbrella term for leading journalists involved with public broadcasting, including those who work for the Public Broadcasting System and the Corporation for Public Broadcasting, the administrative arms of public television; journalists affiliated with WETA, WNET, and WGBH, who actually produce or commission public affairs shows; and independent producers who sell their shows to PBS affiliates (and on rare occasions, to the networks' news departments).

Unlike the other news organizations we sampled, public television represents a loose alliance of central administrators, affiliated stations with their own production units, and independent filmmakers responsible for many of the documentaries aired on PBS affiliates. As a result, public television attracts many journalists for whom the opportunity to make a personal statement with relatively minimal bureaucratic constraints outweighs the high salaries and large audiences available from network television. Such people tend to be both socially concerned and politically liberal (attitudes which apparently carry over into the sphere of Third World relations). In fact, one high-level staffer told us that PBS was "the Peace Corps of the 1970's."

Even aside from PBS, leading US journalists from the commercial networks, news magazines, and prestige newspapers remain far more receptive to Third World complaints than do business executives. Responses of those in all 10 news organizations were found to be more "liberal" on each item than were those in the business elite. That is, journalists at every major news organization sampled are closer to the Third World position than is the average business leader. Despite the diversity from one news outlet to another, these journalists hold views that are sufficiently distinctive to set them apart from corporate America.[3]

CONCLUSION

On five issues dealing with American-Third World relations, leading US journalists were consistently more sympathetic toward Third World

---

[3] To insure that these findings were indicative of journalists' attitudes toward the entire range of Third World criticisms measured in the survey, we created an additive index based on responses to all five statements and examined the differences in the means of the media subgroups analyzed above. Results indicated that the item concerning American exploitation was representative of attitudes toward Third World criticisms. On the index, the PBS sample was most critical of US policies, and their group mean score again accounted for all significant differences in attitudes produced by the structural and functional breakdowns of the media sample.

views than were US business leaders. Three fourths of the journalists rejected the idea that, on balance, the West had helped more than hurt the Third World. In general, the newspeople were somewhat divided, but with a tilt toward pro-Third World positions. Journalists who work with PBS were significantly more likely than their peers to endorse the Third World criticism of American economic exploitation. In sharp contrast, the business leaders rejected most criticisms of the United States by wide margins. Moreover, this division of opinion held across both organizational and occupational boundaries. No news organization or occupational grouping within the media elite supported US policies as strongly as did the business leaders.

This finding should not be especially surprising, because it is known that journalists tend toward liberal attitudes in many areas of life, and businessmen are correspondingly conservative (Sussman, 1976; Rothman, 1979; Lichter & Rothman, 1981). Moreover, businessmen have long complained that the national news media are unduly critical of business practices at home and abroad (Barrett, 1978). Nonetheless, proponents of a "New World Information Order" have contended that the major American news outlets produce a kind of informational imperialism that upholds the interests of Western capitalists.

Ultimately, the issue cannot be settled without analysis of actual news content. But these survey findings show that the allegedly negative press coverage of the Third World cannot be attributed to media personnel being clones of those in big business. Moreover, the journalists we surveyed are at the top of their profession. They are notoriously prickly about outside interference with their news judgments, whether the complaints come from advertisers, their own corporate supervisors, or academic media analysts. Recent history shows that neither major corporations nor American governments can consistently override the judgment of reporters and news organizations in presenting major international stories from Vietnam to the oil crisis. (Whether those judgments are fair or correct is an entirely different issue.) The burden of proof rests with those who seek to portray US news as an organ for capitalist world domination.

REFERENCES

Barrett, Marvin. 1978. *Rich News, Poor News.* New York: Thomas Crowell.

Epstein, Edward J. 1973. *News from Nowhere.* New York: Random House.

Gans, Herbert, J. 1979. *Deciding What's News.* New York: Pantheon.

Gates, Gary Paul. 1978. *Air Time.* New York: Harper & Row.

Halberstam, David. 1979. *The Powers That Be.* New York: Knopf.

Hirsch, Paul. 1977. Occupational, Organizational and Institutional Models in Mass Media Research. In Paul Hirsch, Peter Miller, and F. Gerald Kline, eds., *Strategies for Communication Research.* Beverly Hills, Calif.: Sage Publications, 13–42.

Johnstone, John W. C.; Edward Slawski; and William Bowman. 1976. *The News People.* Urbana, Ill.: University of Illinois Press.

Lefever, Ernest. 1974. *TV and National Defense.* Boston, Va.: Institute for American Strategy.

Lewis, Paul. 1981a. West's News Organizations Vow to Fight UNESCO on Press Curbs. *New York Times,* May 18, 1981, A-1-14.

———. 1981b. Gloves Come Off in Struggle with UNESCO. *New York Times,* May 24, 1981, E-3.

Lichter, S. Robert. 1981. Media Support for Israel: A Survey of Leading Journalists. In William C. Adams, ed., *Television Coverage of the Middle East.* Norwood, N.J.: Ablex, 40–52.

——— and Stanley Rothman. 1981. Media and Business Elites. *Public Opinion* (October/November): 42–46.

Rivers, William L. 1965. *The Opinionmakers.* Boston, Mass.: Little, Brown and Company.

———. 1971. *Adversaries: Politics and the Press.* Boston, Mass.: Beacon Press.

Robinson, Michael J. 1978. Future Television News Research: Beyond Edward Jay Epstein. In William C. Adams and Fay Schreibman, eds., *Television Network News: Issues in Content Research.* Washington, D.C.: School of Public and International Affairs, George Washington University, 197–212.

Rothman, Stanley. 1979. The Mass Media in Post-Industrial America. In S. M. Lipset, ed., *The Third Century.* Stanford, Calif.: Hoover Institute Press, 346–388.

Sussman, Barry. 1976. *Elites in America.* Washington, D.C.: *Washington Post.*

Tuchman, Gaye. 1972. Objectivity as Strategic Ritual: An Examination of Newsmen's Notion of Objectivity. *American Journal of Sociology* 77 (January 1972): 660–679.

Tuchman, Gaye. 1973. Making News by Doing Work. *American Journal of Sociology* 79 (July 1973): 110–131.

Weiss, Carol. 1974. What America's Leaders Read. *Public Opinion Quarterly* 38 (Spring 1974): 1–22.

5

REVOLUTIONS, EARTHQUAKES
AND LATIN AMERICA:
THE NETWORKS LOOK AT ALLENDE'S CHILE
AND SOMOZA'S NICARAGUA

WALTRAUD QUEISER MORALES

How do the three American television networks portray Latin America?
Sparingly and violently. ABC, CBS, and NBC nightly news coverage of the
independent nations of Latin America demonstrates again the appropriate-
ness of the commonplace phrase for US-Latin American relations: "benign
neglect." Television reporting also reinforces stereotypes of the region by
the kinds of issues that are covered and that are omitted. As a geopolitical
unit, Latin America is shown as chronically violent, ungovernable, mili-
taristic, authoritarian, and troublesome. Economically and socially, TV
news depicts a region of poverty, unemployment, backwardness, turmoil,
disease, and natural disaster. From the perspective of international relations, Latin American countries appear as third- and fourth-rate states,
with little role in world affairs other than disobligingly to provoke national
security "itches" on the small of the back of the United States.

The omissions of issues, events, and countries in routine reporting
are as indicative of network world views as are the subjects they do report.
Half of the Latin American countries have been ignored almost entirely.
News from the rest of Latin America has typically required natural disasters, coups, revolutions, or imbroglios with the United States.

Size is not a determining characteristic. Brazil, a large and powerful
Latin American state, had practically no visibility on ABC, NBC, and
CBS coverage during the years 1970–73 and 1978–79. Mexico and Venezuela were relatively ignored until energy and oil were defined as big
issues for American television viewers after 1973. Other Latin American
countries, such as Chile under Allende and Cuba under Castro, were consistently reported from the single perspective of US national security.

Why should stereotyping and ethnocentrism be so apparent in television presentations on Latin America? In part, because the general constraints of the newsgathering process—defining "newsworthiness," time pressures, demands for universal and specialized expertise, and the gray overlap of fact and interpretation—become more pronounced and pernicious when reporting deals with foreign or international news. This is especially true with Latin America, a backwater of broadcast commitment. Crisis reporting, like the US government's crisis policy-making in Latin American affairs, is inherently distorting and difficult.

The tremendous fluctuation in attention and the norm of neglect ensures that media competency and expertise in reporting Latin American events is unlikely to improve unless changes in technique and priority occur. During the 1970's, the television networks appeared not to have the time, expertise, or inclination to report the region differently. ABC, CBS, and NBC may have derived the most convenience, efficiency, and economy in jetting to crises, echoing traditional views and official rationales, and upholding the first instincts of their reporters in the field.

In order to assess coverage of Latin America in a systematic fashion, the *Television News Index and Abstract* was used to identify news stories involving Latin American countries in any manner.[1] There was no sample; instead, every nightly news program on all three networks was examined for a period of six full years—1970–73, 1978–79.[2] Eight hours of this coverage were studied in detail using compiled videotapes loaned from the Vanderbilt Television News Archive. Special attention was given to coverage of Chile and Nicaragua.

LATIN AMERICA ON THE TV NEWS AGENDA

Latin America usually received only about one percent of the total news time on ABC, CBS, and NBC. In the early 1970's, the entire region received less than two hours of attention (144 minutes) annually on the average network early evening news series. (If one adjusts for the fact that one fourth to over one half of all reporting about Latin America concerns

---

[1] The traditional, independent Latin American republics studied here are Argentina, Bolivia, Brazil, Chile, Colombia, Costa Rica, Cuba, Dominican Republic, Ecuador, El Salvador, Guatemala, Haiti, Honduras, Mexico, Nicaragua, Panama, Paraguay, Peru, Uruguay, and Venezuela. Excluded from the content analysis were the British, French, and Dutch-heritage states in and around the Caribbean. The country categories used for coding also included the United States, a category for "other" nations, and the regional categories of "Latin America" and "Caribbean" when no specific countries were mentioned.

[2] Vanderbilt has an essentially complete collection of weeknight newscasts from this period; however, its archive is missing some weekend newscasts before 1979. The unavailability of a few weekend newscasts seems quite unlikely to change the findings of this study with regard to coverage of Latin America.

the United States as much as Latin America, the total allocation of network time would be even lower.) With upheaval in Central America in
the late 1970's, coverage more than tripled by 1978–79 to an average of
almost exactly six hours each year per network.

In the early 1970's, Vietnam was the focal point of international
coverage and by the middle and end of the decade, the Middle East had
come to dominate international coverage (Adams & Heyl, 1981). At no
time was Latin America given such prominence, although there were
brief periods of intense coverage during certain segments of revolutions in
Central America.

Table 5.1 shows the number of minutes each network gave annually
to Latin American coverage. At this level of aggregation there is relative
conformity among the three networks, and changes over time covary. The
chief exceptions were in 1971, when ABC gave the region much less coverage than the other two networks, and in 1972, when NBC had much more
coverage. In 1978–79, the networks stayed fairly closely aligned in their
volume of coverage of Latin America.

Table 5.1
Annual Network Totals of Time Given to Latin America
(Time in Minutes)

	1970	1971	1972	1973	1978	1979
ABC	70	85	74	115	338	284
CBS	89	170	75	131	314	302
NBC	101	177	140	145	306	272

There was also a fair amount of consistency in the priorities of
country-by-country coverage. Table 5.2 ranks and compares annually the
top Latin American countries in terms of network coverage over the content analysis period.[3]

Television networks demonstrated more consistent coverage when
confronted with an indisputable crisis in Latin America or a major diplomatic event. Table 5.2 shows that similar attention was given to stories
such as the fall of Allende in Chile in 1973, the Nicaraguan Revolution in
1978 and 1979, the suspected presence of Soviet combat troops in Cuba in
the same years, the ratification of the Panama Canal Treaties in 1978, and
President Carter's Mexican-energy-oil trip in 1979. A notable exception is
NBC's interpretation of the Panama Canal as the preeminent Latin
American news story in 1978.

---

[3] This ranking excludes the United States, which is always the top ranking country in network
time. The criteria used for selection of countries were as folows: (a) top three countries in a
quarter, or two minutes of total coverage per country per network, whichever is less; (b) five
minutes of total time per country per network; and (c) 10 minutes total time per country for
the networks combined.

Table 5.2
Rank Order of Network Coverage of Top Latin American Countries*

	1970		1971		1972		1973		1978		1979		1970–79	
	Country	Min.	Country	Min.	Country	Min.	Country	Min.	Country	Min.	Country	Min.	Country	Min.
ABC	Peru	11	Cuba	14	Cuba	9	Chile	37	Cuba	52	Other	40	Cuba	118
	Other	6	Haiti	11	Argentina	8	Mexico	12	Nicaragua	49	Cuba	38	Nicaragua	74
			Chile	7	Chile	8	Argentina	9	Panama	49	Mexico	28	Panama	52
					Other	7	Cuba	5	Mexico	6	Panama	11	Mexico	46
CBS	Peru	9	Cuba	27	Argentina	11	Chile	46	Cuba	45	Nicaragua	42	Cuba	124
	Chile	7	Chile	17	Nicaragua	11	Mexico	8	Nicaragua	39	Cuba	38	Nicaragua	92
	Cuba	7	Haiti	11	Cuba	7	Argentina	5	Other	37	Other	37	Mexico	72
	Mexico	6	Other	9	Mexico	6			Panama	30	Mexico	34	Panama	37
			Mexico	8					Mexico	10	El. Salva.	13		
			Peru	5							Dom. Repub.	8		
											Panama	7		
NBC	Chile	15	Chile	28	Cuba	33	Chile	38	Panama	79	Nicaragua	38	Cuba	130
	Peru	13	Cuba	23	Nicaragua	17	Argentina	17	Nicaragua	46	Cuba	34	Nicaragua	109
	Bolivia	5	Other	12	Argentina	13	Mexico	15	Cuba	32	Other	27	Chile	90
			Bolivia	12	Other	10	Nicaragua	8	Mexico	25	Mexico	26	Panama	79
			Brazil	9	Chile	9	Cuba	8	Argentina	5	El. Salva.	11	Mexico	74
			Mexico	8					Venezuela	5	Dom. Repub.	11		
			Ecuador	5										

* Top countries have a minumum of five minutes of news time per network per year. For 1970–79 cumulative, only the highest four countries were included.

82

Periods of "routine" reporting of Latin America can be distinguished from periods of crisis reporting. During the routine reporting period of 1970–72, more network time was distributed to short, spotty, "one-liner" reports of various Latin countries. On the other hand, the crisis years of 1973, 1978, and 1979 concentrated on major Latin American "hot spots." Normally, one might have expected more linking of Latin American events to the United States in crisis periods. However, reporting in crisis years—whether because of the crisis proportions of the story, how the problem was defined, or the greater sensitivity of the reporter—was more likely to emphasize the Latin story per se, and its impact for the country in question and the region. Perhaps during a crisis, Latin America was perceived as more autonomous or newsworthy in itself, and less derivative of US problems and policies.

Table 5.3 presents the amounts of total Latin American coverage broken down into time devoted primarily to US relations, time alloted to those few top Latin American countries receiving the most coverage each year, and the time dispersed among the rest of Latin America. This is typical between one fourth and one third of the coverage focused on the role and interests of the United States. In crisis years, the share of coverage going to the most newsworthy echelon of Latin American countries (as listed in Table 5.2) increased to over half of all coverage.

Almost no reporting was broadcast about purely inter-Latin American issues, or relations primarily between Latin American states. As Adams and Heyl (1981) found with regard to the Middle East, news focused on interactions with the United States, wars and civil wars, and disasters; rarely mentioned were the "peaceful" bilateral relations between other states.

REVOLUTIONS, EARTHQUAKES, AND US SECURITY

The three networks varied little in overall coverage or ranking of the most important issues.[4] The collective network "image" for Latin America was the negative and sensationalist one of "revolutions and earthquakes." Table 5.4 shows that the networks ranked the two issue categories, instability/violence and terrorism, high in "newsworthiness" for Latin American coverage. Cumulatively for 1970 through 1979, violent, political events ranked second or third in network coverage time, and by implication in importance and priority. Ranked fourth was terrorism, defined as acts of kidnapping, hijacking, bombing, and other violence and intimidation by dissident, non-governmental actors. Foreign relations, a some-

---

[4] There were 12 issue categories: non-violent politics, political instability and violence, domestic economy, international economy, energy/oil, foreign relations, drug traffic, terrorism, national security, immigration, natural disasters, and human interest.

Table 5.3
Network Coverage of Top Latin American Countries* and of US-related Issues As a Share of Total Latin American Coverage

	1970			1971			1972			1973			1978			1979			Total		
	US	Top LA	LA Other	US	Top LA	LA Other	US	Top LA	LA Other	US	Top LA	LA Other	US	Top LA	LA Other	US	Top LA	LA Other	US	Top LA	LA Other
ABC																					
Minutes	16	17	37	24	32	29	23	32	19	31	63	21	114	156	68	99	117	68	307	417	242
Percent	23	24	53	28	38	34	31	43	26	27	55	18	34	46	20	35	41	24	32	43	25
CBS																					
Minutes	22	29	38	46	77	47	22	35	18	35	59	37	108	161	45	87	185	30	320	546	215
Percent	25	33	43	27	45	28	29	47	24	27	45	28	34	51	14	29	61	10	30	51	19
NBC																					
Minutes	19	33	49	45	97	35	34	82	24	31	86	28	103	192	11	82	154	36	314	644	183
Percent	19	33	48	25	55	20	24	59	17	21	59	19	34	63	4	30	57	13	28	56	16
Total min.	57	79	124	115	206	111	79	149	61	97	208	86	325	509	124	268	456	134	941	1607	640
Percent	22	30	48	27	48	26	27	52	21	25	53	22	34	53	13	31	53	16	30	50	20

* "Top Latin American countries" each year are those listed in Table 6.2

Table 5.4
Rank Order of Top Issues Covered by Networks Annually*

		1970	1971		1972		1973		1978		1979		1970–79	
	Issue	Min.	Issue	Min.	Issue	Min.	Issue	Min.	Issue	Min.	Issue	Min.	Issue	Min.
ABC	Terrorism	20	For. Rel.	22	For. Rel.	23	Violence	19	Security	123	For. Rel.	75	For. Rel.	238
	Disasters	14	Terrorism	12	Terrorism	15	For. Rel.	16	For. Rel.	96	Security	71	Security	210
	Violence	9	Immigratn.	11	Disasters	10	Intl. Econ.	12	Violence	65	Energy	64	Violence	144
	Security	6	Security	10			Politics	11	Drugs	16	Violence	51	Terrorism	73
	For. Rel.	6	Politics	9			Disasters	8	Terrorism	7	Disasters	31	Energy	64
							Terrorism	6			Terrorism	13	Disasters	63
CBS	Violence	16	For. Rel.	28	Disasters	16	For. Rel.	33	Security	119	Security	88	For. Rel.	218
	For. Rel.	14	Drugs	23	Terrorism	12	Violence	30	For. Rel.	84	Violence	76	Security	213
	Disasters	12	Politics	18	For. Rel.	8	Intl. Econ.	16	Violence	53	For. Rel.	51	Violence	190
	Terrorism	8	Disasters	15	Politics	7	Disasters	14	Politics	14	Disasters	26	Disasters	83
	Security	6	Violence	15			Terrorism	9	Drugs	14	Energy	24		
			Immigratn.	15			Politics	7	Immigratn.	6	Terrorism	16		
			Dom. Econ.	12										
			Terrorism	10										
			Human Int.	10										
NBC	Terrorism	21	For. Rel.	59	For. Rel.	34	Violence	39	For. Rel.	91	Security	79	For. Rel.	259
	Violence	18	Terrorism	19	Terrorism	26	For. Rel.	14	Security	85	Violence	53	Violence	201
	Disasters	13	Violence	17	Disasters	25	Politics	14	Violence	67	For. Rel.	49	Security	178
	For. Rel.	12	Disasters	13	Politics	12	Disasters	13	Drugs	18	Terrorism	17	Terrorism	91
	Dom. Econ.	7	Intl. Econ.	12	Violence	7	Intl. Econ.	12			Disasters	12	Disasters	76
	Intl. Econ.	6	Drugs	11	Dom. Econ.	6	Terrorism	8			Energy	11		
	Politics	6	Politics	11			Security	8			Dom. Econ.	7		
			Immigratn.	7			Drugs	6						
			Security	6										

* Top issues have a minimum of five minutes of news time per network per year. For 1970–79 cumulative top issues have a minimum of 60 minutes of news time per network.

what more "neutral" category, was ranked first by all television stations and was given very similar time coverage. Reporting of foreign affairs concentrated on countries with which the United States had disagreements or disputes.

The negative image of the region was further reinforced by the high and concentrated reporting on national security problems and natural disasters. National security rankings by network and overall news time varied but were roughly equivalent. Of the three networks, NBC downplayed the national security dimension somewhat, and emphasized violence and terrorism instead. In contrast, CBS tended to report less terrorism and more national security. Network coverage of natural disasters, mainly earthquakes, was also a near-constant in reporting time and "newsworthiness," with CBS giving it the most attention.

None of the television networks was very sensitive to the energy/oil issue, at least not in association with Latin America, or during the time period analyzed. However, ABC did broadcast over an hour of energy-related stories in 1979, which compared favorably to less than half an hour for CBS and less than 15 minutes for NBC. One can also note that NBC tended to focus reporting on a broader variety or greater range of issues (over five minutes) than did CBS, and especially ABC.

The networks associated certain countries with particular issues. Tables 5.5, 5.6, and 5.7 crosstabulate the key countries for each network (shown in Table 5.2) by the topic of coverage.[5] Cuba is clearly linked to the national security theme, especially for ABC and CBS. Similarly, Nicaragua, Argentina, Chile, El Salvador, and to a lesser extent, Panama are associated with political instability and violence. Countries which pose the greatest foreign policy challenge for the United States are strongly linked to the foreign relations category, almost in a consistent order of priority of time by the three networks. ABC ranked in minutes: Panama

Table 5.5
ABC Coverage of Top Latin American Countries by Major Issues in Minutes

Issue	Countries							
	Argen.	Chile	Cuba	Haiti	Mexico	Nicar.	Panama	Peru
Foreign Rel.	2	17	30		22	3	47	
Security		1	74	2	3		2	
Violence	7	7			1	69	4	1
Terrorism	3	6	19		3	2		
Energy					6			
Disasters		2	1	1	18	6	1	11
Total	12	33	125	3	53	80	54	12

[5] These tables may vary slightly from data in previous tables because of rounding and converting to minutes.

Table 5.6
CBS Coverage of Top Latin American Countries by Major Issues in Minutes

Issue						Countries				
	Argen.	Chile	Cuba	D.R.	El Sal.	Haiti	Mexico	Nicar.	Panama	Peru
Foreign Rel.	1	17	32	3			24	1	36	1
Security			72			1	1		1	
Violence	9	11		1	14	3	3	77	2	
Disasters		2	2	8		2	16	14		14
Total	10	30	106	12	14	6	44	92	39	15

Table 5.7

NBC Coverage of Top Latin American Countries by Major Issues in Minutes

Issue	Countries												
	Argen.	Boliv.	Brazil	Chile	Cuba	D.R.	Ecua.	El Sal.	Mexico	Nicar.	Panama	Peru	Venez.
For. Rel.	1	1	4	14	33	3	5	1	22	8	43		3
Violence	19	11		50	57	2		9	6	70	3		
Security								1		1	1	1	
Terrorism	5	1	5	3	10			2	1		1		1
Disaster				4	2	5			20	25		13	
Total	25	13	9	71	102	10	5	13	49	104	48	14	4

(47), Cuba (30), Mexico (22), and Chile (17). CBS ranked in minutes: Panama (36), Cuba (32), Mexico (24), and Chile (17). And NBC ranked: Panama (43), Cuba (33), Mexico (22), and Chile (14).

ABC associated the energy issue almost exclusively with Mexico. The earthquakes in Mexico, Nicaragua, Peru, and the Dominican Republic tie those countries into the natural disaster category. Largely because of hijackings, Cuba was strongly related to terrorism by television, and so were Argentina, Brazil, and Chile by one or more networks. Although not presented separately in this summary cross-tabulation, the drug problem tended to be associated with Mexico over the entire period, and also with Panama in 1978 when the brother of General Omar Torrijos was linked with the drug trade during the debate over ratification of the Panama Canal Treaties. Immigration topics focused on Haiti in 1971, and then shifted to Mexico for 1978 and 1979.

As might be expected, the country-issue association follows a distinct time pattern. In analyzing network reporting over the 1970–73 and 1978–79 periods, patterns of single-issue reporting of certain countries become more pronounced. Chile, for example, was covered intensively for 1973 in the categories of foreign relations and political violence; Chile was ignored after the fall of President Allende and the immediate consolidation of the General Pinochet government. As the first Marxist regime in the Southern Hemisphere established by constitutional elections, Chile represented an anomaly and was "newsworthy." As a repressive military regime after 1973, Chile became too "normal" to be major news.

Similarly, reporting on Panama is concentrated almost exclusively in 1978 and dropped from the list of news items after resolution of the Panama Canal question. Nicaragua would have returned to being invisible in Central America after the December 1972 earthquake, had it not been for reporting of the revolution in 1979. While the coverage on Mexico and Cuba is also time and issue determined, of all the Latin American nations, these two countries received the most consistent network attention over time and, relatively speaking, over a mix of issues. The pattern of issues is the most balanced for Mexico in that a wide variety of issues tended to be covered in any one year. This pattern suggests that geographical proximity and the interdependence of problems may encourage, however weakly, more consistent and multifaceted coverage.

Of the three television networks, NBC provided the broadest coverage of Latin American countries, a greater mixture of Latin issues (except for energy), and more coverage in overall network time. Content analysis also indicates that NBC allocated more network resources to coverage and analysis of the Allende years in Chile, and, to a lesser extent, to coverage of the Nicaraguan Revolution. Another example of a higher commitment to Latin American news is the fact that NBC allocated much more air time to reporting of Bolivia, a relatively insignificant country in Latin America from North American perspectives, than did ABC and CBS. NBC covered the leftist coup and political instability of Bolivia in 1970 with more analysis, on-location films, and interviews.

To examine more closely how the networks reported Latin America, two case studies were selected—Chile and Nicaragua. Videotapes of news stories about Chile from 1970 through 1973 and about Nicaragua in 1978 and 1979 were viewed and analyzed. The rest of this chapter reviews coverage of these two major Latin American stories, the election and fall of Salvador Allende and the Nicaraguan Revolution.

CHILE AND ALLENDE

ABC

ABC reported the Chilean elections of September 1970 and the fall and death of Allende three years later in an "I told you so" context. Post-election days were cast in a mood of violence and instability—the assassinations of General René Schneider, long lines of Chileans seeking to leave the country in fear of a Marxist future, the brooding threat of army intervention, and the germinating seeds of economic chaos in Allende's nationalization policy. Charles Murphy's report (10/23/70) from Santiago seemed to sum up the mood, as concluding remarks of reporters in the field usually try to do. Murphy speculated, with an air of serious prescience, that Chile, "relatively peaceful in the past, may be entering a new and violent period, and life will never be the same again."

Chilean internal events were closely linked to Fidel Castro's Cuba when, after seven years, that Marxist head of state left his Caribbean island to visit Chile in 1971. Reporting emphasized the enthusiasm of the crowds, the populist appeal of Fidel, and footage of huge demonstrations in the bright Chilean sunshine. A smiling Fidel was shown with admiring miners in the large copper installations and with students in their radical university strongholds. Nearly every report by Murphy wove into the political and international news the theme of US business interests and implications of this issue for the future of the Chilean economy. He concluded one field transmission with the words that in the long run more capital investments—from which Allende had cut himself off by the expropriations of Kennecott and Anaconda copper multinationals—would make or break the Chilean economy and therefore the Chilean government. Of course the economic theme culminated in the story of ITT (International Telephone & Telegraph) and CIA activities in Chile. The ITT-CIA affair was handled domestically by ABC, as by the other two networks, using brief studio reports and location reporting from the Senate Foreign Relations Committee and the State Department.

Charles Murphy's analysis of the causes of the military coup in 1973 demonstrated the high caliber of his reporting. His September 11 report synthesized the complex socio-political forces that propelled the violent ending of Chilean socialism—as Murphy had suggested three years earlier. Thus, in retrospect, the early reports find logical resolution in the events of 1973.

While Murphy's coverage may have been consistent and analytically sound, the network editorials by Howard K. Smith and Harry Reasoner shifted with the prevailing winds from the South. For example, in an early Smith editorial, when US copper interests had not yet been nationalized and the hope persisted that American pressure might forestall such action, Smith urged the United States to offer the "hand of friendship and help" to Allende so that he would not be forced to turn to the Soviets for assistance. His commentary called for a more imaginative US foreign policy for Latin America, especially for a shrewd policy toward Chile.

After 16 months of Chilean socialism and major business takeovers, the editorial pitch turned hardline. Chilean economic stagnation and chaos were said to be the fault of ideology prevailing over competent administration. At the time of stories about ITT-CIA intervention, launched by Jack Anderson, a Smith editorial concluded that if any government were planning to intervene in Chile it would be "gilding the lily." The mess in Chile, according to Smith's analysis, "grows worse by the month and is entirely homemade" (4/23/72).

After embarrassing revelations by the Senate Foreign Relations Committee in 1972 and 1973, ABC reported ITT activities in Chile more critically. The broadcast of December 4, 1972, featured taped portions of Allende's speech at the United Nations containing a sharp and direct accusation of indirect aggression in Chile by the United States. While the network provided some balance to the charge in the person of George Bush, then US Ambassador to the UN, the Allende indictment was left as a strong one. "I accuse ITT of attempting to bring about civil war in my country, the greatest possible source of disintegration of a country," Allende said. "This is what we term imperialist intervention."

While the complicity of the United States Government remained ambivalent in the broadcast, a critical image of ITT was implied when the network devoted further air time to a history of ITT domestic and international activities and assets. Few critical words were said, but the impression was that of a corporation too big to be blameless.

As was observed in this story, one pervasive network practice that comes through dramatically in repeated viewings of TV news is the frequency with which stories' conclusions are made by unstated implication, by innuendo, and by unrefuted third parties. Rarely do the correspondents explicitly offer more than equivocal concluding remarks. They have, however, refined the art of making rhetorical questions sound like an obvious indictment.[6]

The style of ABC coverage of the ITT affair differed little from that of the other networks. Initially, Jack Anderson's charge was aired in a short, factual statement by the anchormen; it was clearly attributed to Anderson and was presented without supporting evidence. Coverage usually concluded by noting that an ITT spokesman denied the charge. The approach was one of uncertain matter-of-factness: "Well, its news. Who knows if its true."

As the momentum of the issue grew and evidence of involvement surfaced, ITT became the major object of criticism and ridicule more than censure. Tapes were shown of ITT spokesmen contradicting one another before the Senate Committee. Network reporters did not try to resolve these contradictions, but merely left the implication of ITT's lack of credibility. The American public was never told whom to blame, only that "something was rotten in Chile." Following standard network style, ABC drew implications and inferences by the order of direct statements of independent supporters or critics of ITT, by what was left unsaid, and by seemingly unrelated reports which might have been designed to "prejudice the jury."

ABC editorial opinion on the affair continued to be inconsistent, and to mirror the dominant public perspective of the moment. On April 20, 1973, ABC played a tape of Senator Edmund Muskie calling the plot "blackmail." Two days later, Harry Reasoner in a critical but inconclusive editorial pounced upon the "murky story" of ITT.[7] Mixing historical and children's book imagery with moral outrage, he said it was "wrong for an agency of the American government to discuss with an American company the feasibility to bring down or prevent the rise of a legal government with whom we are not at war." For Reasoner, the immorality and the ridiculous incompetency of the conspirators was an insufferable combination: "They act like Captain Hook."

A few months later, the September 12 editorial by Howard K. Smith attempted to exorcise the United States of even a breath of complicity in the Chilean events. Now that Allende's experiment in socialism is over, Smith argued, if we are to blame ourselves, it is only for doing nothing and for being powerless to protect the Chileans from themselves. With the omniscient sadness of a philosopher-king, Smith declared: "Free institutions have broken down in Chile, which until lately was a rare, successful

---

[6] See Michael Robinson's (1981) essay for many vivid examples of the practice as applied to candidates in the 1980 campaign.

[7] A perusal of the tape index indicates that ABC was the only network to take an editorial stand on ITT involvement in Chile.

nation in self-government." He wondered what the United States could do about this. The consensus was nothing. While "benign neglect" sounds reprehensible, he admitted, "we honestly don't know what to do." The "United States has no policy for Latin America"; we have "no clear ends that are desired with specific plans to achieve them." He held that Latin America's problems—Chile was forgotten as he turned to a higher level of philosophizing—were its own. American aid has not helped, as all but four nations are under military rule and the future remains unstable. "Unless South America takes some of these actions on its own, we are truly one helpless giant watching another flounder." The editorial concluded with the rousing assertion that "if ever there is a continent that has to work out its own problems before outside help will help, it is South America."

ABC ended its coverage of Chile by fully reporting the charges of US involvement in the Chilean military coup and summarizing the congressional committee hearings chaired by Representative Dante Fascell. Stories focused on the testimony of Assistant Secretary of State Jack Kubisch who denied US involvement in a manner that was clearly unpersuasive to the press corps. When asked by Representative Fascell if the coup plotters had received any advance encouragement from the United States, Kubisch said "No." However, added Kubisch, there had been much speculation and inquiries from some Chileans about potential US reactions. Fascell pressed on, asking: "The question is whether the United States government directly or indirectly financed in any way the activity of opposition to the Allende government." Kubisch refused to answer, urging the committee to go into executive session. After Kubisch was told by reporters that a non-answer left the impression that the United States had been involved, ABC's Sam Donaldson concluded: "Kubisch said he didn't mean to leave that impression but could say nothing more to clear it up."

ABC also aired an in-depth report about repression by the new Chilean military government (9/21/73). General Pinochet, leader of the junta, was quoted denying any foreign involvement in the events; the coup had been a "national movement, away from all foreign influence." "I want you to know," he said through an interpreter, "that even my wife didn't know what was going to happen." The report vigorously pursued the charges of repression by the military, and focused on the daily round-up of hundreds of people suspected of counter-military or leftist sympathies. A report of September 24 also pursued the charges of military repression. Sources were quoted as saying that the "police brutally treat detainees."

On both days, the transmissions by Murphy ended on the note that the government had something to hide. In the first one, Murphy commented: "the government is not likely to show the press some of those scenes we've been told about—those of course, it does not want the rest of the world to see." Murphy said in the second report that "this sort of thing is bound to bring down criticism on the Chilean army from the rest of the world, or parts of it, but at this point, I don't think the Chilean army really cares what the rest of the world thinks."

The final lengthy transmission by Murphy from Chile (9/26/73) again left the viewer with a strong sense of criticism concerning the new Chilean military regime. Murphy covered the funeral of Nobel prize-winning poet and national hero (and Marxist) Pablo Neruda. The funeral, Murphy explained, represented "an act of defiance" by Chilean intellectuals, students, and Marxists against the government that had overthrown Allende. The videotape from Santiago showed the mass of mourners around the poet's coffin as it was brought through the streets of the capital. Murphy repeated the words of a prominent Chilean intellectual that "a dark and powerful wind has struck our lives." This, he noted was referring to the military takeover as much as to the death of Neruda.

CBS

The CBS style of reporting the Chilean scene differed from ABC only in nuances. Field reporting by Robert Schakne from Santiago was generally more supportive of the Chilean political experiment than that of ABC's Charles Murphy. As with ABC, however, the editorials of Eric Sevareid recited stereotypes of Latin America and demonstrated little insight into Chilean events.

Robert Schakne's pre-electoral reports, while not ignoring the climate of tension in Chile, emphasized "business as usual" and the legality, popularity, and democracy of the Allende administration. Mixed with some skepticism of the long-range consequences, Schakne concluded his reports with more optimism. His transmissions included provocative interviews with major political figures and Latin American specialists. His format was often that of a debator, outlining both the pros and cons. After a barrage of contradictory opinions and analyses, he tended to conclude with either a "moderate," "ever-humble" opinion or the refrain—"no one really knows."

George Nathanson's occasional reports tended to follow Schakne's format with, perhaps, an extra pinch of skepticism. For example, Nathanson ended one report from Santiago with the words: "What his next step will be remains to be seen. If socialism defined by Allende is compatible with democracy—this is a question of the future."

In one early report from Chile, Schakne challenged misconceptions about Allende's election. With the words "normalcy," "order," "legality," "constitutionality," and "democracy," he argued that Allende's accession to the presidency is anything but "how Marxists ever predicted revolutionaries would take power." Using footage of Congressional voting, he aired the polar interpretations that the election begins the inevitable rise of a one-party, communist dictatorship, or the dawn of a new and authentic democracy. Schakne ended: "No one really knows." Another transmission (4/3/71) projected the message that nothing terribly subversive, unnatural or immoral may be occurring in Chile. Happy Chilean children and couples eating and drinking in everyday-fashion were shown, and it was suggested that if Chilean socialism were all that bad, such normalcy would not exist.

A two-part CBS special report reviewed the long history of "correct if not always comfortable" United States-Chilean relations. Viewers were shown goose-stepping Chilean troops and were told of US economic and military assistance to Chile over the years. Deputy Assistant Secretary of State John Crimmins explained that US policy is "hoping for the best," and "not seeking in any way a confrontation with the government of Chile," but rather "normal diplomatic relations." Schakne then analyzed the copper nationalization issue in depth. Again with a pro-con format, viewers were told that high-placed diplomats thought it was only a matter of time before Allende turned Chile into another Cuba, and that they urged a hardline US policy. But, no high-placed diplomat was presented for audience inspection. On the other hand, Schakne devoted more time to the dissenting interview of the very personable Claudio Veliz, a noted Chilean academician, who urged US restraint. After the films of the huge El Teniente mining complex, Salvador Allende's taped interview explained that the Chilean government was "not acting against the Americans." "We are acting in favor of Chile," and "not expropriating the copper out of revenge." The special report ended with Schakne's statement: "In the final analysis for the United States, the issue in Chile is not whether this country is socialist or capitalist, dictatorial or democratic, but how much Chile will pay for the copper properties."

The theme that "Chilean socialism can't be half bad" dominated another Schakne report. Sharply dialectical audio coverage was combined with a visual format supporting the conclusion that Chile is not a revolution in the tradition of a Marx or Castro. Scenes of busy Chilean night life supported the reporter's interpretation that the "rich are still rich with money to spend" and that life, like the press, is essentially free. The issue of whether Chile had become truly socialist was discussed and was resolved by the strong suggestion that perhaps real democracy was not impossible. These interpretations were bounced back and forth between spokesmen on both sides of the question.

Schakne played up the land reform policy in dramatic and dialectical form. Films focused on the poverty and marginalization of the Indians in the countryside and in abysmal squatter settlements like Población Che

Guevara. Amid the radicalism of the poor and the students, Allende contrasted as a moderate.

The audience was also confronted by the personal and human drama of a dispossessed landlord, one with whom they could easily identify. Arthur Lewis, a former North American copper mining engineer, and his wife lived most of their lives in Chile and now, in their old age, were deprived of their farm by the land reform program. The couple was shown at the auction of their possessions and in the emptiness of their house. A sad, personal interview with the elderly Mrs. Lewis was "balanced" with an interview with the Chilean Minister of Agriculture who matter-of-factly stated that 90 percent of the Chilean people support the land reform.

Despite this segment, the overall presentation of the Chilean scene by Schakne was positive. Despite crises in agriculture and other parts of the economy touched off by change, he explained, the future of the Allende government would hang on Allende's political astuteness and the outcome of the local elections. But the issue is "still a matter of elections which make Chilean socialism—if that is what it is becoming—different from any Soviet, Chinese, or Cuban model."

Like ABC's coverage, the fall of Allende was reported by CBS with some sensational visual footage of bombings, fires, strafing from the air, and chaotic sounds. Voice reports from Frank Menitzes in Santiago—networks had lost all but telephone communication with their headquarters—lent a breathtaking air of crisis and immediacy to the evening newscast. Robert Schakne followed up with a thorough and highly accurate background report. Replaying film footage of the 1970 elections with standard campaign fare of crowds and rallies, Schakne assessed why it all went sour. Films of civil violence, long lines of protesting housewives, and army tanks were shown to accompany the analysis of a breakdown in the Popular Unity coalition. The explanations included the fear of communism by the middle class after Castro's visit in 1971, the political polarization of the country into left and right, the end of tolerance, and the intervention of the military after the truckers' strike. Throughout the next days, network reports by CBS, as well as by ABC and NBC, would rerun both the still photos and the same footage of military movements and tanks, gutted buildings, sniper fire, etc. Violence and chaos in Chile were the unmistakable message.

The CBS editorial analysis of what the Chilean elections and the death of Allende in 1973 meant in the overall scheme of things flaunted perspectives quite unlike those from the field. Eric Sevareid in an initial editorial after the Chilean elections, interpreted Chilean events as potentially linked to communist revolution and Cuban subversion in Latin America. Sevareid reported that, with the opening of Chilean relations with Cuba, the Cuban Minister had advised Chile not to be soft on its internal enemies because Castro's mistake had been not to keep his firing squads busy enough. The editorial ended on the grim note that the first piece of advice to Allende from Cuba was a "public urging to start the blood flowing."

One Sevareid editorial (4/12/71) described the "quiet diplomatic vigil" over the events in Chile, stating that the "working premise is that Allende doesn't want totalitarianism, but that events might get beyond his control." After all, the "scenario has a chilling familiarity," as this "traditionally moderate people is more and more infused with the politics of passion." The editorial then concluded with characteristic Sevareid syntax: "The questions are whether this approach to sharing the wealth will not merely share the poverty more equally and after that whether even this peaceful social revolution will leave the people politically free. Whatever the drift, what Washington can do about it remains next to nothing." The broadcast then switched to Walter Cronkite with the inevitable: "And that's the way it is."

In his final editorial on Chile, just after the coup against Allende, Sevareid pursued his favorite theme of Latin American violence and instability. Describing the Latin American scene as one of close to 2,000 civil wars, coups, and palace revolutions, he concluded that this chronic social instability must have roots in "the nature and culture of the people." In comparison, the impact of US policies and economic assistance "must be minor and fleeting." Charges that CIA involvement and an absence of US assistance were among the causes of Allende's fall were dismissed by the phrase "no one can be sure one way or the other" but the odds seem against it. With a lack of historical understanding, he cited the failure of Juan Bosch as an example of how US aid could not make a difference in the Dominican Republic. With apparent sadness, he concluded that the "United States has the power to alleviate only here and there, now and then." The "remorseless dilemma" of Latin America is that economic growth is enjoyed only at the price of individual liberties and that, as Latin American politics polarizes further, the left becomes the only force for human equality, the right the only force of order, and the middle only atrophies.

Sevareid made these comments a day after a broadcast (9/12/73) in which Marvin Kalb, reporting from the State Department, strongly hinted that not only were administration officials not particularly saddened by the demise of Allende and his regime, but that amid "expected denials" there were charges that the US government knew of the coup two days before it happened. Kalb questioned "expected denials" of US involvement or complicity in the coup by noting the fact that Ambassador Nathanial Davis had returned from Chile one day before the coup; that there had been no formal expressions of regret at Allende's death; and that a behind-the-scenes special task force had been established at the State Department before news of the coup was known. Kalb said that he did not intend to suggest that everyone in the government was happy about the coup, but those who deplored the overthrow of a legally elected government were "in a distinct and fading minority."

NBC

NBC coverage of Chile from 1970 to 1973 provided contrast with the style of the other networks. Of the three, NBC was relatively more "silent" and "neutral" about the ITT-CIA-Chile affair, and this study found no formal editorials about Chile by the network. The Senate Foreign Relations hearings were covered in a routine manner by Paul Duke; and some stories, for example the March 20, 1973 report by Duke, replayed tapes of the testimony of William Merriam, head of ITT's Washington office, and the sharp reactions of Senator Edmund Muskie. Whether intended or not, the impression of the film segments was that of a tough and critical news report. However, little was ever said by way of indirect or direct reporter conclusions.

The difference in how this topic was reported was also seen in the all-anchor coverage on March 22 by John Chancellor. He stated that one ITT vice-president had reported that the one million dollars was to have been used to block the elections, but that another spokesman had said that it really was intended to help Allende improve Chile's economic position once elected. Chancellor's report abandoned the two contradictory statements in mid-air. The next evening, his reporting appeared as scrupulously neutral, but left the impression of implausibility and ridicule and ended with a quotation from the committee chairman, Senator Frank Church: "There ought to be a law against this kind of thing." In contrast, that evening's news report by ABC's Reasoner directly criticized the affair in an editorial. CBS also made a more direct challenge (4/2/73) to the claim that the money was to "placate and strengthen" Allende; in the words of reporter George Herman, this was "a fact ITT forgot to tell the government, put into memos, or mention during the first two weeks of hearings."

NBC reporting also differed from the other networks in the selection of news coverage. Some stories that were broadcast by the other networks were not carried by NBC, while some reports that ABC and CBS ignored were covered by NBC. Referring back to Tables 5.5, 5.6, and 5.7, NBC reported Chilean events largely from the issue context of "political instability and violence," five times more than ABC or CBS. The images of "normalcy" or constitutionality of the Chilean political scene projected by CBS and somewhat by ABC were absent on NBC.

Two examples illustrate the point. First, NBC broadcasts on the Chilean nationalization of the US copper multinationals—Anaconda and Kennecott—were in the form of relatively long, special reports. A network film presented the Chilean Congress meeting to ratify the copper nationalization amendment, and it was followed by a detailed background report and news analysis by Tom Streithorst in Santiago and Rancagua, Chile. In contrast, ABC and CBS simply announced that the nationalization had occurred. Second, NBC covered the pre-election days in Chile with grueling thoroughness, but the program was set in the theme "violence around the Chilean elections," and the announced death of eight and injury of 200. The other networks did not emphasize this pre-electoral violence.

While NBC ranked overall as less national security conscious than the other networks, coverage of Chile was an exception. Tom Streithorst's incisive reports from Santiago explored several themes: the national security implications of an Allende victory; the nationalization of US properties; and the likelihood of the failure of Allende's experiment in socialism. Streithorst's analysis was skeptical and critical. More than any other network, it also tended to capture the excitement of "explosive," "revolutionary" changes afoot in Chile by presenting an entertaining mix of film of mass student rallies and Chilean protest songs, free milk distribution centers, radical graffiti on walls and banners ("No Pago Los Yankees," or "¡Ahora Si! El Cobre Es de Chile!"), crowds of ecstatic Chileans, and the ever recurring pictures of the military in dress parade. Streithorst's practical economic analysis complemented these popular scenes.

A week before the Chilean elections (8/30/70), a typical Streithorst report was shown. His coverage began in a radical squatter camp where 90 percent of the people support the Marxist candidate. While observing scenes of poverty and radicalism, he noted the name of the camp—Venceremos or "We shall overcome." Streithorst noted the major socio-political issues facing an Allende victory and the typical network speculations of whether his election will mean continuation of political democracy, and whether the military will actually remain neutral. The report concluded: "Chile's political future is fraught with dangerous 'ifs.' They won't disappear in the elections of September fourth. They will only become clearer."

After the inconclusive elections, the September 6 report concerned fears of a military coup and showed pictures of military troop movements around Santiago. The news analysis ended with Streithorst's summary that if the Allende government "can accommodate Marxist economics with Chilean democracy" it will achieve what no other government before has been able to do. Another report showed scenes of crowds in front of the passport office, panic in the banks, a pessimistic interview with a prominent member of the American business community, and an unidentified man in the crowd expressing fears of a communist government with the words, "they said it wouldn't happen either in Cuba but it did."

The field reports did not create the impression of a radical Allende as much as the explosive, radical Chilean political scene. Streithorst called Allende "a Marxist with charm and a sense of humor." He interviewed and filmed members of radical Chilean political groups to prove his point. For example, one story focused on squatter communities of MIR, the Movement for the Institutionalized Revolution. The film showed a poverty-stricken squatter town populated by radicals who described Allende as a "hopeless bourgeois;" They were said to conduct classes for indoctrination, train urban guerrillas, and harbor fugitives from the law, such as two bank robbers, Comrade Hector and Comrade Joaquin, whom Steithorst interviewed. The communities were named "Vladimir Lenin," "Che Guevara," and "26th of July."

Streithorst's skepticism about the political economy of the Chilean socialist experiment found extensive outlet in his reports. The overall message elaborated was the inevitable failure ahead for Allende economics: wage increases, price controls, unchecked printing of money, rising expectations, declining production, food and consumer goods shortages, and balance of payments and debt problems. Colorful footage of disco dancing in Santiago and reckless spending sprees of the rich and middle classes characterized a modern "Roaring Twenties" before the crash. The good life is good but it's fleeting if there is no one to pay for it. The rest of the analysis was accompanied by standard film fare of food markets, lines for goods, and money rolling off busy printing presses.

With the military coup against Allende, NBC, like the other networks, provided some historical context for the crisis. The September 11 background report reviewed the three years of the Popular Unity government. In a style much like that of CBS, one heard the voice of Eduardo Nunez over the static of the telephone lines. He was visually accompanied by still photos of street fighting and troop movements. The anchor, John Chancellor, narrated the historical summary. He began with the words that Salvador Allende, the first Marxist President, was believed dead and "will be remembered in Latin America." Chancellor concluded the analysis, in which economic chaos, political instability, and violence dominated, with the words: "outside of the backing of the working classes, he had very little else going for him." On the US reaction to the coup, he said: "There is no evidence of gladness that the generals in Chile have finally done him in."

When Streithorst's reports came in from the field, his analysis strongly suggested US involvement. Speaking from Mendoza, Argentina (on the border with Chile), as the audience sees photos of military troops and tanks, he explained that charges against the United States and the CIA had become so frequent that one began to ignore them. However, based on a high ranking official of the Allende government, whom Streithorst trusted, there was said to be proof of CIA activity. In the studio the anchor, John Chancellor, noted that the CIA was unavailable for comment but that a State Department spokesman had said that the coup had been an "internal matter" and "no elements of the United States government were involved."

NBC pursued this involvement lead persistently. Next evening's news ended with Chancellor reporting that the US government admitted that it had been getting coup reports for a year but nothing specific until immediately before it happened. Chancellor noted that the Chilean government had not been warned. To the United States denial, he interjected a strategic "yet," followed by the statement that NBC's reporter in Mendoza had noted increased United States Air Force activity there three days before the coup.

NBC, following the format of the other networks, replayed the "official" Chilean film of the revolution, showing the bombing, burning and strafing of the Moneda, or presidential palace. A few days later, NBC showed an unofficial film recovered from an Uruguayan plane. NBC concluded news reporting of Chile—as did the other television stations—with the installment of the Pinochet regime and coverage of its acts of repression. But by late September, with release of American prisoners held in the infamous soccer stadium, and the diplomatic recognition of Chile by the US government on the 24th, the networks had lost interest in Chile. Reports of repression and brutality of the military regime dwindled. NBC seemed to conclude three years of generally strong field coverage of Chile with a report from Steve Delaney. From Santiago, his summary was that taking sides in Chilean politics has consequences—one might paraphrase —"the winners get to push the losers around a little, and that's what they are doing."

An Assessment

The preceding review of ABC, CBS, and NBC coverage of Chile from 1970 through 1973 suggests several surprising patterns that do not entirely fit with certain schools of thought about US media coverage. To begin with, it is clear that Allende was rarely treated as a serious threat to the United States. He was portrayed as relatively "moderate" in contrast to "radical" elements. Allende's policies were an "experiment" in Marxism in a democracy, rather than the foundation to convert Chile to a one-party socialist state. Allende's motives were not questioned; he was seen as trying to balance competing forces, enact reforms, and sustain democracy, rather than as scheming and desiring to do otherwise. In this vein, if some of his policies were misguided or inflationary, they were not treacherous or malevolent.

Without explicitly endorsing any list of particulars on the ITT-CIA-US role in the downfall of Allende, the networks (with the obvious exception of the editorials noted earlier) repeatedly left the impression of US culpability. The overthrow of Allende was attributed to a reactionary response to upheaval in the Chilean economy (with probable US prodding). Moreover, the Pinochet regime was treated as unambiguously nefarious and oppressive.

In short, even though the negative undercurrents of Chilean economic problems and "another potential Cuba" were treated as legitimate, newsworthy concerns, there was little evidence that the networks acted as apologists for multinational corporations or justified the ouster of Allende. Marxism in Chile was not presented as necessarily evil, and the US government was not painted as an entirely innocent bystander. The absence of a strong "red menace" theme came as a surprise to this researcher and contradicts, at least in this instance, part of the left's critique of TV news.

NICARAGUA AND THE SANDINISTAS

For the reporters who were assigned to cover the Nicaraguan civil war, soon to become a social revolution, the task would challenge their humanity and their duty to impartiality, and would endanger their lives. Network reporting of Nicaragua would call forth united institutional forces, and coverage would often be loaded with sensationalism and emotionalism. There would be an undisputed villain—for no one living in Nicaragua in the months of June and July 1979 would be able to ignore the brutality and stupidity of Anastasio Somoza Debayle. TV news, in abandoning its polite facade, would make its position clearer than in any other recent crisis.

Network reporting of the Marxist Sandinista revolt against Somoza would not be dogged with the complexity and negative concerns that were evidenced in much of the reporting of Salvador Allende's Marxist Chile. Perhaps reporters hoped that their transmissions from the field would help undermine the position of a corrupt and ruthless dictator. Network reporting of Nicaragua was generally homogeneous; only the timing of Somoza's downfall remained in question. All three networks offered descriptions of the conflict that were highly sympathetic to the rebels. Nevertheless, as might be expected under the circumstances, ABC's stories on Nicaragua were the most exceptional.

CBS

A typical Charles Gomez report from Managua (6/8/79) dramatically identified the Sandinistas with the people. Film presented a deserted capital in the grip of a massive general strike, with streets barricaded and manned by guerrilla fighters. The fighters were "los ninos" or young children who had joined the guerrilla cause and believed that "it is better to live as a rebel than as a slave." Gomez explained that "the people are clearly siding with the Sandinista rebels and express fear and resentment to the government forces." The government forces were killing indiscriminately, they claimed. The transmission ended as one rebel said: "Make no mistake about it, we are launching our final drive."

Gomez made other reports with this "war-is-hell" and almost pro-Sandinista angle. As the "battle of Managua" entered the fifteenth day, from Leon, the second largest city, Gomez transmitted this human interest story on June 10. Thousands of homeless, sick, and starving refugees had inundated seven American Maryknoll nuns in a school. He interviewed one, Dona Maria, who told the moving story of how four of her five sons were killed by the government soldiers as they played in the street. "I have to cry when I think about it," he translated from her Spanish. Again the suffering message of the story contrasted sharply with a report of Somoza's charges of international communist conspiracy. Somoza's words lacked credibility to the reporter who ended his report about thousands of people "praying for an end to the fighting and a chance to go home."

On June 12, June 15, and June 17, Gomez returned to the suffering-in-war themes: "A battle many of them have neither the spirit nor strength to endure"; or "one said he was for neither side, his family was just hungry and needed food to keep alive." Graphic videotapes depicted chaos, violence, disease, hunger, looting, death, and constant troop movements. The audience could see the pain and anger in the faces of the people, lying on the floors of fly-infested Red Cross hospitals, the babies sick, and families of eight rationed only two spoons of rice.

The last report by Gomez centered around a church where the "weary and worn" and homeless were "giving thanks for being alive." While in part a cry for international relief assistance for the 63,000 refugees, the coverage also implicated the government in acts of brutality. The report ended with a distraught, sobbing woman who told how the day before she was forced to abandon her wheel-chair-bound nephew to the deserted barrio because they did not have time to get him out on the short evacuation notice. The National Guard of Somoza had since bombed that barrio.

Field reports from CBS's Richard Wagner did not differ significantly from those of Charles Gomez, except for a slightly less anti-government tone. Wagner made a government victory over the guerrillas seem more plausible, perhaps because his reports centered on the National Guard and seemed to rely more on official sources. Despite some sensationalism —for example, his story about a pregnant woman shot in the stomach, wounded children, and a man who "doesn't even know which side shot him" (6/16/79)—his reports were more concerned with the military strategy of the revolution.

Wagner's field transmission on June 18 explained that strategically the Sandinistas had the edge in popular support, but the Somozan forces had greater fire power. Defections to the rebels were increasing, however, and the crumbling solidarity of the Guard posed another problem for Somoza. As Wagner assessed the Sandinista strategy of controlling enough people and territory to win legitimacy as a provisional government, Bernard Kalb announced a "significant shift" in US policy from the State Department (two days before the death of ABC corresopndent Bill Stewart). After Stewart's death the networks would play up this policy change and imply that it was initiated in response to Stewart's death. Kalb at the time described it as the first public indication that the United States had decided to dump Somoza and seek a political solution.

June 19 reports announced Somoza's counter-offensive. Almost immediately, newsmen indicated that it was not working. Wagner, covering the crack General Somoza Battalion, interviewed the leader, Captain Aguilar. He listed reasons why the special force should be effective, but ended the report by reviewing disagreements about how long it might take Somoza's forces to regain control. Events and coverage escalated rapidly when the networks announced the death of correspondent Bill Stewart on the evening of June 20.

Stewart's death mobilized the press corps against Somoza. Although the United States had indicated a policy shift just before Stewart was killed, by the 21st that policy was the only option. TV news capitalized on the foreign policy shift, as if it had occurred solely in response to the death. Walter Cronkite hailed it as a "major new policy initiative," and Bernard Kalb described it as the first time the United States had publicly called for the resignation of Somoza.

With the death of Bill Stewart and his Spanish interpreter, coverage of Nicaragua shifted from Managua to Washington, D.C., where the key decisions were to be made. CBS and NBC weakly tried to remain impartial, although ABC made little attempt. ABC called the death an outright "execution." Walter Cronkite, on the CBS evening news of June 20, emphatically quoted ABC and a State Department condemnation as if voicing his own condemnation. Of the three networks, CBS alone avoided editorial comment; its criticism was expressed indirectly. CBS juxtaposed information, quoted the condemnations of others, and presented critical field reports.

Richard Wagner's June 21 field summary of Somoza's actions after the deaths implied criticism and indignation: "What he called a 'full-scale investigation'"; "the wanton killing of the ABC correspondent"; "the already stunned and angered international press corps"; "his story was not believed"; "only further outraged the press"; and "execution," "murder," and "killing." Walter Cronkite observed in the studio that Nicaraguan radio was still calling the international press "communist sympathizers" despite Somoza's statement that "he does not agree with such characterizations." The order of Cronkite's statements implied duplicity on Somoza's part more than if he had directly called the strongman a liar.

CBS broadcast the silent, un-narrated footage from ABC of Bill Stewart being forced to lie in the dirt, then kicked, and after interminable seconds, shot in the head cold-bloodedly by a Nicaraguan National Guardsman. The audience was shown the terrible horror and shock of the murder, as the gun shot cracked unexpectedly and the reporter's body jerked uncontrollably.

Coverage of Stewart's funeral on June 24 in Ashland, Kentucky, and the oration of an ABC colleague, Frank Reynolds, made Somoza's words —"I will stay to fight to the death against communism"—with which the broadcast began seem ludicrous. The report presented the grief of Stewart's family and friends as they listened to the oratory of Reynolds:

> Dare we grope for consolation today in the hope that the circumstances of Bill's death may hasten the end of suffering in the land where he died. Bill would certainly hope so and I think we can too, for seldom has the world seen so vivid a display of mindless violence.

Subsequent reporting was even more unabashedly critical of Somoza, but was silent about the Sandinista alternative. What the political future of Nicaragua would be after Somoza was a question that was not asked.

NBC

Coverage of the civil war by NBC also took American audiences directly into the war torn experiences of Nicaraguans and into Sandinista strongholds. Reporting about Somoza and the National Guard was characterized as "official" news versus the "real" news uncovered by American correspondents in the countryside and in the barrios. For example, the June 4 report of Bob Jimenez made this distinction: "Contrary to the government account of the fighting, Sandinista rebels are not being pushed back but are advancing."

On location, Ike Seamans took American viewers into a guerrilla stronghold (6/10/79). Seamans' reporting was more measured and less overtly sympathetic to the guerrillas. He quoted one guerrilla who said that he would take great pleasure in killing us because he charged the United States is responsible for all the trouble in Nicaragua." Another report by Seamans (6/19) portrayed José Luis Cruz, a wounded 14-year-old volunteer in the National Guard. The youth said that when he recovered, he would fight for the Guard again.

NBC often juxtaposed statements and images to create the opposite impression. David Brinkley announced (6/13/79) that Somoza, from the safety of his secure compound, locally called the bunker, had said that "in general terms the country is at peace." The network immediately shifted to scenes of shooting and looting in Managua. The audience could draw its "own" conclusions. The next evening's news used the same technique. Somoza had just described Managua as "barely touched" by the guerrilla offensive, and had said the people were "carrying on normal life," when Ike Seamans followed up with scenes of looting, fire fights, and general chaos in the capital city. Seamans' pictures spoke louder than Somoza's words.

Ike Seamans and Sandy Gilmore emphasized the suffering-people angle, which was generally anti-Somoza. The "people are caught in the middle," they observed (6/16/79). A Nicaraguan was quoted as saying (6/15), "Somoza is killing innocent people." News reports continued the refrain that the "rebellion is not going well for President Somoza" and that "the country remains in deep trouble, virtually shut down." Then, Seamans moved to Somoza exhibiting Sandinista weapons and claiming they were bought in the United States. "The United States has betrayed Nicaragua," Somoza charged. "I want the American people to help me like I helped them for thirty years to fight communism."

NBC covered the death of ABC journalist Bill Stewart much as CBS did. With the photo of Stewart behind him, David Brinkley began, "the Nicaraguan government propaganda has taken a viciously anti-American turn." He quoted the ABC statement that "it was an execution." Next, Sandy Gilmore, NBC reporter in Managua, noted that state-owned radio was proclaiming that the "foreign press is in league with the Sandinista communists" and that Somoza had said that international reporters were biased against him. Unlike CBS, NBC concluded the news report with a direct editorial comment. David Brinkley explained that over the years many reporters had been killed in war situations, "but Bill Stewart of ABC news was not killed in a battle. He was murdered and so was his driver. We don't know why."

The next evening Brinkley skeptically presented the government explanation for the shooting. Using short mocking sentences, Brinkley said that the Nicaraguan government first explained that the soldier who had shot Stewart was in custody; then later in the day there was a different story, the soldier was himself killed in fighting. "That's what they say," added Brinkley unconvinced. He noted that the Nicaraguan government had charged that Stewart had been running away—"even though several hundred million people had seen that he was shot lying flat on the ground," he dryly commented. Jessica Savitch later explained (6/24) that Somoza had said that he planned to remain in office "in an effort to maintain order." Yesterday, she retorted, the OAS asked him to resign "for the same reason."

A special "Segment Three" on "The War in Nicaragua" (6/28) culminated this anti-Somoza perspective with the film of John Alpert, an American free-lance journalist. Taped in a Sandinista guerrilla camp and including an interview with famed Nicaraguan "folk hero" and commander of the Southern Front in the Nicaraguan civil war, Eden Pastora (or "Comandante Cero"), the film was the most strongly pro-guerrilla story on any network at that point. Footage was long, lively, and jerky. It personalized the guerrilla struggle by easy banter with ordinary individuals (said to be professors, painters, students, a physicist, and a mathematician) who had joined the Sandinistas. Meanwhile, mortars were constantly falling as the film rolled and twisted. The segment, nearly five minutes long, signaled that the tide had turned against Somoza. On July 5, Ike Seamans wrapped up his broadcast from Managua with this conclusion: "There are some here who believe it is no longer a question of whether President Somoza will resign but when."

ABC

ABC also covered the Nicaraguan revolution with empathy for the rebel cause. Early June field reports transmitted by Bernard Shaw reported, the charges of Somozan terror by the Catholic Bishops' Conference in Managua. The bishops justified opposition to Somoza because of his "gross injustice." As if to support their charges, Shaw's coverage (6/4/79) showed the unembalmed bodies of persons killed when the National Guard indiscriminantly fired high velocity rounds into buildings. In agony, a mother placed a handkerchief over the face of her dead, 8-year-old son, described as an "innocent victim of the fighting." An army officer disputed this claim, insisting that all those killed were Sandinista guerrillas who had fired on his men, killing two. The scene shifted to President Somoza denying charges of government terror, claiming that his government was democratic, and denouncing the guerrillas as "invading communist agents."

Similarly, the reporting of Bill Stewart followed the format and themes described above and by the other networks—especially the bloodshed and suffering of the Nicaraguan people. A pregnant woman shot in the abdomen was shown lying lifeless on a hospital table. With her was a tiny infant with a bloody bandage wrapped around its head. Also shown was an x-ray film revealing a bullet lodged in the child's skull. At a press conference, Somoza displayed captured arms supplied by Cuba and charged Panama with complicity. Stewart's field analysis summed it all up: While the fighting is inclusive, "the fact that rebels have been able to operate this openly suggests that this time Somoza may be in trouble."

Stewart's report of June 12 continued these themes. Amid film of air attacks, the camera centered on the gaping hole in a church roof and the blood on its cement floor. We were told that National Guard rockets hit this church, killing an old man and five children. The weaponry of the National Guard—supplied by the United States and Israel—was contrasted with the makeshift arms of the rag-tag, bandana-wearing Sandinistas, "mostly teenagers." Fire-bombed homes, and crowds of refugees illustrated the concluding evaluation: "These people are refugees, among those hurt most by this fighting, and yet, at this refugee center, everyone we have talked with says he supports the Sandinistas, and would stay and fight with them, if only he had the weapons to do so."

June 18th, ABC announced "an important policy change" by the Department of State, as did the other networks. Bill Stewart's report from Leon ironically foreshadowed the tragedy to come. Reporting from the headquarters of a victorious guerrilla group, Stewart explained that the car of Bob Freeman and Ken Sandborn of the ABC team had been fired upon by Somozan airplanes. The episode demonstrated the danger that dogged reporters during the revolution.

In fact, almost a year earlier (9/15/78), a report on NBC had described the attack on NBC's producer Don Critchfield, and two cameramen by Somozan airplanes in Leon. That coverage had also charged the Somoza government with censorship of the national and international press. At that time, the United States had called for a ceasefire, for Somoza to step down, and for a mediated solution. The shape of events during the first guerrilla offensive of 1978 were not unlike those of mid-June 1979. Given the behavior of the Somoza forces in the past, should what happened on June 20, 1979, have been anticipated?

ABC's coverage of Bill Stewart's death was extensive. The evening broadcast of June 20 made the announcement at 5:22 p.m., CST, and ended the story at 5:28 p.m. The next evening's coverage would be equally long, but it would begin, rather than end, the broadcast. As Bill Stewart's picture inscribed with his birth and death dates was seen off to the side, Frank Reynolds announced that "ABC news correspondent, Bill Stewart, 37 years old, was killed today in Nicaragua." The public is told that a report of "the murder of our correspondent" will follow the news of the fighting in Managua. Later, with field correspondent Al Dale narrating, ABC showed the videotape taken that morning of Stewart and his crew entering a neighborhood under National Guard control.

As the team approached the first checkpoint, Dale explained, the Guardsmen were friendly and eager to dispute the charge of low guard morale. They allowed filming of one guardsman singing and strumming a love ballad on his guitar as other guards sat around him. At this time, continued Dale, Bill Stewart made his last observation about the war he had been covering. "Here are Bill's final words," said Dale, "before the tool of his trade, a news camera." Kneeling in front of the singing guardsman, Bill Stewart concluded his last report "It is said that in every society it is the young men who fight the old men's wars. And that is especially true here in Nicaragua for those who are fighting and dying on both sides are very young indeed."

As the videotape showed Stewart approaching the next checkpoint, Dale found the attitude of the soldiers was entirely different. Next was shown the footage of the killing: Stewart stretching out his hands to show that he was unarmed, lying on the ground "as the soldier kicked him in the side and then shot him." The muffled words of one of the crew, "he killed him," is heard. Nothing more is said.

Coverage shifted to the studio where Frank Reynolds read the prepared statement of Roone Arledge, President of ABC: "This deliberate act by a soldier of the Nicaraguan government on an unarmed newsman, ordered to his knees at a National Guard roadblock, cries out for both full investigation and the penalty of whatever justice is left in that land." Reynolds presented a simple biography of the fallen correspondent. "Bill Stewart was a West Virginia country boy with degrees from Ohio State and Columbia University," etc. Suddenly Reynolds shifted into an angry and emotional tone, which dramatically punctuated the key words in his statement:

> He was good and we knew he was good, and it breaks our heart to admit it now, and that's why we sent him on so many difficult and dangerous assignments. We know of no better way to pay tribute to him and to demonstrate what his loss means to us and to you than to show again his last report from Nicaragua, seen on this network yesterday morning.

Bill Stewart's last report reflected his pro-Sandinista sympathies, which most foreign correspondents had adopted in covering the brutal fighting. As he began, the film centered on young guerrilla fighters behind their make-shift barricades:

> This is the civil war inside barrio Santa Rosa. It is a people's war, led by a few who have training and joined by the people of the barrio or neighborhood, who have behind them decades of hatred of the Somoza family. The guerrillas survive here behind barricades with rifles, Molotov cocktails and conviction, outmanned and outgunned by the National Guard and fearing most the death that falls from the skies, the bombs against which they have no defense.

The film shifted to wounded rebels and rested on the impassive face of one young girl. "She is one of the rebels," explained Stewart, "eleven years old, shot while taking part in the fighting."[8] The June 20 broadcast terminated with final words from Frank Reynolds: "That was the report of a gifted journalist and an extraordinarily warm and sympathetic human being."

The next evening's report was also six minutes long, and began with Reynolds' words: "The terror in Nicaragua was brought home vividly to the American people yesterday in the cold-blooded murder by a National Guardsman of an American newsman who was simply carrying out his journalistic mission." From Managua, foreign correspondent Britt Anderson quoted Somoza's reaction: "I have already ordered a full investigation of this painful, and useless, and hateful incident." Promising just punishment for the killer, Somoza extends "deepest sympathy" to Stewart's companions. As if to question Somoza's sincerity, ABC shifted to an interview with the guardsman who was in charge at that fateful roadblock, but who had not seen the shooting, and who nervously explained that the soldier who had pulled the trigger had himself been killed later that day. Britt Anderson added that the Somozan government had charged that Stewart had been trying to escape, but "that was clearly not the case," and parts of the shooting were reshown.

ABC then aired condemnations by Vice-President Walter Mondale, Senate Majority Leader Robert Byrd, and Senators Howard Baker, Rudy Boschwitz, and George McGovern; McGovern attacked US policy that had over the last decade assisted the very army that had killed Stewart. The condemnations were read as the text was seen on the television screen. This news segment ended with a statement from President Carter. Calling the killing "an act of barbarism," the president added:

> Journalists seeking to report the news and inform the public are soldiers in no nation's army. When they are made innocent victims of violence and war, all people who cherish the truth and believe in free debate pay a terrible price. I know the American people share my sense of outrage and loss at the death of this gifted and dedicated young man.

The report of Stewart's burial on June 24 culminated ABC's catharsis of grief and outrage. The heart of the broadcast was Frank Reynold's funeral eulogy. Attending the funeral were many famous personalities in television broadcasting. Discreetly the camera focused on their faces, and on the mass of funeral flowers; the open coffin was seen in the distance. The funeral text that ABC broadcast was a different excerpt from that used by CBS and NBC. The words and emotion of Frank Reynolds were moving; they also indicated the hope that enough publicity would help oust Somoza:

---

[8] There are two versions of this report; cf. June 18 with June 20, 1979, ABC.

For seldom has the world seen so vivid a display of mindless violence, in a poor country among poor people told by their oppressor who knew it was not the truth that journalists were their enemy. At last Bill's own country has called for the removal of the despot who has misled and misruled his people for so long and so cruelly. And now at last a surge of outrage has spread around the globe and the name of Bill Stewart will forever be associated with the suffering, and, perhaps, the saving of the people of Nicaragua. And now the West Virginia boy who grew up to be what he wanted to be, who saw the world and helped his countrymen to understand it, a noble achievement, has come home.

ABC's reports from Nicaragua next centered on the diplomatic efforts to remove Somoza. On June 29, a memorial service was covered by Lynn Sharer in New York. Again many media celebrities attended, perhaps feeling, commented Sharer, "it could have been me." As the fighting in Nicaragua itself escalated, coverage returned to the field and the last days of the Somoza regime.

An Assessment

The reporters assigned to cover the Nicaraguan civil war, which soon became a social revolution, had a task that challenged their humanity, impartiality, and, in some instances, their very lives. The fighting provided many opportunities for sensationalism and emotionalism.

The overwhelming emphasis on violence and instability again suggests the structural bias of the newsgathering process and the imperatives of television news as entertainment.

The networks abandoned their image of neutrality and opinion conveyed through nuances in order to make their viewpoints unusually candid. Ironically, even the peaceful, legally-elected government of Salvador Allende in Chile had not benefited from such favorable coverage as had the Sandinistas. (Perhaps Allende should have followed Pinochet, not preceded him.)

The Marxist Sandinista guerrillas were projected as so many common people who had become courageous freedom fighters. The death of Bill Stewart may have convinced those not already persuaded of the ruthlessness of the old regime. There was only limited attention to the ideology, funding, and international connections of the Sandinistas. The tenor of coverage on the networks was remarkably similar, with the chief exception being ABC's special attention to Bill Stewart's death. (In contrast to coverage of Chile, all three networks also used Spanish-surnamed reporters to cover Nicaragua during various stages of the revolution—Geraldo Rivera of ABC, Charles Gomez of CBS, and Bob Jimenez of NBC.)

Coverage of Nicaragua refuted the claim that the networks take a conservative status-quo bias and are inherently hostile to the left in coverage of Latin America. Somoza's dictatorship was hardly the beneficiary of favorable stories. The ambivalence that characterized much of the coverage of Allende—wonderment over the elected, moderate Marxist, but qualms about the ultimate consequences of his rule—was rarely present in reports from Nicaragua. Unlike Chile, the intricacy of democratic versus Marxist ideology was not an important factor in the coverage of Nicaragua. The issue was clear: Dictatorship. Nicaragua provided an undisputed villain in the form of Anastasio Somoza Dabayle. The country's uncertain future under the Sandinistas seemed clearly preferable to its misery and oppression under Somoza.

In Nicaragua, searching out and reporting what network news people interpreted as the truth meant destabilizing a corrupt dictatorship and making US support of Somoza increasingly untenable. In plying the tools of their trade, correspondents were making news as well as reporting it. They interacted with the National Guard and the guerrillas, and the killing of one correspondent became a cause célèbre that probably hastened the end of the conflict and marked forever a key event in American broadcast history.

At the New York memorial service for Bill Stewart, US Ambassador to the UN Andrew Young stated: "It is a mark of progress in our civilization that our journalists are our front line of defense, that we have learned to mobilize the power of truth through mass media." Just what kind of truth it is that is mobilized from the front lines continues to be worth understanding more fully.

REFERENCES

Adams, William and Phillip Heyl. 1981. From Cairo to Kabul with the Networks, 1972–1980. In William C. Adams, ed., *Television Coverage of the Middle East*. Norwood, N.J.: Ablex, 1–39.

Robinson, Michael. 1981. A Statesman is a Dead Politician: Candidate Images on Network News. In Elie Abel, ed., *What's News*. San Francisco, Calif.: Institute for Contemporary Studies.

PART

THE WEST
AND
PRESIDENTIAL
DIPLOMACY

6

CAMP DAVID AND THE NETWORKS: REFLECTIONS ON COVERAGE OF THE 1978 SUMMIT

WILLIAM C. SPRAGENS
WITH
CAROLE ANN TERWOOD

The 1978 Camp David Summit of Anwar Sadat, Menachem Begin, and Jimmy Carter created the basis for a peace treaty between Egypt and Israel after 30 years of intermittent warfare. Amid the Mideast turmoil of the 1970's, it stands out as an epic event. This essay reviews how the American commercial networks covered the Camp David Summit on the regular evening news programs, and is based on broadcasts of the early-evening news of ABC, CBS, and NBC during September 1978.

Adams and Heyl (1981) found TV coverage of the Camp David Summit to be one of the key Middle East stories in the 1972–80 period, ranking along with the 1973 war and oil embargo, Sadat's trip to Jerusalem, the fall of the Shah and the Iranian Revolution, the American hostages in Iran, the Soviet occupation of Afghanistan, the Lebanese civil war, and the Iran-Iraq war. TV news attention to the Middle East had grown throughout most of the 1970's and by the year of the Summit, 1978, around 15 percent of the average weeknight news show was devoted to Middle East news. One of the biggest changes was in the coverage of Egypt and its leadership.

Bagnied and Schneider (1981) show some of the ways in which coverage of Sadat's visit to Jerusalem in 1977 catapulted him to widespread recognition and popularity in the United States. One year later, the Camp David Summit provided a second intensive look at Egyptian President Anwar Sadat and Israeli Prime Minister Menachem Begin.

Bagnied and Schneider argued that one crucial consequence of the emergence of Sadat as a media-sanctioned figure was to emphasize the

Palestinian question and to provide a "credible alternative" to Israel's positions. They concluded (1981, pp. 63–64):

> The extension of favorable coverage to Sadat did not come at Israel's direct expense. Instead, television news lifted Sadat, the peace pilgrim, above the other Arabs who appeared to reject any negotiation with Israel...However, Sadat's ascension in television news put into place a highly visible articulate voice that was treated as a credible alternative to Begin. Sadat's image was solidified as a "Westernized," rational, peaceful, personable leader, sufficiently legitimate to appear on a warm, first-name basis with Cronkite and Walters. Having acquired that status, Sadat was then able to speak to Americans, in modulated and moderate tones, on such charged issues as the Palestinian problem. Although he was being attacked by some Arabs for his efforts, Sadat emerged in American television as the first Arab leader able to validate as worthy of discussion most of the key Arab complaints about the state of Israel.

By 1979, Asi (1981) found that Sadat and Egypt were the beneficiaries of strongly positive coverage, more positive in fact than that given Begin and Israel. Adams and Heyl (1981) identified similar trends in US public opinion toward both leaders and their nations.

In the context of these previous studies, this chapter will review coverage of the Camp David Summit as it related to several issues: First, what was the visibility accorded the Summit as well as the Palestinian question in coverage of the Summit? Second, what were the images of Begin, Carter, and Sadat on TV news? Third, how did the networks respond to the news blackout? Before considering these questions, a brief historical sketch is in order.

The Historical Setting

The context and format of the Camp David Summit made it an exciting episode for television news to cover, but it was also clearly a momentous historical occasion. On three occasions following the founding of Israel in 1948, warfare between Arab nations and Israel has raised a threat to one of the critical goals of American policy: assurance of Middle Eastern oil supplied for the United States and Western Europe. The Suez Crisis of 1956 was the first such outbreak. Eleven years later, there were further hostilities. In 1976, Israel fought against Egypt, Jordan, and Syria, and won possession of the Suez Canal, the Sinai Peninsula, the Golan Heights, and the West Bank of the Jordan.

In 1973, Egypt invaded Israel and started another brief war. Israel counter-attacked and was in the process of decisively defeating Egypt when a UN truce was imposed at the urgings of President Richard Nixon, Secretary of State Henry Kissinger, Soviet leaders, and others. Kissinger later conducted extensive "shuttle diplomacy," which was intended to prevent another outbreak of fighting. Both Syria and Egypt made a truce with Israel, but hostilities were not ended by the truce. During this period, the Palestine Liberation Organization appeared to be growing in strength and international support, while the Israelis seemed to be losing ground diplomatically.

With the advent of the new Administration in January 1977, Secretary of State Cyrus Vance and President Jimmy Carter sought some new directions and strategies. Despairing of any movement, the Carter Administration proposed reconvening the Geneva Conference for a general Middle East settlement—an action which would have given the Soviets a greater role in negotiations.

A startling development that preempted this proposal was Begin's invitation to Sadat to visit Jerusalem. Sadat made a dramatic visit to Israel in November 1977, and spoke movingly to the Israeli Knesset of the need for a just and lasting peace in the area (see Bagnied & Schneider, 1981). The first direct negotiations between Israel and Egypt soon followed. These talks began to bog down during the early part of 1978, and, at the request of both Israel and Egypt, the United States once again became more involved in the negotiations as an impartial mediator with friendly relations with both countries. This set the stage for the Camp David Summit of September 1978.

All the participating parties—Menachem Begin, Anwar Sadat, and Jimmy Carter—seized the Summit as a means to begin negotiations to restore normal relations to a region which had been plagued with war and tension. Israel wanted secure borders, safe from attack. The United States desired a peaceful Middle East to guarantee its crucial crude oil supply, to insure Israel's survival, and to further detente with the Soviet Union. Egypt wanted peace in order to improve its economy and preserve internal stability. Egypt also sought the return of all the Sinai and wanted negotiations over the West Bank of the Jordan, the question of a Palestinian homeland, and the status of Jerusalem. President Carter hoped to pursue a new approach to the "peace process," to end the state of belligerency between Israel and Egypt, and to establish a framework for subsequent negotiations of larger questions. The resulting Camp David agreement may have been the most significant foreign policy achievement of Jimmy Carter's presidency.

The Camp David accords announced in September 1978 temporarily halted the growth of Israeli settlements in the Sinai, initiated negotiations about the status and degree of autonomy of Palestinians, and promised future negotiations about the West Bank. Meantime, Israel would give up two air bases in the Sinai, and the United States would replace them with two new air bases inside older boundaries of Israel. Egypt would get back the Sinai lands in stages. After Israel and Egypt had signed a peace treaty, they would exchange ambassadors for the first time; and, efforts would be made to involve Syria, Jordan, and other Arab states in the evolving negotiations with Israel. In the following negotiations, President Carter participated in "shuttle diplomacy" to nail down the details of the accords. A peace treaty was finally signed by Egypt and Israel in Washington in March 1979.

The Summit and the Palestinian Issue on the News Agenda

The Camp David Summit was given extensive and sustained coverage on all three networks during the month of September 1978. The Summit and closely-related developments in the Mideast constituted almost one fourth of all news coverage throughout the month.[1] On some nights, as Table 6.1 shows, news of Camp David consumed almost the entire newscast. In the week of September 18, in particular, coverage was saturated. On ABC that week, over half of the total news time (56 percent) was given over to news of the Summit.

Camp David was the big story in September 1978. While it did not totally dominate newscasts every single night, it did dominate coverage if the month is taken as a whole. Of the three networks, ABC gave the most coverage to the Summit—over 29 percent of total news time in September. CBS was second with almost 24 percent, and NBC was third with about 21 percent. While other stories were not ignored, one fourth of all news time represents a sizeable portion of attention to give to one story, particularly one with a "news blackout."

ABC, giving Summit news the most coverage, relied especially on Frank Reynolds, one of the anchors who was given considerable time on the story, and Barbara Walters, who conducted controversial interviews with Sadat and Begin after the talks ended. Other key ABC personnel included White House correspondent Sam Donaldson; correspondent Bill Seamans; and Peter Jennings, anchor for overseas coverage.

CBS, midway between ABC and NBC in terms of its amount of Summit coverage, relied heavily on diplomatic correspondent Marvin Kalb and White House correspondents Bob Schieffer and Robert Pierpoint, with Walter Cronkite in the major role as anchor. NBC assigned its State Department correspondent, Richard Valeriani, to handle diplomatic coverage, and its White House correspondent, Judy Woodruff, to

---

[1] Vanderbilt's *Television News Index and Abstracts* was used to select relevant news stories to be dubbed and compiled by the Vanderbilt Archive. The collection of weekend newscasts is incomplete for this period and, as Table 6.1 indicates, except for two Sundays on NBC, the analysis is based on weekly coverage during the month. The research assistance of Carole Terwood, Lori Mizer, and Tammy Manähan is acknowledged and appreciated by the author. Material in this chapter is taken from a more extensive unpublished paper, "Network Television Coverage of the 1978 Camp David Summit," by William C. Spragens.

cover activities of the President and his chief aides. David Brinkley and John Chancellor had the anchor spots for NBC.

Several of the studies in *Television Coverage of the Middle East* (Adams, 1981) document the steadily increasing attention given to the Palestinian problem on US television during the 1970's. Coverage of the Camp David Summit stands as one key example of that pattern. During this period, all three networks devoted a significant share of Camp David air time to discussion and news related to the Palestinian question.

Table 6.1
Percentage of Total News Time Devoted to Camp David Coverage
by Day and by Network, September 1978

Date	ABC	CBS	NBC
Sept. 1 (Fri)	.8	.0	.0
Sept. 4 (Mon)	45.0	55.1	20.6
Sept. 5 (Tue)	47.0	30.2	29.5
Sept. 6 (Wed)	40.2	23.4	15.2
Sept. 7 (Thu)	27.6	10.1	8.2
Sept. 8 (Fri)	13.7	12.1	10.5
Sept. 11 (Mon)	20.5	6.5	7.4
Sept. 12 (Tue)	10.2	11.8	8.2
Sept. 13 (Wed)	25.0	6.5	24.8
Sept. 14 (Thu)	21.1	13.0	16.3
Sept. 15 (Fri)	9.7	13.7	11.1
Sept. 17 (Sun)	(NR)	(NR)	8.2
Sept. 18 (Mon)	88.0	79.1	77.0
Sept. 19 (Tue)	60.9	54.6	34.3
Sept. 20 (Wed)	42.3	26.1	28.4
Sept. 21 (Thu)	36.6	29.3	30.6
Sept. 22 (Fri)	53.3	50.4	29.6
Sept. 24 (Sun)	(NR)	(NR)	24.8
Sept. 25 (Mon)	13.5	22.5	13.4
Sept. 26 (Tue)	17.2	3.6	9.8
Sept. 27 (Wed)	31.1	.1	30.8
Sept. 28 (Thu)	21.9	24.7	21.7
Sept. 29 (Fri)	.8	1.4	.8

(NR) = Not Recorded

Not only did Sadat take advantage of forums before and immediately after the Summit to raise Palestinian and West Bank issues, but the networks frequently went to Yasir Arafat, George Habash, and other Palestinian leaders for additional viewpoints. There were some network differences in this area, however. According to our calculations, in the key week of September 18–22, CBS gave the most time to this subject with just over three minutes each night—roughly one third of all CBS Camp David coverage that week concerned the Palestinians. In the same week,

NBC was averaging 2 minutes 20 seconds each night on the same issue, while ABC was typically offering less than 1 minute 25 seconds per weeknight on the Palestinian issue. The networks treated this topic as if it were long overdue for high-level discussion. As Barry Dunsmore said on ABC (9/19), referring with approval to Secretary Vance's remarks: "The Israelis have recognized the legitimate rights of the Palestinians. Vance will note that this is enormous progress from the days when Israelis used to say there was no such thing as a Palestinian." (Dunsmore might have added that it was also a change from the days when the networks acted as if there was no such thing as a Palestinian—other than terrorists.)

Nations Personified

Television news is often accused of trivializing and simplifying complex issues into broadly-sketched and stereotyped conflicts. Symbols are frequently used to provide convenient, shorthand labels and representations of more intricate matters. The time constraints of television make such short cuts useful and the audio-visual, narrative format makes such practices attractive dramatically. One element in this approach can be to treat nations as embodied fully in key leaders.

The personification of nations as men must have been a special temptation in the situation of Camp David. All of the principals were by then known to the American public. Sadat's trip to Jerusalem had received massive media coverage in the United States. He and Begin were among the foreign leaders most well-known to Americans.

In fact, coverage was kind to all three men. Their deep sincerity and good intentions were noted frequently and never questioned. Carter was portrayed as the "honest broker" with virtues of patience, compromise, and interpersonal skill. Despite some different nuances among networks, this picture of Carter was similar in all three. The post-Summit coverage reflected the euphoria associated with one of the high points of Carter's roller-coaster popularity ratings. As for Begin, the crusty, tough, bantam image was there—one reporter compared him to Harry Truman—but other aspects of Begin's personality came through as well. Begin was sometimes depicted as valiantly trying to restrain his combative and righteous instincts in the interest of conciliation.

Coverage of Sadat continued to reinforce the media persona he had acquired during his trip to Jerusalem and the year before. Sadat was treated as a fair-minded, moderate, genuine, and bold leader. In public relations terms, Sadat appeared to be engendering an increasingly receptive attitude on the part of Americans who had been conditioned to be suspicious of Egyptian diplomacy since the Suez crisis and the imbroglio between John Foster Dulles and Gamal Abdel Nasser.

Bernard Kaplan, in an ABC story from Paris on September 4, reported that the Egyptian head of state was stressing to French President Giscard d'Estaing that Camp David might be decisive to hopes for any kind of Israeli-Egyptian settlement. The next day, Doreen Kays of ABC described Sadat as "relaxed and fit" and quiet. She said he was not changing from the view that Israel must withdraw from occupied territories and Palestinians must be given self-determination.

CBS treated the pre-Summit period with similar reverence. On arriving in Washington, according to Bob Schieffer, Sadat "decided to do a little politicking first, but when he came to the microphone, his mood could not have been more serious." Sadat's airport comments referred to the talks as a "tremendous challenge" and added that it was time for "magnanimity and reason."

Coverage of the arrival at Camp David, just as that for the remainder of the Summit, was under the ground rules of the temporary official news blackout. This removed Sadat from direct contact with the news media and made correspondents rely on Egyptian staff members for background information. Beginning with the September 18 newscasts, Sadat was once again accessible to the media.

Sadat told Barbara Walters he felt the Camp David agreements opened the way for other Arab nations to sign. In an interview with Walter Cronkite, Sadat denied that the accord represented a separate peace with Israel and said that Egypt would continue to press its points on the Palestinian issue and other matters. He confirmed that at one point he had almost walked out of the negotiations. He commented, ". . . Carter visited me and we had a quarter of an hour discussion, and whenever I meet with Carter, and whenever we sit together: not more than quarter of an hour to solve any problem, whatever its size."

References to Prime Minister Begin were also most respectful. ABC's September 4 newscast features a Bill Seamans' interview with Begin in New York City. The interview consists mostly of pleasantries and links Begin's walks through the city with those of Harry Truman. The absence of any "hard" news did not seem to be a problem.

The next day, ABC emphasized Begin's view of the upcoming talks as "the most important and most momentous of all" and expressed the hope that "the peace process can continue and ultimately be crowned with peace treaties." NBC described Begin in "high spirits" on the eve of the Summit, and as sensitive to past criticisms (9/4). Similarly, CBS coverage offered no hints of Begin as intransigent or belligerent, or as anything other than a dedicated peacemaker.

In the initial period after the Summit, an especially affable side of Begin was visible. He told Barbara Walters that he and Sadat were "two happy men." Soon, however, there emerged some controversy over the interpretation of the agreement, and the networks differed in how they treated the confusion. Beginning with Walters' interviews, ABC was the leader in stressing this story. CBS picked up the conflict but did not stay with it long; NBC was the most low-key about the whole controversy.

In the interview with Walters, Begin had seemed to indicate that several matters were not open to future discussion after all. He said that there "won't be any repartition of Jerusalem"; he also discussed differences in positions on the West Bank and his unremitting opposition to the PLO and proposals for Palestinian sovereignty. On Capitol Hill, Begin reasserted Jewish rights to "Judea-Samaria" and the Gaza strip. Considerable newscast attention, most notably on ABC, was given to whether Israel was "reneging" on the key element of dismantling settlements. President Carter became personally involved by urging Begin, and Sadat as well, to relax their public statements and to be careful about reigniting old passions and problems. This brouhaha died down and the network focus shifted to such matters as Begin's "triumphant welcome" home.

President Carter was not the object of as much attention as were Begin and Sadat. Carter was discussed, paraphrased, or quoted on the Summit 101 times on all three networks during September, compared to 159 times for Begin and 120 times for Sadat. Like the other two men, Carter was the beneficiary of respectful and positive coverage. The picture of the President was that of a low-key, confident, and calm man experiencing one of the peaks of his term of office. Reporting lacked the cynical and questioning tone that sometimes accompanied coverage of the Chief Executive.

ABC and CBS quoted the President saying on September 4:

> There's no cause for excessive optimism, but there's also no cause for despair. Compromises will be mandatory. Without them no progress can be expected. Flexibility will be the essence of our hopes, and my own role will be that of a full partner.

When the Summit ended, the President was depicted, with awe and acclaim, as diligent, tireless, and shrewd. Even Sam Donaldson adopted this tone, as illustrated by this excerpt from his September 18 story on ABC:

> . . . the two sides studied the American plan and made initial responses and suggestions—and, at this point, an extraordinary thing occurred. President Carter and Secretary of State Vance sat down with an Egyptian and an Israeli to do the work. Not President Sadat, but Sadat's principal foreign policy adviser, Osanna El Bas; not Prime Minister Begin but Begin's legal adviser, Aharon Barak. These four men worked together for eight hours last Wednesday, and many hours thereafter, each day sifting out the differences, and when it was over the final

product was draft number 23—much of the final language written by Mr. Carter himself...

Network reporters fell only slightly short of the enthusiasm showed by Menachem Begin when he exclaimed that the "Camp David Summit should be renamed and called 'the Jimmy Carter Conference'" (ABC, 9/18). When Carter's popularity rating soared upward after the Summit, it was treated as neither unsurprising nor unjustified; it was taken as entirely his due.

Unlike some European conferences where a few key leaders took pleasure in sniping at Carter, both on and off the record, Begin and Sadat seemed determined to outdo each other in praising Carter. Aside from predictable criticisms from the Soviet Union and extremist Arab states, Carter enjoyed an extended period of highly favorable coverage.

No News Is Good Diplomacy

The news blackout was extraordinary. Sam Donaldson told the ABC audience on September 6 that Presidential Press Secretary Jody Powell had "made it clear that one of his principal duties is to see that nothing about the substance of the Summit gets out." Powell, he said, "even declined to characterize the mood."

The Administration believed that the only effective way negotiations could be conducted was by keeping the media away until the talks were concluded. Many people in the media seemed to understand the logic and need of secrecy for the sensitive discussions; but, as several White House correspondents told this author, they were somewhat frustrated nevertheless.

Cronkite announced on September 6 that the "secrecy lid the White House imposed was total." In this period, the networks were obliged to present an unusual number of background stories due to the shortage of "hard" news. As exemplified in Bob Schieffer's September 8 report, some of the coverage resembled a kind of "sociogram" that described who talked to whom that day. Without firm information about the status of the talks, reports were invariably based on speculation. Schieffer's September 12 stand-up alleged that "they were close on some of the issues, but they still don't have a deal." On September 14, Cronkite stated that "yesterday's hopes were dampened today." The next day, Cronkite was using the word "marathon" to describe the Summit.

On NBC, Judy Woodruff talked in similarly vague terms. On September 11, the Summit was thought to have taken on "new momentum;" on the 13th, it has a "faster pace." On ABC, Sam Donaldson said the Summit had entered a "make or break" phase.

The news blackout was remarkably effective. The number of genuine "leaks" were few and largely trivial. September 13th, ABC related a "leak" claiming that the Egyptian delegation had come to Camp David anticipating failure and prepared to push instead for a clarification of UN Resolution 242 in the Security Council. Some other stories representing this same level of revelation were also broadcast.

After the Summit ended, all three networks had long reports of day-by-day accounts of the "13 days and 12 nights of haggling at Camp David" (CBS, 9/18). While the conventional interpretation of this Summit was that the agreements would have been impossible if they had been negotiated under the glare of media spotlights, the networks did not discuss on the air the virtues of their having been kept so uninformed.

The importance of the Summit and the perception of the stakes involved promoted the acceptance of the temporary news blackout. The networks appeared to try to compensate for the loss by extended post-Summit analysis and interviews. President Carter had also tried to discourage heavy media exposure after the talks, lest the entire agreement become unraveled without surviving even the first few weeks.

Despite daily speculations on the progress of the talks, television coverage was more substantive and analytical than it is usually given credit for being. Perhaps in part because of the news blackout, a number of solid background stories were broadcast.

CBS, in particular, offered many analyses of the diplomatic situation. As with the other networks, most of the CBS stories were primarily devoted to reporting or analysis by CBS correspondents themselves, rather than interviews and comments of others. ABC had the most coverage, but a large portion of ABC's extra coverage went to human interest stories.

Each network explained the nature of the issues in some detail, using visual displays of maps and key phrases along with film and tape clips. After the signing ceremony, each network devoted considerable time to the specifics of the text. In addition to the regular nightly news, the networks carried live the President's speech to Congress and other events not normally shown live. Time constraints are one reason that television news tends to be superficial. To the extent that time constraints were pushed aside in the case of the Camp David Summit, the coverage was more substantive as befitted what Begin termed (CBS, 9/28) "the great turning point in the history of the Middle East."

REFERENCES

Adams, William and Phillip Heyl. 1981. From Cairo to Kabul with the Networks, 1972–1980. In William C. Adams, ed., *Television Coverage of the Middle East*. Norwood, N.J.: Ablex, 1–39.

Asi, Morad. 1981. Arabs, Israelis, and TV News: A Time-Series, Content Analysis. In William C. Adams, ed., *Television Coverage of the Middle East*. Norwood, N.J.: Ablex, 67–75.

Bagnied, Magda and Steven Schneider. 1981. Sadat Goes to Jerusalem: Televised Images, Themes, and Agenda. In William C. Adams, ed., *Television Coverage of the Middle East*. Norwood, N.J.: Ablex, 53–66.

7

COVERAGE OF THE 1980 OLYMPIC BOYCOTT: A CROSS-NETWORK COMPARISON

LAURENCE BARTON

Following the Soviet invasion of Afghanistan in December 1979, the Carter Administration worked to construct policies aimed at mounting enough pressure on the Soviets that disengagement would be the most suitable option. One of the economic, diplomatic, and military responses under consideration was a boycott of the 1980 summer Olympic games.

The Olympic proposal was particularly well suited for the American television networks. Unlike two other proposed retaliatory measures—the curtailment of grain shipments and sophisticated hardware—the Olympics have an entirely nationwide "clientele." The Administration anticipated that such a challenge to the Soviet Union would guarantee robust debate, generating widespread support among the populace. Four months of intense, coordinated effort on the part of the President, Congressional leaders, State Department officials, and others eventually proved this to be the case.

The manner in which the White House tested and then ultimately embraced American public opinion on the boycott proposal is a fascinating instance of mobilization and manipulation. A decision was apparently made in late December to have Vice President Mondale first voice a potential boycott concept, as he did in Des Moines on January 10, 1980, in an attempt to prevent public embarrassment for the President, should the idea trigger widespread rejection. In the next several days, a number of nationally-syndicated columnists (including Mary McGrory and George F. Will) enthusiastically endorsed the boycott move, as did a number of House and Senate leaders. Yet, it was not until January 19 that the President himself directly urged a boycott. On NBC's *Meet the Press*, Mr.

Carter said: "Neither I nor the American people would support sending a team to Moscow with Soviet troops in Afghanistan." From that moment on, the three networks traced the boycott story with closer scrutiny, clearly because the proposal now constituted a crusade on the part of Jimmy Carter to embarrass the Soviet Union and solidify Western opposition to the Afghan invasion.

How did the three American networks treat the Carter Administration's proposal for a boycott of the 1980 summer Olympic games in Moscow? The story developed from its early stage as a mere option, a potential "warning" to the Soviet hierarchy in retaliation for that country's invasion of Afghanistan, into a major controversy for the United States and its allies with the curtailment of a popular sports spectacular and the escalation of superpower politics in athletic competition.

In examining coverage of the boycott, it is especially useful to assess the degree of diversity in content among the networks. ABC, CBS, and NBC are frequently accused of adopting nearly identical agendas and story angles—"pack journalism". Media analysts have come to assume a large degree of homogeneity among the networks, since Lemert (1974) found a large degree of overlap in hard news stories. Nevertheless, it is a question worth re-examining. As George Comstock and Robin Cobbey (1978) put it:

> Network diversity in news coverage is a state toward which there is approach-avoidance behavior. When diversity occurs, observers may suspect the deviation represents less than ideal news treatment by one or more networks. Such a conclusion derives from the unrevolutionary homily that not everyone can be right. At the same time, viewers may often demand and hope for differences in coverage so that three such expensive endeavors as network television news are not redundant with one another. . . [After a review of prior research,] one might easily conclude that this body of evidence demonstrates that network news programs are measurably different, but that they seldom exhibit radical differences. . . Taking into account the manufactured nature of news, we cease to consider the moderate differences demonstrated to exist among the networks as minor in importance. Instead, we would suggest that the evidence of divergence, although never by itself proof of distortion at variance with good reporting, should be taken as the starting point for scrutiny. Divergence is not wrong, but it deserves acknowledgment as the products of choice, not happenstance.

In the case of coverage of the Olympics, there are special reasons to be interested in network differences. One of the networks, NBC, held an obvious stake in the story with its 72 million dollar agreement with the Soviets for exclusive coverage from Moscow. NBC was faced with a potential loss of substantial advertising revenue and loss of the ratings bonanza that network president Fred Silverman had been counting on for two years. How would NBC cover a story in which it had a far more immediate and sizable interest than in virtually any other news story in recent memory? How would ABC and CBS cover a story that was laden with potential for melodrama and piousness? In an attempt to discern differences in coverage among the three networks, the author examined a series of compiled videotapes tracing the story from early January through April 1980. The research used resources of the Vanderbilt University Television News Archive and the diligent research assistance of Lori Heyman of Tufts University. (For an analysis of US television coverage of the invasion of Afghanistan, see Kern, 1981).

Outline of the Olympic Battle

Struggles surrounding the proposed Olympic boycott made "good stories" for TV news. Coupled with the embargo of selected products, these measures represented the first overt US actions against the Soviet Union since the 1961 blockade of Cuba. The issue was a relatively simple and straightforward one. Key questions were unambiguous: Should the United States participate in Moscow? And, will other countries follow the American lead and make the boycott truly successful? The games themselves were already a well-known and dramatic sports event. The story was infused with a series of tensions and confrontations—between the US and the USSR, between the President and reluctant athletes, between the Administration and the US Olympic Committee, and between the State Department and US allies. Furthermore, TV visuals had the potential of bringing good pictures of sports scenes into the news lineup. In short, it was no surprise that the subject became a frequent story on all three networks.

In analyzing network coverage between January and April, each segment was coded. In cases where a report interfaced on two or more topics (athlete reaction and a State Department report, for example), the more significant or lengthy aspect of the story was categorized. Findings appear in Table 7.1.

Findings reported in Table 7.1 suggest a high degree of homogeneity among the networks in terms of general subtopics that were covered. The general rank order of the items is highly similar for all three networks. The allies' response was the most frequent story on all three networks. US government actions and policies and the debate within the USOC and IOC were the next two most frequent subtopics. On all three networks, the fourth most common report dealt with the reaction of US athletes and coaches. (The greatest difference came in coverage of NBC's role. ABC ignored the story, but CBS focused on it in two reports; NBC examined the impact of the boycott on itself in five reports.) A closer look at the depiction of the ongoing story will reveal more marked differences across networks.

Table 7.1
Substantive Network Reports
January–April 1980

	NBC	CBS	ABC
Status of US allies in response to Administration boycott proposal	14	17	15
US government action from President, State Dept., Congress	11	12	8
Debate on part of USOC, IOC	12	9	10
Reaction of US athletes and coaches	6	6	6
Soviet government or citizen response to boycott	3	2	5
Impact on NBC Television	5	2	0
Other, including commentary	1	1	3
Impact on American business	0	1	1
History of Olympic game manipulation	0	0	2
	51	50	50

Starting on January 5 and throughout that month, the networks treated the boycott suggestion of the Vice President with skepticism, but three separate events appear to have been used to propel the story into one of major significance. First, during the second week of January, the president of the American Olympic Committee, Robert Kane, was responding with open criticism to the Carter Administration's efforts, thus triggering debate well suited for the nightly news. Each of the networks' broadcast footage of the infamous Goebbels-sponsored 1936 Olympiad in Berlin, interlaced with a historical study of the erosion of non-partisan Olympic competition in the post-war era. Second, the overwhelming enthusiasm for a boycott expressed by the US House of Representatives provided an additional sense of legitimacy and seriousness to the proposal. Finally, President Carter's ultimatum of January that he would implement the boycott within a month if Soviet troops were not withdrawn added a new dimension of confrontation to Soviet-American relations.

In February, all three television networks concentrated upon efforts being made to orchestrate a unified stand on behalf of Western allies, although ABC provided more cumulative time to this area than either NBC or CBS. The mission of former heavyweight boxing champion Muhammad Ali to several African nations in search of support for the boycott was at first generally reported with a sense of hope, particularly by Peter Jennings of ABC. Yet within a week it was clear that the State Department was not entirely pleased with Ali's diplomatic style, and he returned having received only minimal endorsement. The boycott effort appeared to be further embattled in problems when Secretary of State Cyrus Vance brought a personal, unsuccessful plea to the opening caucus of the IOC at the Lake Placid winter games on February 9. (Although all three network evening news programs featured footage of the Secretary's address, ABC provided additional attention to the growing controversy during its prime-time coverage of the winter games themselves. Its general tone suggested frustration on the part of the Administration.)

Initially, priority attention had been given to reports detailing action on the part of the President, the Secretary of State or key Congressional leaders. But, as the month of February unfolded, network coverage tended to drift away from the Administration in order to follow a changing daily count of "who's who in closest allies." This fairly encouraging sign for the boycott proposal made its way into newscasts on a regular basis throughout February and thereafter: the total number of nations which had formally endorsed the boycott was regularly listed for viewers on all networks. This figure increased from only a handful in January to a total of 36 by the time of the opening ceremonies in Moscow on July 19. (Potential over-enthusiasm in categorizing some nations did lead to some confusion, however. At least two networks gave contradictory assessments of West German and Canadian policies.)

During the remaining months of March and April, it was becoming increasingly clear to foreign policy analysts and reporters that the proposed boycott was edging towards reality: the Carter Administration had not waivered in its demand of a troop withdrawal and White House counsel Lloyd Cutler had made soundings regarding punitive action against athletes who intended to circumvent boycott policy. Meanwhile, NBC continued to insist it would abide by the government's intentions and abdicate plans for what one of the network's news releases had termed "the biggest event in television history."

Attention turned increasingly to those young men and women who had been training for years in anticipation of the Moscow journey. Some 46 separate reports were broadcast about this particular issue on the three networks. Correspondents appeared sympathetic regarding the faded expectations of young athletes whose dreams of a potential medal had been erased due to international squabbling. Occasional references surfaced that some athletes would compete in Moscow, regardless of the Administration's policy. (Three Puerto Ricans and a few other Americans who later claimed citizenship elsewhere did compete in Moscow.)

Subtle Differences in Approaches

In the early stages of the boycott story, reports on CBS expressed some skepticism over the feasibility of an Olympic withdrawal. While NBC was interviewing angered athletes and ABC's *World News Tonight* surveyed the boycott's impact on a multitude of American businesses, CBS pressed on with an outlook that seemed to presume the boycott would never get off the ground. On January 5, correspondent Robert Pierpoint emphasized that the President lacked the legal authority to withdraw a US team, and anchor Walter Cronkite reiterated on January 10 that the United States still preferred not to withdraw from the games. Six days later, State Department correspondent Marvin Kalb stressed that while sentiment was growing for the boycott, European allies were only "luke-warm" toward the proposal. Less than one week later, on January 21, a report by Gordon Joseloff reported that "political zigzagging" on the part of Western governments "will not affect the games," although it was noted that Soviet prestige might be tarnished.

Within two weeks, as it became increasingly clear that the American Olympic Committee would probably accede to Administration pressure, CBS News incrementally placed greater credibility in the likelihood of a boycott. A major determinant in this change, no doubt, was passage by the House of Representatives of a January 24 resolution (by a vote of 386–12) supporting the Carter policy. Correspondent Mariya McLaughlin commented that the Congressional enthusiasm embraced these "popular resolutions" which would lead to the similar passage of a Senate resolution five days later. CBS was to place more substantive attention on the Congressional blessing of the boycott than either ABC or NBC.

While CBS hesitated in giving credence to the proposal, NBC was placing serious attention in the likelihood of a withdrawal. Anchor John Chancellor, throughout the first two weeks of January, correlated footage of invading Soviet tanks with the Administration's get-tough policy. He reported on January 10 that "the Kremlin has started a propaganda campaign against President Carter" in response to the Administration's suggested measures. In the weeks following, the content of NBC Nightly News reports presumed that a boycott was probably eminent.

NBC, particularly in the early stages of reporting the story, concentrated more air time on the reaction of American athletes than either of the other two networks. During January, for instance, NBC included interviews with no less than a dozen athletes in training, although correspondent Fred Briggs apparently found it difficult to round up a broad spectrum of sentiment at the USOC training camp in Colorado Springs. Briggs interviewed one athlete, weightlifter Robert Giordino, on three separate occasions in a one-month time frame (Giordino expressed the same sentiment on each occasion) even though Giordino was not a spokesman for the athletes, nor did he receive any attention from either ABC or CBS.

By mid-February, pressure was clearly growing on NBC to determine which course it would pursue: an aleatory "wait and see" attitude which could aggravate the Administration given the growing tide of popular support, or announcement of the difficult decision to withdraw entirely. The network played it safe, pursuing a middle ground of rhetoric and patriotism, announcing on February 20:

> NBC will be guided by the policies and regulations of the US government. There is a higher calling. . . than NBC's interest.

The network did not say, however, that it would pull out of its unprecedented commitment to the Soviets.

Over at ABC, coverage of President Carter's efforts also reflected moments of discouragement. On March 21, for instance, 100 Olympic hopefuls travelled to the White House to listen to a personal explanation by the President of his decision. Correspondent Sam Donaldson gave a pessimistic, low-keyed report on the attitude of athletes and then grimly asserted that when the President entered the meeting room, it was the first time in his Presidency that he was not greeted by applause in public. The effect was dramatic and accentuated the seriousness of the situation.

Two weeks later on April 3, ABC correspondent Bettina Gregory reported a "growing revolt" against the boycott because several athletes again met with White House officials to push their plan whereby American athletes would compete in Moscow but boycott the opening, closing, and award ceremonies. Gregory's comments appear exaggerated, given the fact that by April the boycott was virtually certain and had widespread public approval that would outdistance the anger of a few dozen athletes.

In terms of innovative reporting on the boycott story, ABC's *World News Tonight* took special efforts to regularly secure an accurate determination of the number of nations supporting the President's intentions. While NBC and CBS largely relied on listings of supportive allies released by the State Department, ABC undertook its own poll of foreign governments on at least two occasions. Early in the process on January 17, the network surveyed chief government leaders in 19 capitals and found that seven were anti-boycott while the remainder were divided. Again, on February 1, ABC polled governments of 107 of the 143 nations invited to Moscow by the IOC. Its findings: 32 nations supported the boycott, 55 opposed, and 21 were undecided, a highly accurate indicator of the number to appear in Lenin Stadium five months later. (ABC also more closely followed Soviet reactions.) Unlike CBS and ABC, both of which gave more attention to the political rationale behind the proposal and the jockeying of positions by US allies, NBC opted to spend more time on the human dimension of a boycott: athletes, IOC personalities, coaches, and families.

NBC was, as noted previously, shrewd but fair in reporting its own role and its potential loss of advertising revenue and lost ratings. On January 5, the network had said it would clearly "abide by any decision made by the government." Ultimately, it did not waiver from that stand.

One of the more marked contrasts to emerge in the study were varying degrees of editorializing engaged in by the weekend sports anchors on NBC and ABC broadcasts. Dan Lovett, ABC's sports reporter, offered a series of interviews during the period analyzed that, although emphasizing American athletes' dissatisfaction with their new status as hostages of international politics, were usually balanced with new developments of a political nature.

On NBC, sports anchor Dick Schaap was somewhat less objective in approach. He began a March 1 report by asking athlete Eammon Coghlan what it would feel like to hear the American anthem being played at the July award ceremonies in Moscow. His reporting was emotionally leading at times. (For example, he introduced a March 9 report on members of the disgruntled women's volleyball team by saying: "These American women share a dream of gold medals. Of being the hockey team of the Summer Olympics. And, they also share a nightmare. . . ")

The Soviet Side of the Story

As early as January, there were reports on all three networks linking the upcoming Moscow games with past utilization of the Olympics for propagandistic purposes, either on the part of the host state or by others. On January 16, NBC correspondent Garrick Utley reviewed Goebbels' spectacular guise of anti-Semitism in the 1936 Berlin games and followed this with footage of the 1968 games in Mexico City (where black American athletes protested domestic racial policies) and the Montreal 1976 Olympiad (in which some participating teams protested apartheid policies of certain other states). Utley noted that a boycott of the Moscow Olympics "would be a severe blow to Soviet prestige." Both ABC and CBS included similar file footage in their nightly newscasts, highlighting violence and controversy associated with the Olympics in past years. The sometimes unstated but clearly implied message was that the United States feared the Soviets might muster a substantial propaganda advantage with their Olympic festival—one additional reason not to travel to Moscow.

Network news coverage of the boycott story revealed surprisingly few stories about Soviet reactions to moves by the Carter Administration. In terms of total air time, ABC provided viewers with five major reports detailing denunciations from TASS and party chairman Brezhnev. NBC and CBS both provided two major reports. Yet, considering the fact that the Soviets had been working for four years on elaborate Olympic preparations, had ordered the exodus of 700,000 school children and assorted political dissidents from Moscow proper, and had spent hundreds of millions of dollars on construction of tourist facilities, remarkably little attention was devoted to the economic and diplomatic impact of a Western boycott. It was almost as if—once having instigated the boycott as retaliation—the United States would derive little satisfaction in recounting the damage that the boycott would inflict.

ABC provided the most coverage of this subject. One of the most comprehensive and representative of ABC's airings occurred on January 21 with diplomatic correspondent Ted Koppel reporting that the State Department had sent cables to some 100 nations explaining the President's rationale for a boycott. Koppel indicated that while most Mideast nations were quick to pledge support, European allies were "hedging." Charles Bierbauer concluded with a report from Moscow where American athletes, present for a trial competition, were surveyed for their opinions. Bierbauer also conducted man-on-the-street interviews with Muscovites on their reaction to the boycott as well, sometimes a risky venture in the Soviet capital.

In the many weeks following, ABC regularly interjected reaction from the Kremlin to developments in Washington. Examples of these brief but nevertheless potent elements include Richard Anderson's February 1 interview with Vitaly Smirnov of the Soviet Olympic Planning Committee (who admitted that the boycott "would hurt" the USSR) and the February 10 report of TASS criticism of the President who, the Soviet news agency reported, was utilizing "crude political interference" to destroy the Olympic movement.

On February 20, while NBC and CBS were pursuing themes surrounding the USOC debate and vocal protests by American athletes, ABC surveyed actual damage that the boycott would inflict upon the USSR. Charles Bierbauer indicated that Moscow's estimated $3.5 billion investment in the games would be tarnished if some 100,000 expected Americans dropped their travel plans (only about 1,500 eventually attended in July) and estimated the loss in revenue from American-related efforts alone to be at least $100 million. Bierbauer was quick to point out, however, that American firms would not be immune from losses, including the California firm whose exclusive rights to utilize the mascot bear "Misha" would crumble, costing investors millions of dollars.

ABC pursued this theme into April. On April 13, the network relayed a Moscow newspaper report accusing the FBI and CIA of orchestrating a plot whereby an "anti-Olympic sabotage team" of trained Americans from Harvard and other universities would subvert the Olympics by spreading anti-Soviet propaganda to foreigners. On April 21, correspondent Ann Garrells provided fresh Soviet reaction to Western disclaimers, reporting that the Kremlin was becoming increasingly convinced the CIA would infiltrate the Olympiad.

CBS provided only cursory attention to Soviet response to the boycott movement, but did broadcast segments of an interview with the chairman of the Soviet Olympic Planning Committee on January 21, which neither ABC nor NBC broadcast. Also, on April 4, Walter Cronkite asserted that the Soviets had become more than merely concerned over the ramifications of a US-led boycott. Cronkite noted the Soviets were reportedly considering such tactics as cut-rate travel bargains for Americans, free trips for athletes, and the deployment of Soviet coaches to poorer Third World nations in need of athletic guidance so that their nations could compete in July.

On NBC, Moscow correspondent Gene Pell attempted on two occasions to explain the worry brewing in the Kremlin over the boycott proposal, but may have over-reacted when he reported on January 24 that the boycott had triggered "open alarm" throughout the Soviet capital. In actuality, the boycott did signal a financial loss for the Russians, but at no time did the Soviet hierarchy or its populace express fear that the American boycott would destroy its grandiose plans. NBC colleague Jim Bitterman provided some equilibrium two weeks later (2/20) when he asserted that many Russians were (now only) "mystified" by the Administration's efforts.

One concise report filed by Bitterman (4/13) sampled opinion in Red Square over the USOC decision to abandon its Moscow journey. Bitterman included footage of a Soviet news program critical of President Carter and quoted Radio Moscow's denunciations of the Administration plan.

By the time the Olympic torch was ignited in Moscow in July, much of the Western interest in the games had subsided, proving the potency of a public relations campaign directed by the executive branch on a subject traditionally sacrosanct from external interference. The three networks were to devote relatively little coverage to the two-week-long Olympiad, and the footage that was broadcast came mostly from the overseas Intervision and Eurovision feeds. No discernable pattern emerged for daily updates on medals won or records broken by athletes; in fact, NBC, CBS, and ABC correspondents concentrated content primarily upon political and social controversies rather than the games themselves.

Athletes and Afghanistan

Each of the three networks tended to present the boycott story from slightly different perspectives: CBS was somewhat skeptical, NBC tended to focus on the athletes, and ABC was very interested in international reaction. Despite having already expended tens of millions of dollars toward its Olympics coverage, NBC provided largely balanced reporting. NBC, previously depending on the Olympics to salvage sagging ratings and corporate profits, exhibited a consistent degree of fairness on the boycott issue, although the network did lapse with a few melodramatic accounts of the athletes' discontent. (It has been suggested, of course, that NBC must have recognized that its coverage would be closely scrutinized.) ABC broadcast a more international perspective, providing news about concerns and frustrations of American allies as well as Soviet planners. CBS, more cautious about the likelihood and feasibility of a boycott from the outset, reported the story with a curious tone of moderation, sometimes bordering on paleness.

All three networks gave the Olympic boycott roughly the same amount of attention in early 1980, and all three had fairly similar approaches to the topic (cf. Table 7.1). Much of the reporting overlapped in content and approach, yet there were noticeable differences in the tenor of their coverage, as noted above. In all, the observations support Comstock's conclusion that "network news programs are measurably different, but that they seldom exhibit radical differences" (1978, p. 58).

The dominant emphasis throughout the first four months of 1980 was on the role of the Executive Branch in shaping and leading opinion in the United States and abroad. Television network news was an ideal vehicle through which the Carter Administration could generate support for its proposal, and one can assume that the medium was important in informing millions of citizens as to the rationale and practicality of a boycott. An NBC/AP poll asked Americans the following question: "If the Olympics are held in Moscow in 1980, should the US withdraw its participation?" In mid-January, 49 percent of the public favored withdrawing and 41 percent preferred US participation. Two weeks later, however, after the White House, State Department, and TV networks had dramatized the ramifications of the Afghan invasion and its link to Olympic diplomacy, support for a withdrawal had grown to almost three quarters of those polled. Thus, by early February, 73 percent favored withdrawal, while only 19 percent opposed US withdrawal. The proportion favoring US withdrawal remained high during the rest of the spring.

Images and rhetoric may have contributed to this overwhelming change in public attitude. On all three networks, for instance, in a typical week during February, if correspondents interviewed frustrated athletes at the USOC training facilities, such reporting was usually juxtaposed with newsfilm of developments in Afghanistan. The end effect was a sober reminder of the sacrifices that talented amateur athletes would be forced to make, but an equally chilling reminder of Soviet aggression against a neutral neighbor.

Reports focusing on the agony of the athletes clearly constituted the most damaging evidence against the campaign initiated by the White

House. Scenes were shown of wet-eyed women athletes, clustered near a fireplace in a Colorado Springs apartment, singing newly-written, anti-Carter ballads; articulate boxers lamenting the loss of their Olympic challenge; and coaches almost begging viewers to prevent amateur athletes from being utilized as a pawn in East-West diplomacy—all vivid reminders of the human elements. Yet concurrently, television news acted as a collective conscience, showing Soviet tanks rolling over the fields of Afghanistan in the process of subjugating a poor remote land.

REFERENCES

Comstock, George and Robin E. Cobbey. 1978. Watching the Watchdogs: Trends and Problems in Monitoring Network News. In William Adams and Fay Schreibman, eds., *Television Network News: Issues in Content Research.* Washington, D.C.: School of Public and International Affairs, George Washington University, 47–63.

Kern, Montague. 1981. The Invasion of Afghanistan: Domestic vs. Foreign Stories. in William Adams, ed., *Television Coverage of the Middle East.* Norwood, N.J.: Ablex, 106–127.

8

TERRORISM ON TV NEWS:
THE IRA, THE FALN, AND THE RED BRIGADES

DAVID L. PALETZ
JOHN Z. AYANIAN
PETER A. FOZZARD

Terrorism seems more ubiquitous than ever. It is accompanied by a prolif-
erating industry of often repetitive academic literature. (See, for example,
the massive bibliography compiled by Mickolus, 1980; as well as the works
of Alexander, 1976; Alexander & Finger, 1977; Alexander et al., 1979;
Bassiouni, 1975; Beres, 1980; Burton, 1979; Hutchinson, 1978; *Journal of
International Affairs*, 1978; Trent & Kupperman, 1979; Laqueur, 1977;
Miller, 1980; Stohn, 1979; *Disorders and Terrorism*, 1976; and the new
publication edited by Alexander, *Terrorism: An International Journal*.)

Scattered throughout the terrorism literature are occasional discussions and assertions about the connections between terrorism and the mass
media. The most conventional is that the "success of a terrorist operation
depends almost entirely on the amount of publicity it receives" (Laqueur,
1977, p. 109). Terrorists have indeed been known to undertake activities
with the specific purpose of publicizing their grievances, aspirations, and
demands. For example: "The Montoneros in Buenos Aires kidnapped the
industrial director of Germany's Mercedes-Benz there and released him
after the company *inter alia* published advertisements in newspapers in
Europe, Washington, D.C., and Mexico denouncing the 'economic imperialism' of multinational corporations in developing countries" (Alexander,
1978, p. 103).

In most cases, terrorists act and then depend upon the news values
and perspectives of the media to transmit, present, and interpret their actions. With what effects? According to Norman Podhoretz, "the publicity
that terrorism has received helps to further the aims of the terrorists" (1980,

p. 85). Argues Walter Laqueur: "in the final analysis, it is not the magnitude of the terrorist operation that counts but the publicity" (Laqueur, 1977, p. 109). But publicity is not self-evidently favorable. Why would terrorists benefit from media coverage? Because, writes Laqueur, the media "with their inbuilt tendency toward sensationalism, have always magnified terrorist exploits quite irrespective of their intrinsic importance" (Laqueur, 1977, p. 109; see also Alexander, 1977b; Bell, 1978; Cooper, 1977, Vol. 2, Nos. 1 and 2 of *Terrorism: An International Journal*; and, for a quite different perspective, Davison, 1974).

Alexander expands on Laqueur's argument. "Willingly or unwillingly" the media serve terrorists' "specific or general propaganda and psychological warfare needs" (p. 102). They do so by giving the terrorists publicity. Through this publicity, Alexander explains, the terrorists(1978, p. 102):

> hope to attain essentially one or two of the following communications purposes: First, to enhance the effectiveness of their violence by creating an emotional state of extreme fear in target groups, and, thereby, ultimately alter their behavior and dispositions, or bring about a general or particular change in the structure of government or society; and, second, to draw forcibly and instantaneously the attention of the 'whole world' to themselves in the expectation that these audiences will be prepared to act or, in some cases, to refrain from acting in a manner that will promote the cause they presumably represent.

The conventional view, then, is that media coverage is favorable to terrorists. According to Alexander: "by providing extensive coverage of incidents the media give the impression that they sympathize with the terrorist cause, thereby creating a climate congenial to further violence" (1978, p. 112). Podhoretz goes further, contending that the "regnant assumption in the American press concerning the rise of terrorism is that it is rooted in what may be called 'social causes'" (1980, p. 86). He adds that the "'what are the terrorists trying to tell us' syndrome tends to underlie a good deal of the discussion of terrorism in the American and Western media generally." And he concludes "that the media have been in collusion with terrorism and have helped to make it a successful political weapon in our time...." (1980, p. 86). Alexander summarizes this general argument succinctly: "in the final analysis, the communications purposes which at least revolutionary terror groups seek through the media are attention, recognition and legitimacy" (Alexander, 1978, pp. 103–104).

It is one thing to charge that terrorists enjoy "attention, recognition and legitimacy" through their media coverage, but it is quite another to document the accusation. Here, scholars have so far failed us. Alexander's article "Terrorism, the Media and the Police," which discusses some of the most spectacular sieges and crisis management situations, has appeared, virtually unchanged, in one journal and two books, not to mention its origin as a conference paper (see Alexander, 1978, 1979a, 1979b). One other substantial study of media coverage of terrorism is Philip Elliott's research on how events in Northern Ireland during two three-week periods were reported by the press in England, Northern Ireland, and the Republic of Ireland (Elliott, 1977). With that conspicuous exception, there are no systematic and quantitative studies. For confirmation, see the citations in the bibliographies compiled by Mickolus (1980, pp. 343–349) and by Norton and Greenberg (1979). This chapter is an effort to remedy this neglect.

APPROACH

Terrorism is a widely-used, emotionally-charged term. We define it as politically motivated violence that strikes at symbols and figures of authority in society, seeking to achieve the goals of the perpetrators through intimidation; it is more than a technique, less than a doctrine. From the bevy of contemporary terrorist groups active around the world (Laqueur, 1979), we have chosen three to study: the Irish Republican Army (IRA), the Red Brigades, and the Fuerzas Armadas de Liberacion Nacional (FALN, or the Puerto Rican Armed Forces of National Liberation). The three groups have different histories, ideologies, goals, and tactics.

The IRA

The Irish Republican movement dates from the late eighteenth century; the IRA was formally organized in 1916. It claims to act on behalf of the Catholic minority in the six Protestant-dominated counties comprising Northern Ireland. Its ultimate goal is to end British authority there and to unite Northern Ireland with the 26 counties of the overwhelmingly Catholic Republic of Ireland to the south to form one republic encompassing the entire island of Ireland. Some members of the IRA want that republic to be a socialist state (Bell, 1970, 1976; MacStiofain, 1975).

In 1969, the conflict in Northern Ireland exploded after civil rights demonstrations by the Catholics there. During this crisis, the IRA divided into two factions. The "Provisional wing" has been responsible for most of the IRA violence of the subsequent years (Lebow, 1978; Corrado, 1979, pp. 195–223).

O'Day describes the Provisionals' movement as essentially "nonideological, populist, heavily working-class and sectarian." It is, he writes, "attractive to Catholics in Ulster less because of the goals, which are unlikely to be realized, than because it is in fact the only effective organ of protest available to the Catholic minority with its deep-seated Catholic grievances." The Provisionals' terrorism, based on " half-baked history and ideology" and "genuine economic and social grievances," "is essentially sectarian and ritualistic and helps to maintain Provisional IRA and Catholic morale" (O'Day, 1979, p. 129).

According to Lebow, "The IRA and its components resemble a military organization. . . a formal structure, hierarchical control—albeit not always effective—and a notable esprit de corps. IRA violence reflects these attributes: it has generally been authorized from above, has had specific political objectives, and has been carried out in a comparatively professional manner" (Lebow, 1978, pp. 49–50). Tactics consist of "hit-and-run attacks on military installations and murders of police, informers, and intelligence personnel. . . . Sometimes bombings are indiscriminate, but normally they are directed against specific and strategic targets" (O'Day, 1979, p. 125).

Conflict in Northern Ireland has resulted in appalling carnage: "The average number of deaths caused by political disturbances in Ulster has averaged about 200 a year" since 1968. "Relative to population, this is equivalent to 232,668 deaths in the United States and more than 59,010 in Great Britain. . . . Excluding open warfare, no part of Western Europe or North America has suffered such bloodshed for such a prolonged period over the past century" (O'Day, 1979, p. 122).

The Red Brigades

The Red Brigades have been violently active in Italy since the early 1970s. Most members were hardened in their opposition to the Italian ruling elites at the time of the student demonstrations of 1968. The organization is sustained by frustration with unemployment, corruption in government, overcrowding in universities, and the inability of college graduates to obtain meaningful work. Its members view themselves as authentic communists and revolutionaries, the Italian government as corrupt and oppressive, and the Italian Communist Party as compromised by its cooperation with the Christian Democrats.

The goal of the Red Brigades is to destroy the existing Italian state and replace it with proletarian rule. Tactics consist of attacking political, judicial, and corporate officials, thereby creating a climate of fear among the elite. The Red Brigades try to provoke police state responses by the government to enable people to see the oppressive nature of the state and to revolt against it (Lotringer & Marazzi, 1980). The Red Brigades have been estimated to have between 100 and 1,000 active members, with additional supporters and sympathizers.

Three aspects of the Red Brigades are of special importance for this study. First, the group is located so far to the extreme left of Italian politics that its political theories are probably incomprehensible to most

Americans unless carefully presented. Second, one of the group's tactics has been to maim its antagonists by shooting them in the legs; it is hard to be tolerant let alone understanding of such behavior. Third, the period of our research included the Red Brigades' kidnapping and eventual execution of former Italian Prime Minister Aldo Moro—one of the most extensively covered terrorist episodes in recent history.

The FALN

The FALN wants Puerto Rico to be an independent nation. While violent groups seeking Puerto Rican independence have been active since the 1950s, the FALN first made its appearance during the early 1970s. It views the American government and corporations as exploiting the Puerto Rican people. The group is very small, its exact size unknown. While some terrorist groups pursue a wide range of available tactics (the IRA for example), the FALN specializes. It "consistently chooses to bomb selected targets" (Mickolus, 1979, p. 178). These targets are primarily buildings occupied by governmental agencies, political parties, and corporations in major American cities, particularly the nation's media and financial centers.

According to FBI director William H. Webster, the FALN has claimed responsibility for more than 100 bombings in New York, Washington, D.C., Chicago, Philadelphia, and San Francisco since 1974, including two in which five people died (Webster, 1981, p. 6). Damage was estimated at more than $3.5 million.

Period and Networks

Every story on the ABC, CBS, and NBC evening news programs concerning the three terrorist organizations over the two-year period, July 1, 1977 through June 30, 1979, was analyzed. This period was chosen in order to review recent coverage on a representative and manageable basis. (On the general subject of content analysis, see Holsti, 1969; Graber, 1974; Adams & Schreibman, 1978.) All stories mentioning any one of the groups was coded, as were stories which an informed viewer would logically associate with one of the groups (some stories about the kidnapping of Aldo Moro for example). A few of the news stories were what we call "multi-segments" with reporters presenting different story angles; we coded each reporter's segment separately.[1]

---

[1] Reliability checks were performed on 10 percent of the stories, nearly one year after the initial coding. The results were as follows: Intercoder reliability was .84 for ABC stories; .83 for CBS stories; and .87 for NBC stories. Intracoder reliability was .88 for ABC stories; .87 for CBS stories; and .88 for NBC stories. We used the following formula: $R = 2 \, Pab/Pa + Pb$, where R is reliability; Pa is the number of observations of first coding; Pb is the number of observations of the second coding; and Pab is the number of agreed upon observations.

The videotapes were compiled and provided by the Vanderbilt Television Archive which records the networks' evening news programs.[2] We are grateful to James P. Pilkington, Margaret M. Pritchett, and their cohorts at the Archive for their splendid assistance. Without them, systematic research on television news would be virtually impossible. We also acknowledge the invaluable assistance of Mark Ayanian and Gordon J. Smith of Duke University.

Omissions

This chapter has one notable omission—right-wing terrorism. We searched the Vanderbilt indexes under the categories for groups, countries, cities, and relevant subjects. Over the two-year period on all three networks, we found two stories about the frustrated efforts of members of an anti-Castro Cuban group to go to Cuba to attempt a coup. (They were intercepted by the US Coast Guard.) There were three stories of assassinations by rightist elements in Spain. Some half-dozen stories appeared about prison riots in Argentina. Nothing about right-wing violence in Turkey or elsewhere. Certainly, there was no dearth of violence from the right. Why, then, was this terror absent from the American television networks' evening news?

The IRA, Red Brigades, and FALN are active in Western Europe and the United States, free societies open to the press. The television networks have bureaus and correspondents in London and Rome, and frequently send them to Northern Ireland with relative ease. They have no full-time correspondents in Turkey, however, and usually rely on a handful of reporters for all of Central and South America. To be covered, right-wing violence usually must occur in an open, democratic, technologically accessible Western state.

There is another reason for the omission: Some of the most heinous violence is inflicted by or with the complicity of right-wing governments. On television, there was barely a mention of repression by governments in Chile, Argentina, and other Latin American countries. (Roughly, 6,000 people disappeared during the 1976–79 period in Argentina alone.)

Repressive regimes do not seek publicity for their acts, quite the reverse. They do what is necessary to prevent television coverage of their actions. They are usually successful. Similarly, of course, government-abetted oppression and violence in closed regimes of the left are usually not accessible to US television news.

---

[2] Weeknight network newscasts have been recorded off-air by Vanderbilt's Television News Archive since August, 1968. As is the case in many markets, the Nashville stations have not consistently broadcast the weekend network newscasts, so the Vanderbilt Archive is incomplete in its collection of weekend programs. In December, 1978, the Gelman Library of George Washington University began taping weekend newscasts in Washington, D.C. for inclusion in the Vanderbilt Archive; the weekend collection since that date is essentially complete.

AGENDA

Quantity and Prominence

Terrorism is news. As shown in Table 8.1, during the two-year period investigated, the three networks aired some 193 stories about the three groups on their evening news shows.

Table 8.1
Evening News Stories: July 1, 1977–July 1, 1979

	ABC	CBS	NBC	Total
IRA	17	13	12	42
RB	52	36	53	141
FALN	6	3	1	10
Total	75	52	66	193

These figures gain significance when compared to the entire number of stories about the terrorists' homelands. The 10 FALN stories were 40 percent of all stories (25) relating to Puerto Rico during the two years. The 141 Red Brigades stories constituted 53 percent of the 267 stories from or about Italy; and the 42 IRA stories totaled 63 percent of all stories on Northern Ireland. In other words, just over one out of every two stories (54 percent to be precise) from or about Northern Ireland, Italy, and Puerto Rico concerned the actions of terrorists.

About one third of the terrorism stories were prominently placed in the evening newscasts: 15 percent were the leads on the days they appeared; another 18 percent appeared during the first 10 minutes; and 22 percent lasted longer than two minutes.

These figures are also misleading because much of the news time was derived from a handful of events during the two years. Some 58 percent of the stories about the Red Brigades involved the kidnapping of Aldo Moro and the Turin trial of the group's first leaders. The IRA equivalents were the visit of Queen Elizabeth to Northern Ireland as part of her silver jubilee travels despite IRA threats of a "jubilee blitz," and the Provisionals' daring assassination of a Conservative Member of Parliament, Airey Neave, killed when his car exploded in the Parliament's parking lot in the heart of London during the British election campaign. These stories took up 26 percent of the IRA coverage. The disruption of business life in New York City caused by the FALN's bombs and bomb threats occupied 80 percent of television news about that organization.

Aside from these spectaculars, television news stories on the activities of the three terrorist groups were infrequent. For example, there were no stories about the IRA on CBS for almost one year between October 23, 1977 and October 12, 1978. Over 45 percent of all the terrorism stories lasted less than 30 seconds. These were usually brief descriptions or summaries of an event read by the anchorperson against a backdrop of a map or, less often, pieces of silent film. An NBC story, for example, on June 16, 1979 read in its entirety: "Terrorists threw a bomb and opened fire at the Communist Party headquarters in Rome tonight. Twenty people were wounded." In order of frequency, these brief stories reported acts of violence, arrests, trials.

"Clusters"

One practice that increases the impression of widespread terrorism is the use by television news architects of what we call "clusters." Stories are linked in "clusters" by some more or less logical theme (Paletz & Pearson, 1978, pp. 78–80). Such connections can influence, even determine, viewers' perceptions of an event. Approximately 11 percent of the terrorism stories were adjacent to stories about other terrorist violence: such as the PLO (CBS, 3/9/78), Japanese Radicals (ABC, 3/29/78), and South Moluccans (CBS, 9/5/77). Other "clusters" linked the terrorists with international violence, 15 percent (e.g., the Somalian war, CBS, 3/10/78); or with violence in the group's country, 12 percent (e.g., ABC followed news of FALN activities with the New York killer "Son of Sam," 8/4/77); or with non-violent stories from the same country, 4 percent (e.g., Italy's legalization of abortion over Vatican opposition adjacent to a story about the Red Brigades, 5/18/78). An update on the kidnapping of Aldo Moro was followed by this item: "News today of what may or may not be a massive kidnapping in Rhodesia: 420 students, all black, were taken, perhaps at gunpoint, from a mission school. . . ." (ABC, 3/30/78).

A substantial part of the other bordering material involved international news. ABC with its "foreign desk" used the phrase "In other news overseas" (12/19/78), or "Elsewhere overseas" (1/18/79) to introduce terrorist stories. Much of the connecting international news was unpleasant: a story on the fireman's strike in England, in which the theme was Scotland Yard's warning that the IRA might plant new cassette-type fire bombs in shopping areas in English cities, was followed by a report (with visuals) of a hotel fire in Manilla (NBC, 11/14/77). Other remaining adjacent stories consisted of relatively unrelated topics, or commercials.

DIMENSIONS OF CONTENT

Television news viewers are likely to receive the general impression that terrorism is widespread around the world. Beyond this general perception, how does coverage treat such dimensions of terrorism as violence, victims, terrorists' motivations, perspectives, governmental responses, and reassurance? In this section, we analyze how television news conveys each of these dimensions. Our analysis reveals significant differences in coverage of the three terrorist organizations.

Violence and Victims

Violence perpetrated by the terrorists was the primary subject of 29 percent of all the stories we analyzed. These data were unsurprising: obviously terrorists are engaged in violence and violence is news. A substantial portion of all terrorist stories consist of simple recordings of such violence. Here, virtually in its entirety, is this story read by the NBC anchorman on June 13, 1978 against a backdrop film of flames: "In Belfast, Northern Ireland, ten bombs went off destroying a bus station and twenty buses. It was blamed on the Irish Republican Army. . . ." Similarly, several ABC news stories began with such phrases as "Another terrorist killing in Italy today" (6/6/78) and "There was another terrorist killing in Italy today" (6/21/78).

Terrorists wreak harm; they have victims. The victims are often a key element in terrorism stories. Reports of the FALN's bombs in New York specified the number of people killed and injured (CBS, 8/3/77). Occasionally, an entire story is devoted to victims. One NBC report (5/8/78) began by referring to the "fanatical leftist tactics of the Red Brigades," followed with photographs of hospitalized victims, then featured a victim describing his horrible experience when shot by the Brigades, continued with an interview with an Italian sociology professor who spoke in English against the terrorists, and concluded with a description of the various means of protection many Italians were obtaining.

Terrorists' Motives

Terrorists' violence is prominently featured, and their victims cannot be ignored. What about the reasons for terrorism, do they receive any attention? The four most significant aspects of terrorists' behavior that can be reported within news stories are precipitating social conditions, goals, objectives, and tactics. The social conditions underlying a group's grievances may include poverty, unemployment, discrimination, overcrowded universities, unequal justice, abuses of civil rights, and unrepresentative goverment. Goals are the long-range political, economic, and social changes the group seeks to institute, such as supplanting a foreign ruler or replacing capitalism with socialism. Objectives are short-term gains which the insurgents hope to realize from their tactics. They range from the specific to the general and include the treatment of their jailed members as political prisoners, the exchange of imprisoned members for hostages, gaining adherents, destroying symbols and figures of authority, exposing the alleged repression of the state or alien rulers, and creating disorder and a climate of fear. Tactics are the specific actions that groups undertake: releasing statements, demonstrating, kidnapping, maiming, shooting, and bombing.

Of these four elements, tactics are the most easily explained by television correspondents and understood by viewers. They are an integral part of most stories whose subject is violence. Tactics were thus found to be discussed in passing in 33 percent and emphasized in 24 percent of the terrorism stories. They were not mentioned in the rest.

Underlying social conditions were not mentioned in 94 percent of the stories, and were emphasized in just three percent. Goals went unmentioned in 90 percent of the stories, were discussed in passing in 8 percent, and emphasized in just two percent. There was no mention of the insurgents' objectives in 67 percent of the stories; they were emphasized in 15 percent, and mentioned in passing in the remainder.

Perspectives

It is important to go beneath these data to the underlying perspectives represented in the news stories. Perspective can be expressed directly in an interview, by a quote, or through the direct statements of the network anchors or reporters. We defined stories as "pronunciamento" when their point of view stemmed only from authority figures such as elected officials, magistrates, judges, prosecutors, the police, the military. The networks' evening news provided such a conduit for authority-wielders in 69 percent of the terrorism stories. An additional 10 percent of the stories supplemented or supplanted the state's perspective with reactions or comments from ordinary or not-so-ordinary citizens (Mrs. Moro, the Pope). Only 21 percent of the stories could in any sense be defined as "adversary." That is, while they transmitted the official perspective on events, they also contained information or statements of some sort, no matter how meager, from the terrorists or their sympathizers.

This perspective category revealed dramatic differences in coverage of the three groups. Some 36 percent of the IRA stories were what we defined as "adversary." Corresponding figures for the Red Brigades and FALN were 18 and 10 percent respectively. In virtually every segment story about the IRA (that is, excluding the brief items read by the anchorperson), the group's position appeared. The IRA position was never presented alone—it was invariably accompanied by Protestant or British perspectives, or both—but it was presented nonetheless, and often eloquently.

In one instance, CBS correspondent Mike Lee showed viewers the inside of the Maze prison (9/26/77), home of most IRA prisoners, with film from a camera smuggled in by the IRA. The film showed IRA members being trained militarily to continue their struggle as soon as they were released or escaped from prison. It suggested the weakness of the authorities, their inability to control the prison. Adding to the pro-IRA impression was an interview with the mother of two of the prisoners who denied here sons were criminals. "They're out fighting for their country . . . they fought for the love of their country," she said.

In complete contrast, none of the networks ran a story on the reasons, rise, and political program of the Red Brigades. No member, no family relative, no person-in-the-street sympathizer, not even a scholar who might say a good word in a pro-con appraisal of the Red Brigades was interviewed.

The Moro kidnapping and the Red Brigades' demand that he be exchanged for their colleagues on trial in Turin offered an opportunity for television news to provide a modicum of information about the organization, objectives, goals, even the causes of the Brigades' actions. Why were they shooting people in the knees? What were their thoughts? Was there remorse or guilt? What was their doctrinal logic?

In almost eight weeks of coverage of the Moro kidnapping, viewers could learn little about the Brigades beyond their penchant for violence. Some typical statements of network correspondents: "Their only ideology is destruction" (CBS, 3/16/81); "The Red Brigades don't want to kill Aldo Moro, they just want to disrupt Italy" (ABC, 5/5/78). And when the Turin trial of the Brigades' early leaders ended in their conviction, ABC reported (6/19/78): "From their steel cage in the courtroom the defendants read a final statement praising the murder of former premier Aldo Moro."

With a relatively simple ultimate objective, the FALN was not too difficult to characterize. When the FALN exploded bombs in New York, CBS correspondent Steve Young described the organization as a "terrorist group calling for the independence of Puerto Rico and believed to number just a dozen persons in its ranks" (8/3/77). But, only ABC described at any length the FALN's goals and objectives. Its story carried an excerpt from Police Commissioner Michael J. Codd's interview in which he said:

> . . . aside from the usual rhetoric, there were statements to the effect that this was part of the effort of the FALN to counteract what they call the exploitation by the multinational corporations of the people of Puerto Rico and that they will exact punishment on these corporations in the form of damages to properties.

Then correspondent Geraldo Rivera was called upon to tell viewers who the FALN are and what they want. His conclusion: "No more than a dozen fanatics based here in the United States and committed to murder and mayhem they say will somehow make Puerto Rico independent— whether Puerto Rico likes it or not" (ABC, 8/3/77). Such a description is unlikely to enhance the FALN in the minds of viewers. It is, however, clearer about the group's objectives than the vague phrase "a militant Puerto Rican group" subsequently used on CBS (5/22/78).

Governmental Responses

Viewers of television news in the United States saw and heard about terrorist violence but were told little about the motives and reasons behind it. They were, however, informed of governmental responses to the violence in 37 percent of all terrorism stories. There were statements by officials about the evils of violence and their determination to end it. There were actions and reactions by the authorities: searches, investigations, arrests, new laws, the visit of the Queen to Northern Ireland to symbolize the British commitment. There were judicial activities: inquiries, indictments, trials, convictions.

Most of these government response stories were favorable to the authorities, presenting their perspectives, actions, and reactions. There were two exceptions: stories about governmental incompetence and about repression.

Reported ABC anchorman Peter Jennings on assignment in Rome: "police prestige is suffering." He recounted how police roadblocks were causing massive traffic jams (3/27/78). NBC correspondent Fred Briggs recounted "much bitterness over what many feel to be police incompetence." He observed that "most people expect the Brigades will continue to be one step ahead of the authorities" (5/9/78, the day Moro's body was found).

Yet even the Italian police were redeemed in part. All three networks reported that the massive hunt for Moro and his captors had drastically reduced regular crime in Rome (CBS, 3/22; ABC, 3/27; and NBC, 4/4/78). Walter Cronkite even introduced one story by saying, "Italian police have scored a major triumph in their war against terrorists" (CBS, 4/12/78). However, the actual story dealt with the release of two kidnapped Italians and had nothing to do with the Red Brigades.

Beyond police incompetence was the issue of government misconduct —violations of civil liberties before, during, and after terrorist outbreaks. In reference to this issue from Italy, the most detailed account was by Greg Dobbs of ABC:

> To combat the Red Brigades, the government plans strong new police powers which Americans might think impossible to tolerate. Searches and arrests without judicial warrants; wire-tapping and withholding information from the public; removing the right of counsel; suspension of habeas corpus.

Scary certainly, but Dobbs took pains to legitimize the proposals when he added: "Now such measures do bend the Italian Constitution to be sure, but all major political parties here agree there is no choice" (ABC, 3/21/78).

The most extensive coverage of governmental repression came from Northern Ireland. CBS aired Mike Lee's story on the Maze prison (9/26/77).

ABC reported the decision of the European Court of Human Rights that the British had mistreated suspected IRA members (1/18/78). However, ABC diminished the story's impact by relegating it to the anchorman and following it with a far longer report from correspondent Greg Dobbs about the issue of birching on the Isle of Man. But again it was ABC which, in the person of correspondent John Laurence, featured a British Government Commission's report that prisoners were indeed being mistreated in Northern Ireland. He included in his story an interview with a police surgeon who confirmed the existence of torture (3/16/79).

Reassurance

In conventional stories, reporters often look for and find some reassurance with which to assuage their audience (Paletz & Entman, 1981, pp. 17–18). Terrorism stories are no exception. Certainly, it was not easy to find grounds for reassurance in Northern Ireland. As NBC's Garrick Utley summed up the situation: "In the end, Protestants and Catholics here want peace but each side wants it on its own terms. So there is no prospect of peace. Prejudice on both sides has been passed down through too many generations" (10/10/77). Nonetheless, ABC correspondent Jack Smith managed to reassure viewers a few weeks later (11/25/77):

> The level of violence in Northern Ireland has diminished considerably ...the IRA is running out of cash. ...The will to commit terror does still exist but the means to carry it out with deadly explosives is fast diminishing. So, for the first time since the violence began in Northern Ireland eight years ago there's almost a mood of optimism in the streets of Belfast because, for the first time in eight years, people here believe that the end is at last in sight.

Even with the FALN the news provided reassurance. Reported CBS on the day of the FALN's disruption of New York (8/3/77): "The city's Police Commissioner assured reporters that he had the manpower to cope with this investigation and the continuing search for the forty-four caliber killer." The following day CBS reported that 150,000 people had attended a concert in Central Park and "there were no reported injuries."

All three networks' news departments seemed determined to soften the threat of the Red Brigades with reassurances that the Italian government was holding firm, Italian democracy remained strong, civil liberties were only mildly modified, the police were achieving some success, and life was going on. Thus, in the midst of reports of the Moro case, the NBC anchor introduced a story on an Italian fashion show as follows (4/5/78):

> There has been a tendency these past few weeks or, rather, a great many people have believed that Italy under Red Brigade pressure is coming apart at the seams. Not true. Life, development, progress continues.

Similarly, in introducing NBC's story on the just completed trial of the leaders of the Red Brigades in Turin for crimes committed before 1974, NBC's John Chancellor said (6/23/78):

> After one of the most turbulent trials in Italian history, a verdict was rendered in Turin today on members of the terrorist Red Brigades: long sentences in prison. The Red Brigades and their urban guerrilla allies had tried to stop the trial through threats, shootings and the kidnapping of Aldo Moro, but it was not stopped.

Here is what CBS correspondent Bert Quint said after reporting the death of Aldo Moro (5/9/78):

> As painful as the moment is for Italy there is some consolation. The Red Brigades did not accomplish what they set out to do when they seized Aldo Moro. They had hoped to gain freedom for jailed comrades; they failed. They had hoped to force this country, where fascism was born, to abandon its democratic institutions and adopt repressive security measures. . . . If anything, the Red Brigades have helped to bring Italy's rival political groups together.

Reported ABC's Lou Cioffi (5/9/78):

> If the Red Brigades had hoped to split the new political alliance it has failed. The Communists, who have dropped revolution for respectability, have joined with the Christian Democrats in condemning the actions of the Red Brigade. In a real way it has brought the political alliance closer together in its desire to end violence and get on with the business of running the country. Even in the role of a helpless victim, Aldo Moro still managed to be the master of conciliation and compromise.

Back in the United States, ABC News anchorwoman Barbara Walters asked Haywood Asham of the State Department whether a Moro-type event could happen here. And she said, answering the question herself, "Your feeling is, yes, it could happen here; but, no, the terrorists would probably not get away with it." He agreed.

Networks

There were differences between the three networks' news programs. NBC had a section entitled "Briefly" near the broadcast's end during which the anchor read a group of one or two sentence reports from around the globe. Consequently, NBC had more short stories and aired more stories during the last 10 minutes of its news than its rivals.

On the other side, ABC used more multi-segment reports than the other two networks. The result was that its stories focused less on group violence (CBS 40, NBC 32, and ABC 21 percent), gave more attention to the political situations in the countries considered (CBS 4, NBC 9, and

ABC 21 percent), and discussed social context to a greater extent than the other two (CBS 1, NBC 3, and ABC 11 percent).

Despite these differences, the three networks' coverage of the three groups was extremely similar. They reported the same events, and depicted them similarly. Violence and governmental response were emphasized; terrorists' goals, objectives, perspectives were neglected. Tactics received a modicum of attention. The IRA was depicted far more favorably than the FALN, and the Red Brigades were condemned.

SOME EXPLANATIONS

In this section, we want to try to explain why terrorism occupied a majority of the stories from and about Northern Ireland, Italy, and Puerto Rico; why the stories contained their particular content; and why the three insurgent groups were depicted differently.

Similarities

Terrorism is unexpected, disruptive, often dangerous. It is the stuff of news. That is why a majority of all television news stories emanating from or about Italy, Northern Ireland, and Puerto Rico during the period studied recounted terrorism. Yet, many of these stories were brief, giving only momentary mention to the terrorists' activities.

To obtain extensive coverage, terrorists need to undertake dramatic actions: to threaten violence during a Queen's jubilee visit, to plant bombs in major buildings in New York City. The Moro story, in particular, contained the classic ingredients of news, with the daring, daylight kidnapping and the perpetrators disguised as airline pilots. All of his bodyguards were killed, yet Moro miraculously was taken alive. The victim was several times prime minister, a leader of the major party, and the leading candidate for the Italian presidency. Dramatic questions recurred with varying intensity during Moro's captivity. Would the police find him? Would the government exchange hostages for Moro? Would the Red Brigades kill him?

As Moro's captivity continued, it was punctuated by events which roused media coverage above the routine. There was the claim by the Red Brigades that Moro had been killed and dumped in an icy lake north of Rome to which police and media rushed. There were photographs of Moro, the most dramatic showing him holding a daily newspaper the day after he allegedly had been killed. There were Moro's letters, perhaps written under duress. There were deadlines and ultimatums. And the final bullet-ridden horror was followed by statements from world leaders, eulogies, funeral, remembrance ceremony, and speculations about the effects of the events on Italy's forthcoming municipal elections. Most terrorist actions are one-shot events lacking the continuing dramatic qualities of the Moro story.

Even when terrorists' activities were extensively covered, as with Moro, the coverage was characterized by governmental perspectives, and infused with both repugnance and reassurance by reporters. Governmental perspectives are stressed because the violence occurs usually without the presence of television correspondents and equipment for obvious reasons. The authorities arrive first and are there to provide details, explanations, and their interpretations to the press.

Repugnance is manifest at the horrors of the violence by newspeople who value human life and dignity. The sentiment was eloquently expressed by Michael Elkins, long-time CBS correspondent in Israel, now with the BBC (1980, p. 96): "We need to generate in the world passionate revulsion to terror and terrorists; and we need always and everywhere to deny them acceptance, to deny them dignity, and to deny them victory." Reassurance is also expressed because there is no substantial evidence that the established institutions are crumbling, and because Western reporters usually have a tacit commitment to democratically elected authorities, and an aversion to violent bands of revolutionaries.

Another similarity was the absence of attention to possible funding and international support for any of the three groups. In recent months, debate has begun about the extent of external connections of indigenous terrorist groups. Claire Sterling claims to document such connections in *The Terror Network* (Sterling, 1981); Dan Schorr and some others are skeptical (Schorr, 1981, pp. 13 and 20; *New York Times*, 3/28/81, p. 4). Intriguingly, in the 193 stories covering a two-year period, there was hardly any mention that the IRA, the Red Brigades, or the FALN might be connected to terrorist groups active in another country, or to a foreign government, or even to private citizens abroad who might be providing training and support. Only ABC commentator Howard K. Smith had the temerity to suggest that the Red Brigades had received training from Czechoslovakia and/or the Soviet Union (ABC, 5/19/78). More such stories would have cast the terrorists in an even more ominous light.

Differences

Beneath the three groups' common dedication to violence and concomitant similarities in television news coverage lie distinct differences in their portrayals. The IRA challenge appeared primarily as a conflict between the Catholic people of Northern Ireland on one side and the British government and army, abetted by Protestant militants in Northern Ireland, on the other. The IRA Provisionals emerged as a people's movement engaged in civil war. Also, activities of the IRA are interesting to Americans because of both the close relationship between the United States and Great Britain and the millions of Irish-Americans, many of whom tacitly (and sometimes financially) support the IRA.

The Red Brigades appeared as an extreme fringe group, devoid of the slightest semblance of popular support, and dedicated to the proposition that Italian democracy must be destroyed by the exercise of senseless violence. The FALN briefly emerged on television as a nuisance, savagely disrupting the lives of New Yorkers.

There are four main reasons for these differences in coverage—the group's histories and perceived support, revelations, sources, and visuals.

History and Perceived Support. The IRA has a long history; clear nationalistic goals; the presence of relatively credible, peaceable, politically active figures; and supporters and sympathizers in the United States. There is a comprehensive literature describing the group's history, organization, objectives, and tactics. These factors helped the IRA obtain coverage of its actions, somewhat balanced between reports from the British authorities and its own accounts and explanations.

The FALN is new and novel, active in the media heart of the United States. Its more incendiary actions were covered, with some mention of the group's underlying grievances and goals. Subsequent stories depended on the group undertaking even more spectacular events, which it apparently did not. Stories about police investigations and court cases relied entirely upon public pronouncements by US officials. During the period studied, they were not forthcoming.

The Red Brigades are a relatively recent arrival to revolutionary action. They appear to enjoy little support among Italians—or at least those Italians known to the networks' television correspondents. The group's ideology is incomprehensible to most Americans. Consequently, stories about the Red Brigades, more than the IRA and even the FALN, emphasized the group's violent activities and the responses of officials, while ignoring the Brigades' purposes.

Revelations. History and perceived support are reinforced by revelations. One reason coverage of the IRA was more sympathetic than that of the Red Brigades and FALN was that the British Government was unable to conceal its repressive measures. Between them, the networks carried the European Court of Human Rights' ruling against the British Government, the conclusions of the Government's own commission confirming the mistreatment of prisoners, and material smuggled out of the Maze prison.

Sources. Correspondents going to Northern Ireland can find legitimate sources able to articulate the IRA and the Provisionals' point of view in English. There are ordinary people to be interviewed who have lost parents, sons, and daughters, in the conflict.

In contrast, coverage of the FALN occurred over a few days, was intense while it lasted, then ended. Thus, reporters had no established contacts who might present the insurgents' viewpoints. Nor, obviously, did they know anything about the Puerto Rican independence movement, or much about Puerto Rico for that matter. They relied on police sources to state what occurred and then on eyewitnesses for the human interest accounts.

The members of the Red Brigades are in prison, in hiding, or out killing and maiming. The Red Brigades, moreover, do not appear to possess many sympathizers who might be willing to be interviewed for American television. Nor do the members' relatives seem to seek coverage. There are apparently no English-speaking academics willing to articulate the Brigades' views or defend their position. Ethnocentric American television does not stoop to subtitles. Other sources are unavailable or unsought.

Visuals. One does not have to be a devotee of the visual determinism theory of television news to realize that stories on the evening news, aside from brief wire service items read by the anchors, are tied to pictures (see Adams, 1978). Television cameras cannot produce pictures of events at will; they have to be present at the action. Their presence is facilitated when an event is known about in advance, or when it occupies enough time for cameras to be brought to the scene. Otherwise, pictures are not of the event itself, but of its aftermath, or there are no pictures at all.

This picture process helps explain some of the characteristics of the coverage of the three different groups. The IRA holds funerals, stages demonstrations, conducts marches (which often culminate in clashes with the British troops). Most of these events are known in advance and attract ample television coverage. The resultant visuals often support the IRA's claim that it is engaged in a war with the British. Nothing supports this contention better than picturesque scenes of Irish Catholic (one assumes they are Catholic) youth throwing stones at antediluvian-looking British tanks. (Meanwhile, there are the drab, desolate streets of Belfast graphically illustrating the social and economic backdrop to events.)

Attitudes towards the Red Brigades might be different if viewers were privy to their plans and passion, or their ideological discussions. Obviously, the Red Brigades do not confide in the media, nor do they provide advance warning of their intentions. As a result, the pictures in the networks' news stories are primarily of the scenes where events have transpired. Members of the Red Brigades were only shown in mug shots or in their cage in the courtroom in Turin where they were on trial for crimes against the state.

With the FALN, all viewers saw were the results of the group's actions: the debris, the crowds of people evacuated from some of New York City's largest and most renowned buildings. They heard interviews in which New Yorkers described their experiences and expressed anger and shock at the bombings. Viewers were exposed to police assurances of ability to cope and brief critical references from correspondents about the purposes of the FALN.

IMPLICATIONS

It is hard if not impossible to demonstrate specific media effects. Let us, nonetheless, reconsider the conventional view that terrorists attain attention and legitimacy from news coverage of their activities.

Certain facts are reasonably clear. We know that television news communicates a special impression of credibility and authenticity. In part, this is consciously crafted because news personnel want to be believed (Paletz & Pearson, 1978, p. 80). It also stems from the format of television news. The brief wire service items are read with conviction by anchors who give the impression they have themselves uncovered the material. The appropriately changing backdrop adds confirmation. The longer, segment stories are even more persuasive: the anchors set the framework with their introductions, followed by the correspondents' narration against a backdrop of various, moving images. Using the cluster approach, terrorists' violent actions and authorities' reactions (a majority of the news stories from and about the countries concerned) are juxtaposed with other terrorist violence, with international violence, or violence-connected news in the United States.

Attention

Television viewers, then, have grounds for believing that terrorism is a world-wide phenomenon and that terrorist groups are palpably threatening. Terrorists kidnap and assassinate a leading Italian statesman, blow up an English MP in the House of Commons' parking lot, disrupt New York City—conveyed dramatically via television news. Terrorists are violent; they strike suddenly; their tactics are shocking. Coverage inevitably focuses on the immediate event; otherwise, it would not be timely and would lose much of its news cachet. Consequently, officials are forced to respond to the shooting, to the kidnapping, to the bombing, well before there is much chance of capturing the perpetrators; government picks up the pieces. Then the pursuit itself often languishes and the insurgents remain at large. If suspects are apprehended, the result lacks the visual excitement of the original crime, and the cameras are rarely there to catch the capture at all.

So terrorists do receive media attention. No doubt as a result, 90 percent of the US population consider terrorism a very serious problem (De Boer, 1979, p. 412).

This diet of media-carried violence may ultimately deprive the terrorists' acts of their power and resonance, compelling them to turn to even more flagrant and outrageous deeds. It is doubtful, however, that such escalations can continue indefinitely. Indeed, two of the three groups discussed here have faded from the news since their spectacular actions; they are now relegated to routine wire service items, if that. Only the IRA remains, sustained by the hunger strikes of several of its jailed members.

Legitimacy

Terrorists enjoy attention, but they are not endowed with legitimacy by television news. With the occasional exception of the IRA, the justness of the terrorists' causes are denied. Most of the stories about the insurgents' actions are provided by the authorities and concern governmental responses to the violence, or the actual terroristic acts themselves. The underlying objectives of the violence are rarely explained, almost never justified. Terrorists' tactics are stressed in television news. When tactics are emphasized without discussion of motives, objectives, goals, or precipitating social conditions, then context is discarded, and political justifications are denied. The terrorists are identified with criminal violence and seen simply as bent on terror.

Terrorists appear not as Robin Hoods but as people dedicated to destruction. The screen is filled with wrecked trains, crumpled buildings, frightened and injured people. The violence seems irrational and intolerable. Most people committed to the sanctity of human life can only react with abhorence. Rather than viewing terrorism as "acts of desperation, brought on by sustained exclusion" (Hacker, 1981, p. 16), normal people are likely to share Margaret Thatcher's reaction upon hearing of the murder of Airey Neave: "They must never, never, never be allowed to triumph; they must never prevail" (CBS, 3/30/79). Rather than legitimize the terrorists, television coverage of their actions probably increases governmental loyalty and undermines the cause of radical social change.

REFERENCES

Adams, William. 1978. Visual Analysis of Newscasts. In William Adams and Fay Schreibman, eds., *Television Network News: Issues in Content Research*. Washington, D.C.: School of Public and International Affairs, George Washington University.

——— and Fay Schreibman, eds. 1978. *Television Network News: Issues in Content Research*. Washington, D.C.: School of Public and International Affairs, George Washington University.

Alexander, Yonah, ed. 1976. *International Terrorism: National, Regional, and Global Perspectives*. New York: Praeger.

———. 1977a. Communications Aspects of International Terrorism. *International Problems* 16 (Spring 1977): 55–60.

———. 1977b. Terrorism and the Media in the Middle East. In Yonah Alexander and Seymour M. Finger, eds., *Terrorism: Interdisciplinary Perspectives*. New York: John Jay Press, 166–206.

———. 1978. Terrorism, the Media and the Police. *Journal of International Affairs* 32 (Spring/Summer 1978): 101–113.

———. ed. 1979a. Terrorism and the Media: Some Considerations. In Yonah Alexander, David Carlton, and Paul Wilkinson, eds., *Terrorism: Theory and Practice*. Boulder, Col.: Westview Press, 159–174.

———. 1979b. Terrorism, the Media, and the Police. In Darrell M. Trent and Robert H. Kupperman, eds., *Terrorism: Threat, Reality, Response*. Stanford, Calif.: Hoover Institution Press, 331–348.

——— and Seymour M. Finger, eds. 1977. *Terrorism: Interdisciplinary Perspectives*. New York: John Jay Press.

———, David Carlton, and Paul Wilkinson, eds. 1979. *Terrorism: Theory and Practice*. Boulder, Col.: Westview Press.

Bassiouni, Cherif, ed. 1975. *International Terrorism and Political Crimes*. Springfield, Ill.: Charles C. Thomas.

Bell, J. Bowyer. 1970. *The Secret Army*. New York: John Jay Press.

———. 1976. Strategy, Tactics, and Terror: An Irish Perspective. In Yonah Alexander, ed., *International Terrorism: National, Regional, and Global Perspectives*. New York: Praeger.

———. 1978. Terrorist Scripts and Live-Action Spectaculars. *Columbia Journalism Review* 17 (May/June 1978): 47–50.

Beres, Louis René. 1980. *Terrorism and Global Security*. Boulder, Col.: Westview Press.

Burton, John. 1979. *Deviance, Terrorism and War: The Process of Solving Unsolved Social and Political Problems*. New York: St. Martin's Press.

Cooper, G. L. C. 1973. Some Aspects of Conflict in Ulster. *Military Review* 53 (September 1973): 86–95.

Cooper, H. H. A. 1977. Terrorism and the Media. In Yonah Alexander and Seymour M. Finger, eds., *Terrorism: Interdisciplinary Perspectives*. New York: John Jay Press, 139–156.

Corrado, Raymond R. 1979. Ethnic and Student Terrorism in Western Europe. In Michael Stohn, ed., *The Politics of Terrorism*. New York: Marcel Dekker, 191–258.

Davison, W. Phillips. 1974. *Mass Communication and Conflict Resolution: The Role of the Information Media in the Advancement of International Understanding*. New York: Praeger.

De Boer, Connie. 1979. The Polls: Terrorism and Hijacking. *Public Opinion Quarterly* 43 (Fall 1979): 410–418.

Dick, James C. 1979. *Violence and Oppression*. Athens, Ga.: University of Georgia Press.

Disorders and Terrorism. 1976. Report of the Task Force on Disorders and Terrorism. Washington, D.C.: National Advisory Committee on Criminal Justice Standards and Goals.

Elkins, Michael. 1980. Caging the Beasts. *Political Communication and Persuasion* 1 (1980): 96–99.

Elliott, Philip. 1977. Reporting Northern Ireland. In *Race, Ethnicity and the Media*. Paris: United Nations Educational, Scientific and Cultural Organization.

Graber, Doris A. 1974. Approaches to Content Analysis of Television News Programs. Paper presented at the Annual Conference of the American Association for Public Opinion Research, Lake George, N.Y.

Grabosky, P. N. 1979. The Urban Context of Political Terrorism. In Michael Stohn, ed., *The Politics of Terrorism*. New York: Marcel Dekker, 51–76.

Hacker, Andrew. 1981. Up for Grabs. *New York Review* 28 (April 30, 1981): 8–16.

Holsti, Ole R. 1969. *Content Analysis for the Social Sciences and Humanities*. Reading, Mass.: Addison-Wesley.

Hutchinson, Martha Crenshaw. 1978. *Revolutionary Terrorism*. Stanford, Calif.: Hoover Institution Press.

Journal of International Affairs International Terrorism. 1978. 32 (Spring/Summer 1978): 1–125.

Katz, Robert. 1980. *Days of Wrath*. New York: Doubleday.

Laqueur, Walter. 1977. *Terrorism: A Study of National and International Political Violence*. Boston: Little, Brown.

———. 1979. Forward. In Darrell M. Trent and Robert H. Kupperman, eds., *Terrorism: Threat, Reality, Response*. Stanford, Calif.: Hoover Institution Press, i–xviii.

Lebow, Richard Ned. 1978. The Origins of Sectarian Assassination: The Case of Belfast. *Journal of International Affairs* 32 (Spring/Summer 1978): 43–61.

Lotringer, Sylvere and Christian Marazzi. 1980. The Return of Politics. *Autonomia* 3 (1980): 9–20.

MacStiofain, Sean. 1975. *Revolutionary in Ireland*. Edinburgh: R. and R. Clark.

———. 1979. *Transnational Terrorism*. In Michael Stohn, ed., *The Politics of Terrorism*. New York: Marcel Dekker, 147–190.

Mickolus, Edward F., comp. 1980. *The Literature of Terrorism*. Westport, Conn.: Greenwood Press.

Miller, Abraham H. 1980. *Terrorism and Hostage Negotiations*. Boulder, Col.: Westview Press.

New York Times. 1981. Soviet Aid Disputed in Terrorism Study. March 28, 1981, 4.

Norton, Augustus R. and Martin Greenberg. 1979. *International Terrorism: An Annotated Bibliography and Research Guide*. Boulder, Col.: Westview Press.

O'Day, Alan. 1979. Northern Ireland, Terrorism, and the British State. In Yonah Alexander, David Carlton, and Paul Wilkinson, eds., *Terrorism: Theory and Practice*. Boulder, Col.: Westview Press, 121–135.

Paletz, David L. and Robert M. Entman. 1981. *Media Power Politics*. New York: The Free Press.

Paletz, David L. and Roberta E. Pearson. 1978. "The Way You Look Tonight:" A Critique of Television News Criticism: In William Adams and Fay Schreibman, eds., *Television Network News: Issues in Content Research*. Washington, D.C.: School of Public and International Affairs, George Washington University, 65–85.

Podhoretz, Norman, 1980. The Subtle Collusion. *Political Communication and Persuasion* 1 (1980): 84–89.

Redlick, Amy Sands. 1979. The Transnational Flow of Information as a Cause of Terrorism. In Yonah Alexander, David Carlton, and Paul Wilkinson, eds., *Terrorism: Theory and Practice*. Boulder, Col.: Westview Press, 79–95.

Salomone, Franco. 1975. Terrorism and the Mass Media. In Cherif Bassiouni, ed., *International Terrorism and Political Crimes*. Springfield, Ill.: Charles C. Thomas.

Schorr, Daniel. 1981. Tracing the Thread of Terrorism, Review of *The Terror Network: The Secret War of International Terrorism*, by Claire Sterling, *New York Times*. May 17, 1981, 13, 17.

Sterling, Claire. 1981. *The Terror Network: The Secret War of International Terrorism*. New York: Holt, Rinehart and Winston.

Stohn, Michael, ed. 1979. *The Politics of Terrorism*. New York: Marcel Dekker.

Terrorism: An International Journal. 1979. Vol. 2, Nos. 1 & 2: Terrorism and the Media.

Trent, Darrell M. and Robert H. Kupperman, eds. 1979. *Terrorism: Threat, Reality, Response*. Stanford, Calif.: Hoover Institution Press.

Webster, William H. 1981. Meeting the Threat of Terrorism. Excerpts from a speech before the Contemporary Club of St. Louis, Missouri, November 7, 1980. Reprinted in Center for National Security Studies, *First Principles* 6 (March/April 1981): 5–6.

Wilkinson, Paul. 1979. Terrorist Movements. In Yonah Alexander, David Carlton, and Paul Wilkinson, eds., *Terrorism: Theory and Practice*. Boulder, Col.: Westview Press, 99–117.

9

AUSTRALIA ON AMERICAN TELEVISION NEWS: COVERAGE OF THE INVISIBLE CONTINENT

MYLES P. BREEN

Roger Mudd has confused Australia with Austria (CBS, 9/10/74). Walter Cronkite has done a story on Prime Minister Fraser with a picture of someone else (1/12/76), has called a prime minister a premier and called a premier a state minister (1/15/76). Two US networks do not know how to spell the name Sydney, the largest city in Australia (CBS, 2/12/78; ABC, 12/27/74). The author has seen the anchor on WBBM-TV in Chicago solemnly presenting a story, while behind him the map of Australia was upside down, with Sydney prominently labeled on the coast of Western Australia.

This Monty-Pythonesque portrayal of their country is a continuing source of amusement to Australians living in America, and each expatriot's repertoire can be expected to be replete with such examples. (With casual acquaintances, the Australian-Austrian confusion is not infrequent, as in "my ski instructor is Australian.") The "obvious" blunders on television news would routinely pass unnoticed by most American viewers. How does US TV news usually cover other countries?

The purpose of this chapter is to examine how American network television news has presented a single foreign country. The country chosen is Australia, but the method of analysis is universal and the findings may be extrapolated to a wider context.

Prior to the publication of this volume, few studies had investigated the way American television covered foreign nations generally (Adams, 1981; Almaney, 1970; Larson, 1978, 1979; Warner, 1968), or examined in detail the way a particular country is portrayed. Robinson (1978, p. 206)

167

has pointed out that the FCC's Fairness Doctrine, which obligates news-casters to balance reporting of American political issues, does not apply to coverage abroad, and thus foreign news may be an area where political value would be likely to influence news judgment directly. Quite apart from political attitudes, Robinson agrees with Epstein (1973, pp. 246–247) that foreign news is also collected by the organization to fit audience stereotypes, a theory with social and cultural implications.

Both Gans and Fisher have expounded on American ethnocentrism in the media. Gans (1979, p. 42) puts it at the top of his list of enduring values in the news. Fisher (1979, p. 34) claimed that Americans have taken enormous self-assurance from a kind of "validated ethnocentrism" which sustained and invigorated Americans in their communication with foreigners. "The end result," wrote Fisher, "has been something of a one-way flow of communication in the moral and ideological dimension, and Americans have come to accept their role in this as a matter of course." Fisher sees a need to change this state of affairs for America's sake, as the United States has perhaps the largest stake of all the nations in the two-way flow of communications.

Gans (1979, p. 383) has a colorful, if macabre, example of how newswriters at a network measured the newsworthiness of stories from different countries with a simple quantitative scale. It consisted of the minimum number of people who had to die in airplane crashes in different countries before the crash became newsworthy. "One hundred Czechs were equal to 43 Frenchmen, and the Paraguayans were at the bottom." Gans (1979) quotes Schlesinger as reporting that the BBC journalists use a similar scale in which "one thousand wogs, fifty frogs, and one Briton" are equivalent.

Galtung (1965, p. 66) claims that the more distant a nation is, the more dramatic an event will have to be to capture attention, the less am-biguous it will have to be, and the more consonant it will have to be in fit-ting a pattern of expectation. Today, TV news can be disseminated by the distance-insensitive satellite, so "distance" has come to mean the percep-tual distance of the people who decide what is news.

In the case of Australia, the perceptual distance must be the crucial factor in the selection of the relatively low number of stories. In his study of foreign news on television, Larson (1978, p. 145) suggested that "countries closest to the United States in terms of trade, level of economic develop-ment, political ties or perceptual distance receive the most news cover-age." Australia is very close to the United States in trade, political ties, and in the level of economic development, so the deciding factor must be "perceptual distance."

PROCEDURE

Every news story from 1970 to 1979 on the three networks, ABC, CBS, and NBC, which mentioned Australia or Australians was examined. Vanderbilt's *Television News Index and Abstracts* was used to find the relevant stories. Following Larson (1979, p. 136), any news story that mentioned the country, regardless of its thematic content or dateline, was considered an Australian story and duly counted. As Larson has pointed out, this definition produces an inflated measure of the total amount of international news when compared with the more conventional definitions based on thematic content or story datelines, although it ensures complete coverage.

The individual news story was the basic unit of analysis. Stories were coded into 10 thematic categories: legal and political; economy and business; environment (including natural and other disasters); art, music, and show business; crime; religion; sports; science and education; human interest (including obituary and society); and sensation (bizarre events reported to emphasize the sensational).

When one subject was clearly dominant, no secondary topic was coded. For example, Frank Sinatra's celebrated quarrel with the journalists and unions in Australia was largely a show business story, although it had aspects of human interest, legal, and economy and business as well. However, in stories where no one subject was dominant, two categories were coded. (See Deutchmann, 1959, and Masterton, 1977.) With three other coders checking the reliability of the main coder, the inter-coder reliability was .88.

AUSTRALIA AND US TV

Australia is an 80-year-old English-speaking democratic nation occupying an island continent the size of the continental United States. With a population of 14 million people, it has a little over half the population of Canada, twice the population of Sweden, and four times the population of Israel. With a gross domestic product of approximately $109 billion, its citizens earned a per capita GDP of approximately $7,000 (1977), the same as France, and 1½ times more than the United Kingdom. (The US per capita GDP was $8,670.)

Australians have been American allies in two world wars, and in Korea and Vietnam. The American connection goes back to colonial days when an American trader *The Philadelphia* sailed into Port Jackson in 1792 to commence the profitable trading relationship that has never stopped. (In fact, the connection goes deeper because the American Revolution prevented the English from continuing to export their convicts to America, so they set up a penal colony in Australia.) Americans have been involved in building Australian cities, especially Melbourne and Canberra; and the Californian Rangers Revolver brigade, a group of politically-minded gold miners, injected Republican sentiment into the only armed insurrection in Australian history in 1859 when nine people were killed. The history of American involvement in Australia over the past two centuries is as rich as it is unknown to Americans, yet today Australians know America well as American corporations, life-styles, products, and media (notably films and TV programs) are all-pervasive in Australia.

In practical terms, for US television news and audiences, Australia did not exist in the decade of the seventies. Australia was featured in only a handful of stories. If a stereotype was available to match expectations, it was a very faint image indeed.

To get a picture of the coverage, it is worthwhile looking at the beginning and end of the decade in some detail. In 1970, the total time devoted to the news of Australia or Australians was only 8 minutes 56 seconds, out of the hundreds of hours of regular evening news broadcast by the three networks during that year. The two biggest stories in 1970 were occasioned by visitors from overseas. Australia was thrust into the American TV limelight when Vice President Agnew visited Australia in January and the Pope visited in December. Other briefer mentions concerned the purchase of the American F-111 fighter-bomber; a story on an unemployed American worker who was emigrating to Australia to find a job; a few seconds on CBS about a bridge collapse; and a short story on NBC about the death of a 14-year-old boy in an airplane's undercarriage.

These six topics yielded 17 stories on all three networks. The average story duration was 32 seconds. Five stories were filmed or taped, 4 of these came from Australia, and there were 12 studio-delivered (talking head) stories.

Using the non-exclusive categorization system, (that is, a story may fall into two categories, and in this study did 27 percent of the time) the Australian stories in 1970 were 47 percent on religion (the Pope's visit was responsible, although no story from Australia concerned religion for the rest of the decade); 24 percent on legal and political matters; 18 percent on economy and business; 12 percent on human interest; 6 percent sensational or bizarre; and 5 percent on environment and natural disasters.

The decade closed with much the same pattern of inattention. There were 19 stories in 1979 compared with the 17 in 1970, and 7 different topics were covered in 1979 compared with 6 in 1970. In 1979, the newsworthy "visitors" to Australia (who had garnered over half the total time) came from neither Washington nor Rome but from space. The big story in

January concerned a UFO sighting, and in July, Skylab was brought down by NASA over Australia. In addition, there were two five-second mentions of refugees to Australia, a short story of a teenage defector from a communist country (a girl who jumped off a boat), a 10-second mention of Australian birds being smuggled into the United States for profitable resale, and for the obligatory disaster component, pictures of a brush fire near Sydney in December.

The total news time given Australia was 2½ times as great in 1979 as in 1970—22 minutes 37 seconds compared with 8 minutes 56 seconds. While this increase may seem significant, compared with the total amount of evening news time, the time devoted to Australia remained miniscule, not yet reaching a tenth of a percentage point of the total broadcast time (see Table 9.1).

The influence of the satellite link, which was introduced by 1970, along with ENG cameras, which became operative in the latter half of the decade, was evident. (See Table 9.2.) In 1979, there were 14 taped or filmed stories and five studio-only stories, reversing the pattern of 1970 when there were only five filmed stories and 12 studio stories. Nine of the stories originated in Australia in 1979, compared with four in 1970. Thus, from the point of view of production, the pattern had changed considerably.

Further analysis of the data confirms the impression derived from taking the extremes of the decade and also shows the variability inherent in newsgathering. The prominence of America's Cup events in 1974 resulted in a relatively high proportion of (nonstudio) filmed or taped stories. UFO sightings and the Skylab descent, a natural television story given the visual and instantaneous nature of the medium, gave the impetus for the somewhat higher share of TV coverage using tape and film in 1979.

KANGAROOS, CYCLONES, CROOKS, AND THE US CONNECTION

Kangaroos appear to prompt instant merriment to Americans, if one can judge by the media. To take an example, one of Charles Kuralt's "On the Road" segments was about a kangaroo named "Sydney" (10/10/71). In another example, a mysterious kangaroo running wild in Chicago in the mid-seventies inspired unlimited local media coverage until the subject finally grew stale. To Australians, kangaroos lack such humor; they are sometimes thought of as pests and are often officially considered vermin.

US television covered more than kangaroos, however. Table 9.3 shows the subjects that were covered over the 1970–79 period. Legal and political stories were most common. Natural disasters and sports were the second and third most frequently reported topics.

Table 9.1
Number of Stories, Number of Topics, and Duration of
TV Stories on Australia, 1970-79.

	No. of Stories	No. of Topics	Total Duration		Average Story Duration
			Mins.	Secs.	Secs.
1970	17	6	8	56	32
1971	27	12	22	55	51
1972	17	11	4	55	17
1973	9	9	6	35	44
1974	38	10	44	25	69
1975	28	14	21	45	47
1976	10	8	6	05	38
1977	23	9	25	40	25
1978	9	7	2	20	16
1979	19	17	22	37	71
TOTAL	197	103	2 hrs.	45 min.	41 Av.

Table 9.2
Taped/Film and Studio Stories about Australia, 1970-79

	No. of Tape/Filmed Stories	No. of Studio Stories	Ratio Tape-Film/ Studio Stories
1970	5	12	.42
1971	10	17	.59
1972	1	16	.06
1973	2	6	.33
1974	16	22	.73
1970-74 Mean	6.8	14.6	.43
1975	7	21	.33
1976	1	9	.11
1977	12	11	1.09
1978	3	6	.50
1979	14	5	2.80
1975-79 Mean	7.4	10.4	.97
1970-79 Mean	7.1	12.5	.69

Legal and Political

From 1970 through 1979, almost one third of the stories had a legal or political theme. Usually an American connection could be found in the story. Examples include: the American-Australian commitment to Vietnam, the visit of an American spokesman such as John Connally, and President Carter's claim that the CIA did not operate in Australia. Examination of stories in this category shows that there was no attempt to survey the news of Australia's role in the world, but rather that stories were selected that appeared to have a direct connection with a perceived American interest. To illustrate this point, when the Australian Prime Minister travelled to Moscow to meet Leonid Brezhnev in January 1975, he made the national news because Brezhnev did not meet with him, thus arousing speculation as to the Soviet leader's health. By contrast, the visits to Washington by Australian prime ministers are routinely ignored by US TV news.

Environment and disasters. The next most prevalent category of stories from Australia concerned always-newsworthy disasters (see Table 9.3). A bridge collapse in 1970 was considered newsworthy by ABC. From 1971 through 1973, there were no Australian stories in this category, but 1974 had 10 stories because a cyclone devastated the city of Darwin, the French tested nuclear devices in the Pacific, and an eclipse was observed in Australia. While the Darwin disaster made all three networks, the other stories were each covered by one network. The Darwin story continued until December 1975; it was joined that year with a hotel fire and a report that American experiments in chemical warfare had killed several people off the Australian coast during World War II. (This CBS story was later reported as repudiated by the Pentagon.)

Table 9.3
Topics of TV News Stories about Australia, 1970–79

	No.	%
Legal and Political	77	30.6
Environment/Disasters	38	15.1
Sports	26	10.3
Economy and Business	25	9.9
Crime	23	9.1
Sensation	23	9.1
Science and Education	16	6.3
Human Interest	8	3.1
Religion	8	3.1
Art/Music/Show Business	7	2.7
TOTAL	251	

Note: 27.4% of the stories fell into two categories.

While 1976 was quiescent in the disaster classification, an earthquake and a train wreck garnered eight minutes in 1977. Also, along with stories of freezing temperatures within the United States in January, the summer temperature in Sydney was reported as a counterpoint to the main story. In 1978, a plane was reported missing in Australia; in 1979, 10 stories were afforded the Skylab descent and one story was devoted to a Sydney fire. Thus again, in the environmental category which encompasses natural and other disasters, the American association is evident with the Skylab story, the reputed chemical warfare experiments, and the trivia component of a comparison of temperatures.

Sport. Sports, economy and business, crime, and sensation all received about the same number of mentions (see Table 9.3). While most years had no mentions of Australian sports, the years of the America's Cup yachting race (1974 and 1978) were heavily weighted towards sports with 12 and 8 stories, respectively. The photogenic yachts captured long filmed stories. While yachts of many nations competed, the Australian yachts, having made the finals, received significant coverage in this rich man's sport.

If there is a stereotype of the Australian in the United States, it includes a tennis-playing swimmer. In 1971, the national news had two stories on an Australian at Wimbledon, and in 1972 there were three mentions of an Australian Olympic swimmer. One story in 1971 was also classified in the political realm. It concerned the protests in Australia regarding a visiting South African rugby team. The protests concerned South Africa's racial policy.

As Gerbner and Signorelli (1978, p. 189) have pointed out, "television is a regular ritual of which news is a minor part." Because the networks have sports departments and programs separate from news departments and programs, it is not in the national news programs where one looks for "news" of sports. It seems unlikely that 10 percent of the regular network news concerns sporting themes, so the Australian factor must be affecting this relatively high measure. Should archives of sporting programs be available for analysis, Australian golfers, tennis players, racing drivers, and other sportsmen would probably be found to be featured more frequently than are Australians on the general news programs. Also, undoubtedly, the ritual of television imparts images and stereotypes just as forcibly in its dramatic, sporting, and other programming as it does in the formal "news."

Economy and business. Stories about economics and business concerned the purchase of US aircraft, Americans and Englishmen emigrating to Australia looking for work, the effect on the American wheat market on Australian wheat production and sales abroad, Australian-Japanese trade, an American refusal of landing rights to Qantas, depression in the Australian wool industry, the effect on meat prices in the States because of the importation of Australian beef, effects of inflation and the high price of Saudi Arabian oil, and uranium and arms sales. There were a total of 25 stories during the decade.

One of the longest stories, 4½ minutes in length, occurred as the lead story on CBS (1/6/77). The story concerned a prominent Australian, Rupert Murdoch. Murdoch's take-over of *New York* magazine occasioned some controversy, especially in the media centered in New York. For example, he appeared on the cover of both *Time* and *Newsweek* simultaneously. Perhaps the specter of an Australian capitalist acquiring properties in America had the appropriate role reversal requirement epitomized in the classic definition of newsworthiness: "man bites dog!"

Crime. The first Australian crime story of the decade occurred in May 1971 when Walter Cronkite gave 150 precious seconds in his lead story to an extortion bomb threat on a Qantas jet. Illustrating again the impact of the media on real life, the criminals followed, almost to the letter, a Rod Serling script for a movie which had been shown on TV. (Neither ABC nor NBC covered the story.) In August, CBS reported the criminals' capture.

In 1972, three crime stories from Australia covered a kidnapping and one story concerned letter bombs mailed to Israeli diplomats in Australia, putting the story also in the legal-political category. The one crime story in 1973 concerned the bomb threat to Prince Philip. In 1974, the six Australian crime stories were about the Englishman John Stonehouse, who also acquired five stories in 1975. In September 1975, there was one other Australian crime story, the hijack of an Australian jet in Timor. There were no crime stories in 1976 or 1977. A bomb exploded at a summit meeting of Asian and Pacific nations in Sydney in February 1978. Both NBC and CBS noted the explosion. CBS also very briefly noted a bank robbery in November. In 1979, the one Australian crime story concerned the smuggling of rare birds into the United States.

Even in crime, Australian stories concerned Americans, Israelis, Englishmen, Timorese, and Asians in or traveling to Australia. Except for the brief bank robbery story in 1978, the only indigenous Australian crime story of the decade concerned the Qantas extortion, and that escapade followed a script written by an American and propagated by American media. Even the lowest form of notoriety is denied the invisible continent.

Sensation. The "sensation" category included such items as the 1978 story of a pilot who, just before disappearing, radioed a description of a plane he said was following him. The 1979 stories on the UFO sighting were classified as sensational, but, because of the explanation that they were images of the planet Venus, the stories were also coded as "science and education."

In 1970, a sensational story concerned the boy who hid in an aircraft's undercarriage and fell and died when the landing gear lifted. Three stories in 1971 reported a multiple birth of nine babies, all of whom later died. In 1972, a sensational story (also "legal/political") concerned a BOAC aircraft with 125 passengers aboard flying from Sydney to Honolulu while the entire crew fell asleep. (The British Pilots Association claimed they flew too many hours per month.) The 1974–75 Stonehouse criminal stories were also coded as sensational. CBS reported in 1976 that an Australian clairvoyant forecast a tidal wave and earthquake.

Science and education. The 16 stories which were classified under "science and education" were what might be better described as general knowledge of popular science. The first and sole entrant of 1972 was a 30-second description of Singapore's Prime Minister Lee Kuan Yew sending communist students to school in Australia to disperse them and open them to new ideas. In 1974, CBS had a five-second mention of an eclipse. In 1976, NBC reported that the Victoria flu in Australia caused no deaths. The UFO and Skylab stories of 1979, which between them made 12 mentions, were also classified as "science and education." Thus, the decade escaped with practically no mention of Australian science or education in any acceptable sense of these terms.

Human interest. The human interest category was designed to include such items as society and obituary, but the eight stories that made the news hardly met the intent of the category. In 1970, the story of the boy who hid in the plane's undercarriage and died was classified as human interest, as was the story of the American emigrant to Australia. The 1971 story of multiple births qualified, as did the 1979 stories of a Brazilian newborn named Skylab and the Australian winner of a San Francisco contest for Skylab debris. There were no mentions of the demise of any Australian statesmen, scholars, scientists, writers, actors, or other notables during the decade; nor were there any profiles of notable Australians from a human interest angle. "Human interest" elements did emerge in a few other stories—for example, the "earthy parties" of Australian yachtsmen competing in the America's Cup (9/12/74).

Religion. The "religion" category contained no stories about religion in Australia during the seventies other than the eight stories of a few minutes duration reporting the Pope's visit in 1970.

Art, music, and show business. Two stories about Australian "arts" were aired when ABC devoted 150 seconds and CBS 30 seconds to a story on the song "Waltzing Matilda" (5/4/76). In Australia in July 1974, Mr. Frank Sinatra described women journalists unflatteringly and his subsequent union problems made the network news four times. In September 1975, Marlene Dietrich broke her leg (literally) on a stage in Australia. Sic transit ars Australiae!

Commentary. Twice in the decade, Australia was mentioned briefly by the then more-prominent species of newscaster, the resident pundit. Howard K. Smith proposed a solution to inflation such as that adopted by the Australian National Wage Arbitration Commission (8/18/71). Eric Sevareid saw a worldwide conservative movement in many countries including Australia (10/29/76).

News from Nowhere?

"News from Australia" is really, to extract another meaning from Edward Jay Epstein's phrase, "news from nowhere." It is merely a reflection of what news executives are conditioned to think is appropriate from such an insignificant region. Whether or not American commercial television panders to the nation's ethnocentrism is perhaps debatable, but given the enormous resources of treasure and time bestowed on the medium by the populace, the idea that the people deserve much more intelligent and complete world news can hardly be questioned. The large question does not even concern Australia at all, except as a representative of all the other countries, which, because they are relegated to the obscure regions of the mind in the collective unconscious of the news executives, hardly appear to exist as far as American television is concerned.

One might assume that foreign affairs do matter to the electorate of the world's leading democracy, but apparently TV viewers learn about a foreign nation only when a crisis has occurred, for example, in Iran or Vietnam. On June 18, 1980, for example, Walter Cronkite reported that the Australian Olympic team was attending the Moscow games. If this seemed to be unexpected behavior from the English-speaking democracy that had supported the American initiative in Vietnam with military force, it might have been interesting to ask the journalistic "why?" Alas, the inscrutable Cronkite proceeded to another headline and a commercial.

The biggest, most important Australian story of the decade was a constitutional crisis and the ensuing fall of the Whitlam Labor government. The New York Times featured the story on the first and second pages (11/12/75). The crisis was ignored by the networks. The results of the December election immediately after the constitutional crisis was mentioned by only one network (ABC) and then only as a post-script to a story of the anniversary of the Darwin cyclone. The December election changed the course of Australian national policy and influenced the social structure, economic policy, industry, arts, and education—possibly for decades. However, the constitutional crisis and its aftermath were of little interest to the US networks.

As is often the case, the words of Winston Churchill are appropriate. On learning of the unexpected fall of the "impregnable" fortress of Singapore to the Japanese who entered via the land route while the British guns pointed out to sea, he asked, "Why didn't someone tell me?—Why didn't I ask?" For the American populace, then, the question is, "If television news is not going to tell us, is someone going to ask?"

REFERENCES

Adams, William C. and Fay Schreibman, eds. 1978. *Television Network News.* Washington, D.C.: George Washington University, School of Public and International Affairs.

Adams, William C. ed. 1981. *Television Coverage of the Middle East.* Norwood, N.J.: Ablex.

Almaney, Adnan. 1970. International and Foreign Affairs on Network Television News. *Journal of Broadcasting* 14 (Fall 1970): 499–509.

Deutschmann, Paul J. 1959. *News Page Content of Twelve Metropolitan Dailies.* East Lansing, Mich.: Michigan State University.

Epstein, Edward Jay. 1973. *News from Nowhere: Television and the News.* New York: Random House.

Fisher, Glen. 1979. *American Communication in a Global Society.* Norwood, NJ: Ablex.

Galtung, Johan and Mari H. Ruge. 1965. The Structure of Foreign News. *Journal of Peace Research* 2: 64–91.

Gans, Herbert J. 1979. *Deciding What's News. A Study of CBS Evening News, NBC Nightly News, Newsweek and Time.* New York: Vintage.

Gerbner, George and Nancy Signorelli. 1978. The World of Television News. In William C. Adams and Fay Schreibman, eds. *Television Network News.* Washington, D.C.: George Washington University, School of Public and International Affairs, 189–196.

Haupt, Robert. 1979. The Best of Enemies. *National Times* (March 3, 1979): 45.

Larson, James F. 1978. America's Window on the World? U.S. Network Television Coverage of International Affairs, 1972–1976. Ph.D. dissertation, Stanford University.

Larson, James F. 1979. International Affairs Coverage on US Network Television. *Journal of Communication* 29 (Spring, 1979): 136–147.

Masterton, Murray S. 1977. A Comparative Analysis of the Effects of Daily Satellite News Transmissions on Australian Television Newscasts. M.Sc. thesis, Ohio University.

Renwick, George W. 1980. If Australians are Arrogant, Are Americans Boring? *The Bridge: A Review of Cross-Cultural Affairs and International Training.* 5 (Summer, 1980): 2–4; 33.

Robinson, Michael J. 1978. Future Television News Research: Beyond Edward Jay Epstein. In William C. Adams and Fay Schreibman, eds. *Television Network News.* Washington, D.C.: George Washington University, School of Public and International Affairs, 197–212.

Warner, Malcolm. 1968. TV Coverage of International Affairs. *Television Quarterly* 7 (Spring 1968): 60–75.

PART

IV

SOUTHEAST
ASIA

10

THE WAR IN SOUTHEAST ASIA: TUNNEL VISION ON TELEVISION

ROBERT M. ENTMAN
DAVID L. PALETZ

Our objective is to explore the nature and political implications of the American television networks' nightly coverage of the war in Southeast Asia from late 1964 through early 1975. Our argument is that coverage followed four phases, each one mirroring the state of elite dialogue on the war. Our hypothesis is that, dovish reputation notwithstanding, television news did more to contain than to spread opposition to the policies of Presidents Johnson, Nixon, and Ford. This chapter is a literature review that tries to make some theoretical sense of existing fragmentary research findings; to illuminate the ways elites and television operate to influence each other and public opinion; and to suggest a framework for understanding television coverage of America's foreign interventions.

First, some caveats are in order. Our analysis must be treated as preliminary and tentative. The amount of published research on television coverage of the war is surprisingly small, and our ideas are based on the available data; new studies may amplify or alter them.

In addition, it is often impossible to separate the content of television news from that of elite and mass daily newspapers, weekly news magazines, and other media; nor is it completely possible to chart the public's responses. It is equally difficult to identify the intricacies and the shifts in media coverage of American involvement in Southeast Asia. Stories, for example, could relate to one or more of several issues that together comprised public opinion on the war. Among the most significant questions repeatedly posed and implicitly or explicitly answered in the coverage were:

- Is the president's policy the wisest one?
- What is the purpose of US intervention?
- Who is winning?
- Is US success possible at an acceptable cost?
- What are the costs to the United States in men and money?
- How soon will American involvement be terminated?
- Was getting involved in the conflict a mistake?
- Are Vietnamese civilians suffering and at whose hands?
- Are the South Vietnamese contributing effectively to the fight?
- How does the American public feel about the war?
- What is the dovish position on the war? The hawkish? The moderate?
- How representative of the public are opponents of American policy?

Complicating matters further, the context in which these issues were discussed changed as the war persisted. The stated purpose of American involvement went through several phases and the meaning of American "success" differed accordingly. In the middle years, the South Vietnamese were not supposed to be bearing the brunt of the fighting; earlier and later in the war they were. Being a "dove" in 1965 usually meant calling for a bombing halt to stimulate negotiations; in 1970, "doves" sought an immediate withdrawal of all American forces.

Public opinion is the result of a "complex combination of the different characteristics of source, medium, messages, and audience. The opinions themselves are often fickle, even contradictory..." (Paletz & Entman, 1981, p. 185). In the case of Southeast Asia, opinions were also influenced by expectations raised by earlier media coverage and the depiction of new events as they unfolded. The expectations raised and responses evoked by media coverage could differ greatly among viewers because people had varying notions of what constituted successful policy, reasonable costs, and acceptable parameters of dissent.

Further, Vietnam was associated in many minds with other ideological issues including loyalty to traditional American values and respect for the law and the military. Numerous Americans oriented themselves toward Vietnam on the basis of the position of the president or their political party rather than on the policy questions raised by the Vietnam conflict (Mueller, 1973, Chap. 5).

Given all these distinctions, we focus on the most consequential aspect of public opinion—support of presidential policy. Embracing a president's actions meant different things as the war went on, but it was the bottom line. Whether people disliked the South Vietnamese regime or believed that the original American intervention had been a mistake was less significant for the course of the war than whether they favored the actions of the current administration. It is especially important to distinguish support of the war from support of presidential policy. Many people disliked American intervention, yet favored the president's actions. Others thought the United States was right to become involved, but opposed presidential policy for its failure to pursue the war vigorously enough.

PHASE I: OPTIMISM, 1963-67

During the first phase, the problem in Vietnam was defined as stopping communist aggression. The leading question was: When will Hanoi be forced to negotiate? US officials were the prime sources for war news; they had a stake in the success of the policy and realized the significance of favorable media coverage. Sometimes this led them to mislead. For example, casualty reports were often wrong. Yet, networks labeled them as estimates only about two percent of the time, according to a study of reporting in the years 1965–70 (Bailey, 1976b, p. 323).

The whole tone of coverage was set by the overly optimistic pronouncements of officials whose jobs depended on optimism. There was always light at the end of the tunnel. At the time, there was very little dissent on this prognosis—in public at least—among the powerful people in Washington. Most criticism of American activities was linked to tactics (Knightley, 1975, p. 380). Basic American goals and the assumptions underlying them were essentially undisputed. Journalists went along. The questions asked by journalists and the way they defined the Vietnam problem presupposed the validity of American aims. The result was to legitimize further American involvement (cf. Hallin, 1980, pp. 201–204, 243–247).

Walter Cronkite's comments in a late 1965 documentary typify the early coverage. He was summing up his impressions from a visit to Vietnam earlier that year:

> ...having made the courageous decision that communism's advance must be stopped in Asia and that guerrilla warfare as a means to a political end must be finally discouraged, we had fully committed ourselves to a war to the finish, to throwing in whatever was required in men and material. It seemed clear over there, on the ground of Vietnam, that we were prepared for another Korea, or, if the communists insist that this is the time and this is the issue, another World War.

Combat Stories. "The networks assigned full-time film crews and correspondents to Vietnam in mid-1963" (Epstein, 1975, p. 214). However, television news did not then bring the war in all its horrific detail into the living rooms of Americans. The more gruesome scenes were usually sanitized (Warner, 1968; Bailey & Lichty, 1972; Epstein, 1975; Knightley, 1975; Hallin, 1980). One effect was, as Michael Arlen has observed, pictures of men three inches tall shooting at other men three inches tall (Arlen, 1969, p. 8). Vietnam may have seemed tame, even tedious, when compared to television's fictional violence and big screen war and gangster movies.

We would speculate that television combat coverage may have tended to distance the war by inhibiting the audience's identification and empathy with soldiers. Although fictional, World War II movies encouraged American audiences to identify with the experiences, suffering, and successes of their fighting men. By contrast, the television news soldiers in the Vietnam war were usually anonymous. Television reporters covered different soldiers and different battles all the time; the fighting men on the screen were virtually interchangeable.

Language. Language used on television news also supported the war and the perspective of "stopping communist aggression." In Bailey's study (1976b) television used the following words to describe the people the United States was fighting: "enemy" (in 21 percent of the stories); "Hanoi" or "North Vietnamese" (20 percent); "Vietcong" or "VC" (16 percent); and "communist" (14 percent; we have combined some of Bailey's categories). Terms such as "enemy" and "communist" automatically fit the conflict into pre-established patterns of opinion and trigger automatic responses supporting American involvement. More neutral terms were abjured. Very rarely did the label that the other side used for itself— National Liberation Front (NLF)—appear, nor were the South Vietnamese forces called capitalists. (See also Diamond, 1975, pp. 117–119; Hallin, 1980, pp. 346–348.)

Length of Items. Another source of television's contribution to the early legitimacy of presidential policy can be found in the brevity of many of the items read by anchormen. The median length of such items was 31–45 words on ABC and NBC, 46–60 on CBS. Less than 5 percent of the stories had more than 150 words—which would be only four column inches in a newspaper (Bailey, 1976a, p. 154). Thirty-two percent of these items concerned ground combat; 16 percent, air action; 12 percent, official statements; 9 percent, the instruments of war; 7 percent, who won the battles and how many died. Only 4 percent dealt with the impact of the war back home (Bailey, 1976a, p. 155). Almost no stories examined the political and historical context of the war (cf. Hallin, 1980, pp. 367–369). Therefore, television news may have tended to dilute complex reality into quickly conveyed stereotyped snippets.

Documentaries. What of the networks' documentaries? Some were querulous, critical; most shared the assumptions of the nightly news. At

CBS, documentaries underwent careful production scrutiny and editing first by an executive producer, then by the news division vice president. According to McNulty's study (1975, p. 177) of these documentaries,

> The effect of executive editing decisions is essentially to curb extreme attitudes, shifting them more toward the center of the opinion spectrum. This is not the same as saying that a news special or documentary cannot have a stance or position, but rather that opinion extremes tend to be shifted toward "tolerable" limits which depending on the perspective of the viewer could be termed "more conservative" or "more responsible."

PHASE II: SURPRISE AND OPPOSITION—TET

In Phase I, television news appeared as an appendage to the war effort, or a channel of official reassurance in the face of growing frustration. Most of the news legitimized the war. However, television's role changed quite suddenly in early 1968 when the NLF launched its Tet offensive. For a time, television obtained some substantial independence from its elite informants.

Tet news on television produced itself. The war was happening literally in the streets, and in front of the reporters and camera crews. Normally, officials frame the visual images television conveys by their verbal explanations, from which journalists construct their voiceover narratives. Tet disrupted—for a time—this close relationship between sources and television messages; the visual overwhelmed the verbal.

As Braestrup (1977) points out, the values and practices of TV news enhanced the pessimistic slant. The sight of American soldiers battling to defend their embassy, an uncontrollably potent symbol of the lack of progress America had made in "pacifying" Vietnam, was irresistibly attractive to television news, as were the scenes of battle devastation throughout the country. Less amenable to graphic reporting was the failure of most of the population to rise up alongside the NLF; and the slow battles that eventually led to the recovery of most of the territory seized by the NLF were difficult to convey.

Tet coverage confirmed the long festering personal doubts held by many reporters that they had been deceived. The administration had claimed, not so long before, that most of South Vietnam was invulnerable to enemy penetration. Tet brought NLF cadres onto the very ground of the American embassy compound in Saigon. Some news coverage may well have been animated by guilt, outrage, and desire to correct the record; moreover, previously insulated editors back home were finally moved to doubt government assurances (Halberstam, 1979, p. 511).

Tet also destroyed the accord that normally pervades foreign policy leadership circles. Important senators—some of whom had already been expressing doubts—were emboldened to dissent by the news out of Saigon; criticism was increasingly and regularly voiced in official Washington. Even members of the Johnson administration (Defense Secretary Clark Clifford for example) conducted agonizing reappraisals. With legitimate elite sources forcefully expressing dissenting views, reports could no longer convey so unified a picture (cf. Kail, 1973).

Television—like the print media—is strongly attracted to policy conflicts among the powerful. Disputes among the elite individuals who are customarily the chief subjects and sources of news (see e.g., Gans, 1979, pp. 11, 119) are indeed quintessentially newsworthy. When the dissension is within a president's own party and his own administration, media interest seems particularly intense. During wartime, such conflict is especially unexpected and hence newsworthy.

The administration's sanguine assurances soon became savaged by expressions of dismay and doubt about American policies coming from some powerful officials, by journalists confronted with what many took to be evidence that they had been bamboozled by the administration (or at least not dealt with straightforwardly), and by television close-ups of the previously shadowy and elusive Vietcong and North Vietnamese fighters. Coverage of Tet was suffused with a new pessimism and a sense of the war's futility. (Cf. Hallin, 1980, pp. 165–169.)

A striking example of journalistic response to Tet came from Walter Cronkite. He is reported to have said, when he first saw the wire reports coming in, "What the hell is going on? I thought we were winning the war!" (Oberdorfer, 1971, p. 158). He subsequently hosted a documentary in which he blatantly editorialized, calling for an end to American escalation and swift negotiations with the other side (Oberdorfer, 1971, pp. 268–269).

Responses such as Cronkite's were not entirely based on an extensive and unemotional understanding of the war or of the meaning of Tet. In fact, the other side's gains were less substantial than portrayed and many of their "victories" were ephemeral. (See the exhaustive treatment by Braestrup, 1977.) Probably more than the print media, television is drawn to the newest of the news and eschews second looks or updates.

Although not entirely ignored, stories of Tet's aftermath were overshadowed by its domestic reverberations. Television news' favorite show, the presidential election campaign, was beginning simultaneously with Tet. A little-known dove, Senator Eugene McCarthy, had nearly beaten President Johnson in the New Hampshire primary; Johnson withdrew and the best-known dove, Senator Robert Kennedy, entered the race. The Democratic primary contest gave considerably and often favorable pub-

licity to dovish sentiments being voiced by attractive and legitimate elites
—and, crucially, to apparent popular endorsement of those beliefs in
primary elections.

Opinions Change.   The result was a striking change in public opinion within a few months. Lunch and Sperlich (1979, p. 22) conducted a
survey of surveys and found public sentiment for escalation peaked during
late 1967.

One question that may have tapped this sentiment was asked several
times: "People are called 'hawks' if they want to step up our military effort
in Vietnam. They are called 'doves' if they want to reduce our military
effort in Vietnam. How would you describe yourself. . ." In December
1967 hawks outnumbered doves 52–35 percent. The first reports of Tet
apparently ignited a rally-round-the-flag response: the early February
1968 poll put hawks over doves 61–23 percent (Mueller, 1973, p. 107).
Another poll in February found 53 percent in favor of intensifying the
war effort, 24 percent for cutting it back (Mueller, 1973, p. 90). A survey
also found in early February a 70–15 percent majority against a bombing
halt (Gallup, 1972, p. 2106).

The changes wrought by Tet began to emerge in March. Hawks
went down to 41 percent, doves up to 42 percent (Mueller, 1973, p. 107).
By April, approval for the bombing halt (now official policy) was 64–26
percent (Gallup, 1972, p. 2121). A June poll revealed 35 percent for intensification of the war and 49 percent for cutting it back (Mueller, 1973,
p. 91; also see Roper, 1977).

It would be wrong to believe that television news alone caused these
drastic shifts. Certainly, the Johnson administration's sudden adoption of
the (moderate) dovish platform of ceasing the bombing and beginning
negotiations had much to do with the new public sentiment. But the administration's decision itself was, if not caused, at least encouraged by
television's picture of disaster (cf. Braestrup, 1977, Vol. I, p. 671). After
all, if TV news had accepted the administration's official line that Tet was
a stunning defeat for the NLF, the pressures on the administration would
have been quite different. However, the expectations established by the
administration—until then faithfully relayed by the media—undermined
that claim. The administration's own optimism set the stage for the conversion of journalists like Cronkite, whose own sentiments were now in-
compatible with the attempt to put a favorable gloss on Tet, as well as for
the conversion of hawkish Americans in the television news audiences.

The Tet experience suggests that television gains institutional autonomy in covering foreign policy mainly where the evidence appears clear,
massive, overwhelming, and *visual* that the usual network of elite sources
has been misleading journalists. The less obvious and overt the evidence,
the more likely television will be tied to its informants' perspectives, data,

and explanations. In overseas reporting especially, the evening news shows are generally not suited for journalism that independently seeks out the unaccustomed persons and printed sources of information that could undermine official US pronouncements. (For further discussion of this point, see Paletz & Entman, 1981, pp. 214–221).

PHASE III: NIXONIZATION

Arguably, television's legitimation of anti-war criticism, its independence of elite sources, ended with the 1968 Republican convention, where even GOP stalwarts announced their distaste for continued fighting and further promoted the move away from escalation (Mueller, 1973, p. 57, fn. 10).

Stopping further escalation and ending the war were two different goals. Here we believe television returned to its earlier course, contributing to public support of the persistence of war. Richard Nixon won the presidency by a thin plurality in 1968 after promising he had a "secret plan" to end the war. Hubert Humphrey was saddled with the previous Administration's failed policies, of which he had been a stout public defender; he spent the campaign obfuscating and hinting he was a closet dove. Meanwhile, Nixon was allowed to appear as an unsullied if inscrutable peacemaker. Aggressive journalism might have forced a genuine debate between the candidates on Vietnam. Instead, research shows that the major issue facing the country, one about which most people had strong opinions, was not of major importance to presidential voting. It could not be; information on candidates' stands was not available (Page & Brody, 1972). Television's acquiescence in Humphrey's vagaries and Nixon's ploy of a secret plan essentially took Vietnam off the campaign agenda.

The Domestic vs. the Foreign Story. By early 1969, what had a year before been the most dovish of positions became official announced policy. Soon after he took office, President Nixon promised to begin withdrawing troops and to conduct serious negotiations with the other side. With television's contribution, the hawk-dove continuum moved. Now the conflict centered on the speed of withdrawal and the flexibility of US negotiators. But, if official administration policy after 1969 was hawkish in these new terms—slow withdrawal and rigid negotiating stance—so too, on balance, was television coverage.

More than during the previous phases, television coverage during Phase III was distinctly divided into domestic political conflict (over the pace of withdrawals, expansion of the war into Laos and Cambodia, and negotiating stances) and reporting of events in Southeast Asia. Coverage of the first aspect was generally balanced as befits domestic political journalism. The news respectfully and dutifully recorded the dissent of reputable members of Congress and other elites, as well as the administration's responses. This coverage inevitably militated against Nixon's efforts to portray himself as the leader of a consensus policy. Leadership clashes over Vietnam, however, made television news primarily when Nixon escalated sharply, violating the tacit understanding that he was at least winding down the war, even if not fast enough for some. At these times (e.g., the Cambodia "incursion"), criticism and concomitant television attention were substantial. However, such domestic stories were neither frequent, sustained, nor inflammatory. (See Hallin, 1980, pp. 205–242, cf. pp. 361–363.)

The Southeast Asia part of the story was certainly different than it was before Tet. There was skepticism about claims of military progress, and cynicism about the ability or will of the South Vietnamese to beat back the NLF. The volume of reporting from Vietnam dropped precipitously at this time. Television news rarely highlighted or repeated Indochina stories belying Nixon's claim of moderately but deliberately paced de-escalation. It was largely by omission that television failed to arouse public opposition (or even awareness) of what was in some respects a prolonged and even widened conflagration after 1969 (on diminished public concern with Vietnam after 1969, see MacKuen & Coombs, 1981, pp. 72–73, 84–86).

Interest Declines. In a 1972 interview, Robert Northshield, who had been executive producer of the Huntley-Brinkley Report on NBC in the 1965–68 period, said (Hodgson, 1976, p. 378):

> By early 1969 that feeling [of boredom with Vietnam stories] was very marked. The trend was away from Vietnam. About the time, in early 1969, when we got tired of combat footage, we said, "Let's get some pacification footage," and that was soft stuff, so it went out at the tail end of the show. So straightaway people got the impression that the war was less important. The American voter is willing to vote for Nixon now [in 1972] because the voter, who is also the viewer, thinks Nixon has ended the war. . . . And he *has* ended the war, because you don't see the war on the tube any more.

The executive producer of the ABC Evening News, Av Westin, wrote to his Saigon bureau in March 1969 (Epstein, 1973, pp. 48–49):

> I think the time has come to shift some of our focus from the battlefield, or more specifically American military involvement with the enemy, to themes and stories under the general heading: We Are On Our Way Out of Vietnam. . . .

The other networks "also altered their coverage in late 1969 from combat pieces to stories about the 'Vietnamization' of the war" (Epstein, 1975, p. 228).

As evidence of the decline in television's interest, the percentage of CBS and NBC evening news shows containing Vietnam stories fell from around 85 to 90 percent during 1965–68, to about 70 percent during

1969–70. The average number of stories in that sample was 29 per week in 1965–68 and 18 in 1969–70, although they were longer in the latter period. (See Bailey, 1976a.)

After 1968, the scope of the conflict expanded to include Laos and Cambodia and there were many more casualties, and three million more refugees (Knightley, 1975, p. 398). Nonetheless, coverage declined and reports of casualties were infrequent (Hallin, 1980, pp. 330–340; Frank, 1973, pp. 48–49).

There are several reasons for the decline in television (and other media) attention. Nixon and Kissinger switched American concentration from bloody ground combat to the less deadly (for Americans) air war. With diminished American casualties, the war became less interesting to American television audiences (or so network news executives appear to have assumed) as well as much harder to cover. Television news may inadvertently have helped shape military strategy. Nixon surely realized air war coverage would be more difficult and its tenor less critical than coverage of the ground fighting had become—even though the air strategy was as frustrating and ultimately unsuccessful in achieving US aims as ground combat had been.

As for the ground war, television journalism's limitations trapped correspondents into producing many boringly repetitive stories. Coverage of Southeast Asia was often limited to a few stereotyped images—helicopters, tall grass, soldiers shooting at invisible targets, postcombat devastation. Narration, which usually had to fit these pictures, was limited to a few variations on repeated themes. If news values had been more diverse and journalistic sources more various, stories might not have aged so rapidly after 1968.

The Nixon administration may have also contributed to the decline in coverage, as it apparently made intimidation of the media a part of its war policy planning. It reportedly succeeded in substantial measure (Porter, 1976; Wise, 1973, pp. 375–405; Hodgson, 1976, Chapter 19; Gitlin, 1980; Schorr, 1977; Barrett, 1975; Halberstam, 1979). No less an authority than Walter Cronkite charged the Nixon administration with a "grand conspiracy to destroy the credibility of the press" (quoted in Wise, 1973, p. 379). Although we cannot be sure of their motives, it is conceivable that business-oriented, profit-conscious network executives espoused aggressive news reporting less enthusiastically in the fearsome atmosphere Nixon and his men promoted.

A final explanation lies in the media's love affair with the chief policy planner in Phase III, Henry Kissinger. Throughout the first Nixon term, Kissinger was quite possibly the subject of more fawning adulation than any political official since John Kennedy (Morris, 1974, 1975). Nixon by himself might not have been as adept at minimizing and parrying negative coverage. Kissinger's presence as that policy's major expositor, with his reputation for brilliance and moderation, helped legitimize the administration's decisions.

There were three other kinds of news stories reported during Phase III which in combination might have devastated support for American involvement in Southeast Asia; they concerned atrocities, the Pentagon Papers, and the anti-war movement.

Atrocities. We should be careful not to assume that heavy coverage of American atrocities would have provoked a mass demand for immediate withdrawal. Hodgson (1976, pp. 389–393) distinguishes two streams of anti-war sentiment. The first was "moralistic;" it was concerned with the bad effects of the war on the Vietnamese as well as Americans. This kind of opposition was centered among students and liberal intellectuals. The second stream was much, much larger. Its focus was on the losses being suffered by Americans, and on the unacceptable cost to the United States of winning. The "pragmatic" nature of most Americans' judgment of the war meant atrocity reports swayed few.

The pragmatic context helps explain the media's coverage of the events of My Lai in which 100 or more civilians were gunned down by American soldiers. The first report on September 6, 1969, was a brief item of less than 100 words from the AP reporting Lt. William Calley's indictment by the Army. It did not give the number of deaths he was charged with. The *New York Times* ran it on page 38. Not a single reporter called the AP for amplification of the sketchy story of the first officially-admitted atrocity. Only when Seymour Hersh dug up details and aggressively promoted the story did it become prominent. That was over two months later. Then attention waned. Finally, photographs of the incident's aftermath taken by a soldier who was there became available. Then, the major national media, including the networks, devoted significant space to it in December (Knightley, 1975, pp. 391–393; cf. Hersh, 1970).

Television's reporting of civilain casualties tended to stress the responsibility of the other side. Hallin (1980, pp. 331, 340–345) reports 230 mentions of civilain casualties; 44.3 percent were attributed to the NLF or North Vietnam, and 30.4 percent to the US. Most of the rest were unattributed. According to Hallin, the stories made it appear that much of civilian suffering was inflicted by the other side as part of a deliberate terroristic strategy. The smaller amount of American-caused suffering was portrayed as resulting from stupidity or accident (Hallin, 1980, pp. 32, 36). This reporting set a "pragmatic" context for the revelations of American atrocities. The frequent response was that war is always evil; at least the American policy was to avoid killing civilians when possible. The impression left by the media's coverage was that My Lai was an aberration.

Bombing and Secrets.   The story of the secret bombing of Cambodia was treated with even greater diffidence by television news, which thereby helped conceal the substantial escalation of the air war. Apparently, the denials by the President and Secretary of State of any American bombing of Vietnam's neutral neighbor were accepted. The *New York Times* described the bombing in one story during early 1969. *Newsweek* had a brief blurb in its "Periscope" section. That reportedly was all, until the Watergate revelations made it fashionable to focus on Nixonian duplicity (Branch, 1975).

Television news was similarly circumspect in its coverage of the Pentagon Papers—release of the previously-secret Defense Department report on the history of American involvement in Vietnam. When the first installment of the Papers was published in the Sunday *New York Times*, NBC led with the story; but the other two television networks virtually ignored it that weekend (Diamond, 1975, pp. 134–137). Indeed, Diamond contends that a CBS interview with Daniel Ellsberg, the man responsible for releasing the Papers to the media, was television's "sole original contribution" (Diamond, 1975, p. 144). As the story grew, the news emphasis was on the Nixon administration's attempt to suppress publication, not on the Papers' disclosures about official duplicity during the planning and early execution of war policy. The dramatic confrontation between the freedom of the press and a government at war took precedence over the substantive content of the Papers. Historical information and analysis are almost always secondary to the compulsions and definitions of breaking news on television (see Knoll, 1972; Hallin, 1980, pp. 358–359).

Protesters.   Finally, there was television news coverage of the post-Tet anti-war movement. In 1968, of all the political groups, "Vietnam war protesters" were by far the most negatively evaluated by Americans polled in the University of Michigan's nationwide survey. Even respondents favoring the then radical idea of immediate withdrawal from Vietnam felt negative about demonstrators by more than 50 percent (Converse et al., 1969, p. 1087). This finding is presumptive evidence that the media in general and television in particular reported neither the demonstrations nor their participants sympathetically. And the occurrence of protests did not seem to boost anti-war sentiment among the public at large (Schreiber, 1976).

The more disruptive and radical of the anti-war groups were generally denigrated throughout the war period. After Tet, however, moderate and peaceably petitioning anti-war groups received some sympathetic television coverage (Gitlin, 1980, Chapter 7). Overall, Daniel Hallin found critical statements about the anti-war movement in his sample of television news stories outweighed praise 2 to 1 (Hallin, 1980, pp. 318–319; cf. Pride & Richards, 1974).

Although there are no definitive data on the subject, we suspect television, reflecting its usual limitations, did not focus on conveying the (abstract) ideas and critical arguments of the protesters but rather high-lighted their actions (e.g., how many marched where, with what degree of conflict with police). Such coverage provided little cognitive ammunition for opposing the administration's policies, although it probably aroused awareness of the very possibility of protest and helped recruit some viewers into the movement (Hallin, 1980, pp. 320–326).

Opinion Surveys. Gallup often asked the public to react to Richard Nixon's handling of the Vietnam situation. Over the first year of his administration, the president did well indeed. In April 1969, 44 percent said they approved, 24 percent disapproved and 32 percent had no opinion of his policies. Approval steadily increased: 53 percent in July and 65 percent in January 1970 (24 percent still disapproved). Lyndon Johnson's approval had never topped 58 percent. It appears that, at the least, media coverage did not hurt the standing of Nixon's Vietnam policies in 1969. There was little elite dissent the first year. Most Americans were giving the president the benefit of the doubt, a chance to make good on his secret plan. Television coverage of the domestic side of the story passively promoted the legitimacy of Nixon policy.

Between January and April 1970, the president's Vietnam rating declined steeply, to 48 percent. Approval thereafter hovered around 50 percent; it reached a low of 41 percent in early 1971, and a high of 59 percent just after the 1972 election. (For data, see Gallup, 1972, pp. 2190–2291; Gallup, 1978, pp. 13–93). The main reason for the decline and fluctuation appears to have been the administration's well-publicized expansion of the land conflict into Laos. A war that was supposedly cooling off suddenly spread into new territory (or at least the expansion was acknowledged publicly for the first time). Nixon violated the expectations his pronouncements had engendered and members of Congress responded with criticism and pressure. Television reported this domestic side of war coverage as it became a thorn in Nixon's side, pressing deeper or lighter as elite opposition flowered or withered.

Despite recrudescences provoked by the administration's land attacks in Laos and Cambodia, television coverage from Southeast Asia continued to drop. At the same time, the Nixon administration seemed to be able to escape blame for the war. One indication of the media's limited role in undermining Nixon can be found in a comparison of public opinion on troop withdrawal and on George McGovern. In September 1970, a proposal to bring home all troops by the end of 1971 was endorsed by 55 percent in a Gallup poll. By February 1971, the figure had risen to 78 percent (Gallup, 1972, pp. 2266, 2301). Yet, in 1972, the public by 58 to 26 percent felt the president who had failed to withdraw the troops in 1971 would do a better job on Vietnam than the candidate who promised unequivocally to end the war at once.

The press was not the sole cause of these sentiments; many Americans genuinely felt McGovern's policies would lead to a communist takeover, which they widely feared (cf. Mueller, 1973, p. 97; cf. also Frank, 1973), and of course opposed McGovern on other grounds. Perhaps McGovern was identified with moralistic opposition to the war and Nixon was seen as the pragmatist. In any case, the idea that television coverage contributed heavily to deterioration of confidence in Nixon's Indochina policy seems unfounded.

The end of Phase III was associated with Nixon's overwhelming reelection. Then, Nixon ordered a series of unprecedentedly heavy bombings of North Vietnam to force Hanoi to terms. He later claimed that the networks strongly attacked him for this decision, attributing to the networks such phrases as "tyrant, dictator, he's lost his senses, he should resign, he should be impeached." Actually, a study of all three networks' coverage every day during the bombing shows only two such assertions. One was attributed to Radio Hanoi and one to Senator William Saxbe (R. Ohio) whom Nixon later appointed Attorney General. The 79 assertions supporting the decision to bomb were only slightly outnumbered by the 90 negative ones (Lichty, 1973a, pp. 2, 5). The treaty signing brought Phase III to a close.

PHASE IV: SADNESS WITHOUT LESSONS

Television news coverage of Southeast Asia declined even more after the treaty signing and full withdrawal of American combat troops. The two major post-treaty stories were the return of the American prisoners of war in February 1973 and the final defeat of the South Vietnamese in April 1975. (For the data and quotes in this section see Lichty, 1975).

The POW return was played by the president largely for its propaganda value. The networks cooperated with saturation coverage. During the period February 12–16, Lichty found more than 60 percent of all their news stories were on the POW homecoming. During this period, this degree of concentration on one subject was unequaled (except for the week of Nixon's resignation, 8/5–9/74), according to Lichty. The POW show distracted from Nixon's burgeoning Watergate troubles and from the failure of the United States to achieve its original war objectives.

POW coverage retrospectively legitimized American help for the South Vietnamese by providing a list of atrocity stories about the other side. Analysis of the treaty itself might have shown that the final result of America's involvement was to restore the political situation back to 1963, calling the wisdom of US policy into serious question. Any probing of this type was subordinated to the human interest and patriotic fervor inherent in the welcoming home of American war heroes—a healing ritual previously missing from this war.

Fighting in Vietnam lasted another two years. Television occasionally carried brief reports about the conflicts and charges of treaty violations by both sides, but few were filmed. By October 1973, during a 30-day period, only five filmed reports from Southeast Asia were shown on the three networks (Lichty, 1973b).

Coverage of the swift end of the regime in the South concentrated on visual drama. The hurried, helicopter-clinging desperation of Americans and Vietnamese to leave produced exciting footage. The event was depicted more as the fall of the South than as America's (delayed) first loss of a war. The theme of the coverage was sadness and the implication drawn was about the faulty process and tactics—not the substance and goals—of American policy. That theme fit journalism's usual commitment to procedural cures for official mistakes of malfeasance and its dependence upon elites who share that commitment.

No blame, let alone guilt, was assessed. There was no analysis of the foreign policy consensus or the assumptions and aims that led officials to enter the war in the first place. Walter Cronkite's benediction on CBS was typical:

> And perhaps that is our big lesson from Vietnam: the necessity for candor. We the American people, the world's admired democracy, cannot ever again allow ourselves to be misinformed, manipulated, and misled into disastrous foreign adventure. The government must share with the people the making of policy, the big decisions. In Vietnam we have finally reached the end of the tunnel and there is no light. What is there, perhaps, was best said by President Ford: a war that is finished. And ahead, again to quote the president, the time has come to look forward to an agenda for the future, to unify, to bind up the nation's wounds, and to restore its health and its optimistic self-confidence.

Notice how Cronkite relied upon the elite source, President Ford, to frame the war's end. Notice too how he shifted blame for his own institution, which after all was an instrument through which officials misled, manipulated, and misinformed Americans. The language used in reporting events, the questions posed, the ways the problem of American involvement was defined, the reliance on American governmental sources, and the technological limitations, made television news a conveyor of much misinformation. This occurred despite the bravery, dedication, ingenuity, and personal skepticism of so many of the men and women who covered the fighting.

CONCLUSION

Again, we emphasize the limited data upon which our analysis is based, the complications to which we could only allude without developing, and the obvious need for more research. Nevertheless, assuming our analysis is on balance valid, the impact of television on foreign policy during and since the Indochina war needs reassessment. Television news is widely credited with bringing the war in all its cruelty and futility into Americans' living rooms. It is said to have spurred anti-war sentiment, forcing leaders to end the war sooner than they might otherwise have done. Our analysis indicates television's contribution to undermining official policy was limited mainly to the first half of 1968. Generally, before and after that, it legitimized presidential actions. Television helped generate public support for ever deeper entrapment in the quagmire and then served to mute opposition to the pace of Nixon's four-year policy of extrication (cf. also Arlen, 1976, p. 160). At the end, it went along with the concerted efforts of American leaders to stifle consideration of the guiding policy assumptions that had led the country into Vietnam in the first place.

Recent evidence indicates that television and the rest of the press have not assimilated many lessons from their Southeast Asian experience (see, e.g., Paletz & Entman, 1981, Chapter 13, on coverage of American involvement in Zaire; Dorman & Omeed, 1979, on Iran; Morris, 1980, pp. 27–31, on Afghanistan; Maslow & Arana, 1981, on El Salvador). Television's limitations and habits persist. They include its insistence on short, visually appealing stories; its inability or unwillingness to devote many resources to independent, investigative reporting; and its reliance on a certified group of customary sources of foreign policy explanations and descriptions. These characteristics seem to compose an inherent rhythm in coverage of US intervention in foreign countries. The four-phased pattern we found in the Southeast Asia case may be typical of coverage of active US foreign policy involvements. We believe it fits the more recent reporting of US activities in Africa, Iran, Afghanistan, and El Salvador for example.

Generalizing now, Phase I is *homogeneous support* of administration policy. At early stages, time and information are short; both television and potentially dissenting official news sources rely upon the State Department and White House. The uncritical news sows the seeds of the second phase—*diversity of views* and some undermining of administration positions. More information is developed by journalists' elite sources and by reporters themselves. The new information almost inevitably shows mistakes, gaps, or outright lies in the original web spun by the administration. Elite opponents are mobilized, provide new interpretations, and a newsworthy political controversy ensues.

There are limitations on how long Phase II news diversity can last. Two factors operate to create the third phase—*support by omission*. First, in response to the criticism, the administration changes its rhetorical line and its publicly-acknowledged policy tactics (presumably without modifying its essential strategic goals). The idea is to mollify administration critics, cool the controversy, and thereby remove it from the evening news (and public consciousness) as much as possible. During its early months in office, the Reagan administration followed this strategy successfully on El Salvador.

Second is the natural entropy of the television news story. Critics of administration policy can make their cases seem fresh only a limited number of times; new developments constantly compete for air time. Attacks on the administration become old news, briefly noted in the waning minutes of the newscast (if at all). The administration carries out its policy in the relative absence of television attention, unless a dramatic new development stimulates a burst of unexpected information and opposition.

Of course the phases differ in length and quality for different issues. Some stories persist in Phase III indefinitely; sometimes enough surprising developments and elite disputation occur to keep a story oscillating between Phases II and III. But often there is a fourth phase—*return to consensus*. Once again, coverage is homogeneous, although the sameness can take different forms. On occasion, the foreign policy issue may virtually vanish from the news (e.g., Quemoy and Matsu, the Panama Canal). Often, the final chapter is framed as an episode whose ending should be cathartic and emotional rather than analytical. Recently, elites have tended to shy away, at least in the foreign policy realm, from challenging each other's basic premises or explicitly drawing harsh historical judgments. Reflecting this, television tends to offer the kind of paeans to patriotism and unity that accompanied the return of the POWs, the fall of Saigon, and the homecoming of the Iranian hostages.

We can speculate that this four-phased cycle has paradoxical implications for public support of American foreign policy. With its oversimplifications of what is almost always a complicated foreign policy dilemma, Phase I coverage—while initially promoting specific support—may reinforce a continuing, diffuse public sense of confusion, even anomie. This is because Phase II challenges usually do emerge, raising doubts, and Phases III and IV leave the questions unresolved. If Vietnam was truly a noble cause (Phase IV), why did so many members of Congress and ordinary Americans come to oppose US policy there (Phase II)?

With rare exceptions, television seems ill-equipped or ill-prepared to explore such puzzles. Historical analysis, context, and aggressive probing of underlying premises of US involvement are not the forte of television news. In the short run, Phase I reporting promotes public support for government policy; in the slightly longer run (by Phases III and IV), it yields passive acquiescence—acceptance based on ignorance or confusion.

If one assumes that their policies are truly congruent with America's highest ideals and interests, foreign policy elites might actually enjoy greater public support and faith if television developed greater autonomy. If Phase I and the dialectical reactions it spawns in Phases II–IV were reduced or eliminated, citizens might be educated. They could learn to accept the frequent intractability of foreign affairs for great powers; to handle sacrifices and setbacks maturely; and to cope with the existence of other peoples who are as devoted to their visions of truth and justice as Americans are to theirs. Such a citizenry might have deeper feelings of security and control and underlying trust in US political leaders who made wise policy choices. That basic support in turn could diminish the need reigning administrations seem to feel for manipulating television so it conveys Phase I simplicities, quiets Phase II doubts, creates Phase III vacuums, and orchestrates Phase IV incantations of virtue that only set the public up for more confusion and irresolution the next time the United States stumbles. The Southeast Asia war story and its journalistic progeny seem to indicate, however, that such independence—when it emerges at all—arises only briefly and sporadically.

What of the future? Certainly, the conflict in Southeast Asia affected elites, journalists, and the public. Media coverage of the war's opponents circulated an analysis of American foreign policy missing during the cold war. Public skepticism about the necessity and benefits of armed American intercession abroad rose. Many reporters learned to be suspicious of official pronouncements. Nonetheless, most of the organizational goals, practices and limitations that subjected the media, especially television news, to the manipulation of foreign policy makers remain deeply entrenched. In the main, television is locked into a symbiosis with foreign policy elites that may ultimately serve the highest aspirations of neither partner.

REFERENCES

Arlen, Michael J. 1969. *Living Room War*. New York: Viking Press.

———. 1976. *The View from Highway 1*. New York: Farrar, Strauss and Giroux.

Bailey, George. 1976a. Television War: Trends in Network Coverage of Vietnam, 1965–1970. *Journal of Broadcasting* 20 (Spring 1976): 147–158.

———. 1976b. Interpretive Reporting of the Vietnam War by Anchormen. *Journalism Quarterly* 53 (Summer 1976): 319–324.

Bailey, George A. and Lawrence W. Lichty. 1972. Rough Justice on a Saigon Street: A Gatekeeper Study of NBC's Tet Execution Film. *Journalism Quarterly* 49 (1972): 221–229, 238.

Barrett, Marvin. 1975. *Moments of Truth?* New York: Thomas Y. Crowell.

Braestrup, Peter. 1977. *Big Story: How the American Press and Television Reported and Interpreted the Crisis of Tet 1968 in Vietnam and Washington*. Boulder, Col.: Westview Press.

Branch, Taylor. 1975. The Scandal that Got Away. In Richard Pollak, ed. *Stop the Presses, I Want to Get Off: Inside Stories of the News Business from the Pages of MORE*. New York: Random House.

Converse, Philip E.; Warren E. Miller; Jerrold G. Rusk; and Arthur C. Wolf. 1969. Continuity and Change in American Politics: Parties and Issues in the 1968 Election. *American Political Science Review* 63 (1969): 1083–1105.

Diamond, Edwin. 1975. *The Tin Kazoo*. Cambridge, Mass.: The MIT Press.

Dorman, William A. and Ehsan Omeed. 1979. Reporting Iran the Shah's Way. *Columbia Journalism Review* 17 (January/February 1979): 27–33.

Epstein, Edward Jay. 1973. *News From Nowhere: Television and the News*. New York: Vintage Books.

———. 1975. *Between Fact and Fiction*. New York: Vintage Books.

Frank, Robert S. 1973. *Message Dimensions of Television News*. Lexington, Mass.: Lexington Books, D.C. Heath.

Gallup, George H. 1972. *The Gallup Poll, Public Opinion 1935–71*. Volume Three. New York: Random House.

———. 1978. *The Gallup Poll, Public Opinion, 1972–1977*. Volume One. Wilmington, Del.: Scholarly Resources, Inc.

Gans, Herbert J. 1979. *Deciding What's News, A Study of CBS Evening News, NBC Nightly News, Newsweek, and Time*. New York: Pantheon Books.

Gates, Gary Paul. 1978. *Air Time*. New York: Harper and Row.

Gelb, Leslie H., with Richard K. Betts. 1979. *The Irony of Vietnam: The System Worked*. Washington, D.C.: The Brookings Institution.

Gitlin, Todd. 1980. *The Whole World Is Watching*. Berkeley, Calif.: University of California Press.

Halberstam, David. 1979. *The Powers That Be*. New York: Knopf.

Hallin, Daniel. 1980. *The Mass Media and the Crisis in American Politics: The Case of Vietnam*. Ph.D. dissertation, University of California, Berkeley.

Hersh, Seymour M. 1969–70. The Story Everyone Ignored. *Columbia Journalism Review* 8 (Winter 1969–1970): 55–58.

Hodgson, Godfrey. 1976. *America in Our Time.* Garden City, New York: Doubleday.

Kail, F. M. 1973. *What Washington Said.* New York: Harper Torchbooks.

Knightley, Phillip. 1975. *The First Casualty.* New York: Harcourt Brace Jovanovich.

Knoll, Steve. 1972. When TV Was Offered the Pentagon Papers. *Columbia Journalism Review* 10 (March–April 1972): 46–48.

Lichty, Lawrence W. 1973a. Network Evening News Coverage of the Bombing of North Vietnam, December 1972. Unpublished paper, University of Wisconsin-Madison.

———. 1973b. The War We Watched on Television. *AFI Report* 4 (Winter 1973): 29–37.

———. 1975. The Night at the End of the Tunnel: How TV Reported the End of the Indo-China War. *Film Comment* 11 (July–August, 1975): 32–35.

Lunch, William J. and Peter W. Sperlich. 1979. American Public Opinion and the War in Vietnam. *Western Political Quarterly* (1979): 21–44.

Maslow, Jonathan Evan and Ana Arana. 1981. Operation El Salvador. *Columbia Journalism Review* 20 (May/June 1981): 52–58.

MacKuen, Michael Bruce and Steven Lane Coombs. 1981. *More than News, Media Power in Public Affairs.* Beverly Hills, Calif.: Sage Publications.

McNulty, Thomas M. 1975. Vietnam Specials: Policy and Content. *Journal of Communication* 25 (Autumn 1975): 173–180.

Morris, Roger. 1974. Henry Kissinger and the Media: A Separate Peace. *Columbia Journalism Review* 13 (May/June 1974): 14–25.

———. 1975. Kissinger and the Press—Revisited. *Columbia Journalism Review* 14 (September/October, 1975): 49–52.

———. 1980. Reporting for Duty: The Pentagon and the Press. *Columbia Journalism Review* 19 (July/August 1980): 27–33.

Mueller, John F. 1973. *War, Presidents and Public Opinion.* New York: John Wiley.

Oberdorfer, Don. 1971. *TET.* New York: Avon Books.

Page, Benjamin I. and Richard A. Brody. 1972. Policy Voting and the Electoral Process: The Vietnam War Issue. *American Political Science Review* 66 (1972): 979–995.

Paletz, David L. and Robert M. Entman. 1981. *Media Power Politics.* New York: Free Press.

Porter, William E. 1976. *Assault on the Media: The Nixon Years.* Ann Arbor, Mich.: University of Michigan Press.

Pride, Richard A. and Barbara Richards. 1974. Denigration of Authority? Television News Coverage of the Student Movement. *Journal of Politics* 36 (August 1974): 637–660.

Roper, Burns W. 1977. What Public Opinion Polls Said. In Peter Braestrup, *Big Story*, Volume I, Chapter 14. Boulder, Col.: Westview Press.

Schorr, Daniel. 1977. *Clearing the Air*. Boston, Mass.: Houghton Mifflin, 1977.

Schreiber, E. M. 1976. Anti-War Demonstrations and American Public Opinion on the War in Vietnam. *British Journal of Sociology* 27 (1976): 225–236.

Warner, Malcolm. 1968. Television Coverage of International Affairs. *Television Quarterly* 7 (Spring 1968): 60–75.

Wise, David. 1973. *The Politics of Lying*. New York: Random House.

11

TV'S BATTLE OF KHE SANH:
SELECTIVE IMAGES OF DEFEAT

PETER C. ROLLINS

Three major stories from Vietnam during the 1968 Tet Offensive came to create a composite picture of American confusion and defeat. The manner in which these events were conveyed contributed to this portrait. These three major stories of Tet were first, the attack on the US Embassy in Saigon; second, the execution of a suspected Viet Cong officer on the streets of Saigon by General Loan, Chief of South Vietnam's national policy force (Bailey & Lichty, 1972; Culbert, 1978); and third, the defense of Khe Sanh by a Marine regiment against a surrounding force of more than two divisions of North Vietnamese Army regulars. In each case, dramatic events were interpreted to be emblematic of the broader meanings of Tet.[1]

THE ART OF TELEVISION NEWS IS THE ART OF SELECTION

During early May of 1975, I attended the annual TV Newsfilm Workshop of the National Press Photographers Association. For the fifteenth

---

[1] This study has made extensive use of numerous sources including the following: The best narrative history of the Tet Offensive is Don Oberdorfer's *Tet!* (1971). A monumental study of media in the Indochina war is Peter Braestrup's *Big Story: How the American Press and Television Reported and Interpreted the Crises of Tet 1968 in Vietnam and Washington* (1977). The official Marine Corps history of the battle is Moyer S. Shore, *The Battle of Khe Sanh* (1968). White House responses to Tet are best described in Herbert Y. Schandler, *The Unmaking of a President: Lyndon Johnson and Vietnam* (1977). A February 1978 conference—titled "The Tet Offensive and Escalation of the Vietnam War, 1965–68"—brought experts on Tet to the University of North Carolina, Chapel Hill, for screenings of television newsfilm, lectures, and discussions. David Culbert, Townsend Ludington, and Peter Rollins conducted film interviews with selected participants. Both conference remarks and interviews were used in preparation of this study.

consecutive year, cameramen from local stations across the country came to the University of Oklahoma campus to learn the art of television news. Network news professionals and award-winning cameramen lectured, displayed their work, and evaluated student pictorial assignments.

In addition to information about film stock, lighting, and equipment, basic aesthetic guides were provided. First, the professionals stressed that a television news story is a "story" in a literary sense: a form with a beginning, a middle, and an end. For this reason, one of the most significant tasks for camera people is to decide what the real "story" at a given event is; only after making what professionals call a "commitment" do they begin to collect shots. Later editing should follow the inherent visual logic of materials gathered. Even the shortest film stories are attempts to interpret; they are essays written with a cine-pen.

A second major precept of the workshop was that a television account must tell its story visually. Camera crews should strive to give their stories visual integrity; any words supplied later will amplify the visual narrative. As a result, news stories are eligible for the same kind of detailed analysis customarily applied to documentary and fiction films. There is a reason for each shot; there is a viewpoint behind every edited assemblage of shots.

"Microcosms" can also be found for stories. Recognizing that the camera sees only externals, the camera operator looks for surfaces and textures which reflect an understanding of the inner "meaning" of an event. Consider approaches to reporting a fire. Lecturers and practitioners at the workshop stressed that long shots of burning buildings and crowds of tenants were ineffective. The goal before shooting, they said, was to uncover an "inner story" representing the larger experience. In the case of a fire, the camera might follow the travails of a tenant, reporting the traumatic effect of this disaster with close-ups of facial expressions and of the few objects saved from the blaze. Once moved to empathize with the suffering of a particular victim, viewers can then extrapolate to a broader story. Microcosm will be related to macrocosm.

Three key episodes of Tet were interpreted as representative microcosms and became so implanted in the American imagination that they could not be modified by subsequent reports. Redolent with drama, the episodes supplied a series of icons to which later information would cling. The putative "penetration" of the US Embassy in Saigon, General Loan's "gratuitous" execution of a Viet Cong suspect, and the "hopeless" battle at Khe Sanh seemed to summarize both the meaning of the Tet Offensive and the significance of the entire US intervention effort in the Republic of South Vietnam.

KHE SANH, THE NETWORKS, AND DIEN BIEN PHU

To the chagrin of the Communists, none of the military objectives of the Tet Offensive were attained: the South Vietnamese army fought bravely, the Saigon government maintained a semblance of authority, and civilians refused to rally to the Viet Cong cause. As dust settled in Saigon, the mood shifted from initial shock to qualified optimism. At Khe Sanh, however, dust was still in the air, and there was room for speculation. No one could divine the enemy's intention or strength. While facts increasingly contradicted prophesies of doom elsewhere, Khe Sanh still offered a picture of the allies in trouble. The networks shifted their spotlight to Khe Sanh.

For many observers, Bernard Fall's popular book, *Hell in a Very Small Place*, seemed to suggest a compelling analogy between the 1954 French defeat at Dien Bien Phu and the battle developing at Khe Sanh. As Michael Herr put it (1977, p. 99–100):

> . . . as the first Marine briefings on Khe Sanh took place in Marine Headquarters at Da Nang or Dong Ha, the name Dien Bien Phu insinuated itself like some tasteless ghost hawking bad news. Marines who had to talk to the press found references to the old French disaster irritating and even insulting. Most were not interested in fielding questions about it, and the rest were unequipped. The more irritated they became, the more the press would flaunt the irritant. For a while it looked like nothing that had happened on the ground during those weeks seemed as thrilling and sinister as the recollection of Dien Bien Phu. And it had to be admitted, the parallels with Khe Sanh were irresistible.

For reporters, the ironic part of the Dien Bien Phu analogy was that American military leaders seemed ignorant of the parallels and therefore were walking into a trap. Correspondents visiting Khe Sanh attempted to probe Marine Commander Colonel David Lownds about the similarities, but with little success. Because Lownds was taciturn, reporters assumed that the Colonel was therefore as unaware of the obvious perils of his position as the blind men who ordered him to defend such a precarious outpost. Even Walter Cronkite, on the evening news of January 26, sat before a display comparing Khe Sanh with Dien Bien Phu and assured his audience that the *prima facie* likenesses between the two battles were "plain for all to see."

Apparently, few correspondents listened closely to what Colonel Lownds, General Robert Cushman, and General William Westmoreland explained about the differences. General Westmoreland had ordered a staff study of Dien Bien Phu; he had even talked with one of the French commanders. These studies convinced Westmoreland that American advantages in artillery and air support more than compensated for differences in troop strength.[2] Even if the NVA had as many as 2½ divisions in the Khe Sanh area, superiority of supporting arms gave 5,000 Marines of RLT-26 a considerable tactical advantage. Despite these assurances, reporters saw everything through Dien-Bien-Phu-colored glasses. That the fourteenth anniversary of the end of the earlier great battle was in May, just a few weeks away, did not help to clear the airwaves.

Lyndon Johnson was also obsessed by the Dien Bien Phu analogy. To keep up with developments at Khe Sanh, the President had a three-dimensional replica of the battleground made on a 1/50,000 scale, the same map scale used by troops in the field. Whenever the President visited the White House War Room during Tet, he inspected the Khe Sanh mock-up (Schandler, 1977, p. 69). As Doris Kearns has noted (1976, p. 286), objects such as the relif map gave Johnson a sense of control when he felt challenged by intractable problems.

The nervous President sought other assurances that Khe Sanh could be held. In an unprecedented move, Johnson forced the Joint Chiefs of Staff to sign a written guarantee. That President Johnson should go to such extremes over a single battle was less an index of his distrust of the military than it was an indication of the power of historical analogies on both actors and observers. (See also Schandler, 1977, pp. 87–88; and Kearns, 1976, pp. 324–350).

The press was not alone in declaiming the "obvious stupidity" of the military's decision to fight at Khe Sanh. Scholarly observers joined in the clamor. Arthur Schlesinger, Jr., pleaded that "a humane or intelligent leadership would have arranged for the immediate evacuation" of the outnumbered Marines at the isolated air strip. Schlesinger saw the decision to fight at Khe Sanh as a result of poor planning rather than as an aggressive ploy by General Westmoreland. According to the professor, Westmoreland had been so discredited by the Tet Offensive that he hung on to Khe Sanh for lack of any more effective strategy. The inaction was leading to useless casualties: "We stay because Khe Sanh is the bastion, not of the American military position, but of General Westmoreland's military strategy—his 'war of attrition' which has been so tragic and spectacular a failure." (Quoted in Westmoreland, 1976, pp. 335–336.) Echoes of Dien Bien Phu were reverberating everywhere but on the battlefield: press, President, and pundits were obsessed by an historical analogy.

---

[2] Chapel Hill interview. See also General William C. Westmoreland (1976, pp. 337–338). Colonel David Lownds (RLT-26 Commander) and Lt. Colonel James Wilkinson (C.O., 3/26) both report having read works by Bernard Fall and remember discussing Dien Bien Phu "lessons" with small-unit commanders in December, a month prior to the 1968 battle. (Both were interviewed in 1979 and 1980).

With the Dien Bien Phu precedent in mind, reporters who visited Khe Sanh spoke as if they were under a dark cloud of disaster. In a report for the evening of January 24, Don Webster asked troops within the Khe Sanh perimeter how they felt about the way the battle was shaping up. Universially, troopers and officers evinced optimism, but Webster chose to conclude the story on an ominous note: somewhere out in the hills were adversaries in sufficient strength to overrun the doomed base. Walter Cronkite immediately following the Webster report asserted that Khe Sanh was a "miniature Dien Bien Phu" and that wily General Giap was once again directing the attack.

Ed Needham of NBC covered the evacuation of Khe Sanh village on January 24. Military commanders had decided that a final battle could be better conducted if civilians were out of the Khe Sanh area. Rather than interpret the evacuation as a result of humanitarian concern, Needham explained that the North Vietnamese had won an initial victory: we were too weak to fight. Clips of frightened refugees entering the Khe Sanh perimeter seemed to corroborate Needham's claims. While refugees awaited helicopters, some incoming rounds hit the base. The resulting panic was filmed and aired; not so the orderly airlift of civilians from the battlefield.

Two days later, Ron Nessen of ABC reported that Marines could not leave the airfield's perimeter because they were so greatly outnumbered. While Nessen noted that Marines joked about comparisons with Dien Bien Phu, his report concluded with serious doubts about the high spirits: morale of the Marines was ebullient "despite their position."

In a CBS report for January 26, Igor Ogennessof stressed the hazards of flying fixed-wing aircraft to and from the encircled airstrip. (Ogennessof said nothing about the availability of airdrops). Hazards to troops at Khe Sanh were further underscored when program format was unintentionally disrupted. During his "stand-upper" Ogennessof was seriously wounded by fragments from an incoming mortar round. At the moment of impact, the reporter was standing beside the ramp of a C-130 being loaded with the day's dead and wounded. Commentator Walter Cronkite then came on to fill in details. He explained that Ogennessof had been operated on at Khe Sanh and was recuperating at a Da Nang hospital. The medium supplied a significant part of the message. The vertiginous camera, the loss of perspective, and the need for the anchor to intervene during the remote report all added visual and aural confirmation to explicit statements about men in jeopardy.

In a particularly tendentious report (1/29), Don Webster interviewed troops along Khe Sanh's perimeter in an obvious attempt to coax complaints. Some of the questions asked were: "Why don't you have enough protection?" "Does the lack of overhead in the bunkers make you scared?"

"How did you Marines ever get into this fix?" All of the Marines interviewed shrugged off these invitations to grouse. Their commander, Colonel Lownds, refused to talk about Dien Bien Phu. The closing scene of Webster's report was taken at a familiar spot, the ramp of a C-130 into which the bodies of dead and wounded were being loaded. The correspondent intoned, "There will be more such cargo if the battle joins." The implication was clear: every day Marines were dying unnecessarily and their commanders were uninterested in mitigating the dangers.

Murray Frompson contributed to the gloom. At the conclusion of his Khe Sanh story (1/15), he surmised that "the North Vietnamese determine who lives and who dies at Khe Sanh." David Douglas Duncan succumbed to pessimism in a montage of stills for ABC (1/23). Duncan suggested that camaraderie, humor, and heroism were all part of the Khe Sanh experience, but he added his mite to the theme of vulnerability. Duncan knew that only four major aircraft had been shot down at the airstrip; yet, speaking to his photos of a burning C-130, he observed: "sometimes they make it, sometimes they don't." This stress upon the tenuousness of supply lines to Khe Sanh recalled the Dien Bien Phu analogy.

Television is a visual medium that thrives on interesting and representative pictures. Every photojournalist attempts to find physical details and actions revealing the inner meaning of events. Drama sometimes wins out over intelligent discussion so that false or distorted impressions are conveyed. In the case of Khe Sanh, of course, the outnumbered Marines were ultimately victorious, although the viewer of TV news might never have anticipated that outcome. The microcosms selected by reporters consistently excluded many valid alternative pictures of Khe Sanh.

UNREPORTED MICROCOSMS

The wisdom in defending Khe Sanh is still under debate. Some observers think that it was merely a feint by the North Vietnamese army to draw troops away from urban areas. A few believe that it was initially scheduled to be a major confrontation, but that plans were changed. General Westmoreland and the Marine Corps maintain that Khe Sanh was a major allied victory. (See Westmoreland, 1976, pp. 345–346; and Shore, 1968, pp. 148–151.) Whatever the larger importance of Khe Sanh, coverage of the battle ignored important microcosms.[3]

---

[3] A two-hour video program entitled *Television's Vietnam: The Impact of Visual Images* explores the character and impact of news reports during the Tet offensive and includes interviews with Johnson administration officials, troops and commanders, reporters and producers, and scholars. For information about the availability of *Television's Vietnam*, which is designed for classroom use, write Humanitas Film; Attn: Prof. Peter C. Rollins; Dept. of English; Oklahoma State University; Stillwater, Okla. 74078.

The Battle Takes Shape. On the night of January 2, 1968, a Marine listening post outside the Western perimeter of Khe Sanh observed a small squad of intruders heading for the base. When challenges were not answered, Marine automatic weapons fire cut down six of the figures. A search of the bodies revealed the startling information that the North Vietnamese soldiers were all high-ranking officers, and their presence seemed a harbinger of a major operation.

Over the next few days, the Twenty-Sixth Marine Regiment at Khe Sanh was reinforced. The perimeter of Khe Sanh base was strengthened, and some battalions were helilifted to dominant terrain features. Although hilltop battles were seldom reported, they were integral to the Khe Sanh defense. As Shore has noted (1968, p. 31), commanders "were well aware of what had happened at Dien Bien Phu when the Viet Minh owned the mountains and the French owned the valley." In addition to dispelling the Dien Bien Phu analogy, media attention to hilltop battles would have depicted Marines in a posture more traditionally associated with the Corps. Although repeated confrontations between infantry units forced the young Americans to display their mettle, it would seem that only Department of the Navy records remember the heroic hilltop struggles.

Hill 881N. On January 17, a Marine reconnaissance team was ambushed by North Vietnamese Regulars southwest of Hill 881N. Two days later, India Company of the Third Battalion moved out through thick morning fog to uncover enemy in the ambush area. As the fog began to lift, advancing Marines were caught in a deadly crossfire, and within seconds 20 Marines were out of action. Forward observers called in artillery support from the valley. The effectiveness of the 155mm howitzers was so great that the third platoon could resume its advance. Second Lieutenant Brindley, the third platoon's commander, urged his men forward, and took the lead as they advanced. Unfortunately, enemy defensive fires were fatal. As the platoon moved into position, the lieutenant and all squad leaders were killed. Responding to this emergency, a ranking corporal assumed command of the platoon and supervised consolidation of the defense.

During the battle, the Marines showed concern for their friends. When Second Lieutenant Michael Thomas learned that one of his squads was in jeopardy somewhere forward of his position, he ran to lend assistance. About 10 yards from the platoon command post, the lieutenant was stopped by a mortal head wound. But the lieutenant's example inspired actions. Led by Sergeant David Jessup, men of the platoon fought their way to the injured squad and brought the wounded back to safety.

An hour before sundown, India Company was ordered to return to its original position on Hill 881N to prepare for a major night assault by the North Vietnamese. As they moved back to their foxholes, members of the company could take pride in their dangerous work. While seven of the attacking Marines had been killed and some 35 wounded during the day, the North Vietnamese had lost over 100 infantrymen. A day of violence, courage, and sacrifice, this "microcosm" never reached American living rooms.

Hill 861. During India Company's assault, a North Vietnamese officer surrendered to the Khe Sanh base. The prisoner revealed that a major attack was planned for that evening, and it was this news that prompted RLT-26 Commander Colonel David Lownds to pull back India Company to a defensive position. Shortly after midnight on January 21, the defector's prediction materialized. After 30 minutes of preparatory fires, a company-sized attack was launched against Hill 861. Enemy demolitions experts led the way, exploding pathways through the Marine protective wire. Behind them, assault troops followed in sufficient numbers to penetrate the company perimeter. This incursion was countered by a Marine assault from both sides of the penetration. Fighting broke down into hand-to-hand struggles. A body count at dawn revealed that four Marines had been killed while the ground was strewn with 47 attackers.

A number of Marines showed special discipline during the evening. In early fire, the company command post was hit directly by a mortar round. The company commander was taken out of action by three shrapnel wounds, the company gunnery sergeant was killed instantly, and the first sergeant was bleeding profusely from a pierced jugular vein. Amid all of this and completely blinded by powder burns, the company's radio operator continued to conduct all necessary communications. A battalion level officer who received these messages later commented that the radio man was "as calm, cool, and collected as a telephone operator in New York City" (Shore, 1968, p. 41).

Other Marines on Hill 861 found ways to express their cool under fire which no Hollywood director would dare invent for a fiction film. Somewhat dazed by his wounds, and attempting to stem the flow of blood spurting from his neck, a first sergeant stumbled upon a strange scene. Somewhere near the mortar pits, the sergeant heard the sound of music. The veteran of two wars said he was incredulous as he looked down into a gun pit to find men singing the "Marine Corps Hymn" as they loaded the mortar shells.

Khe Sanh Base. The shelling of Khe Sanh base began just after the fight for Hill 861. A little before sunrise, the base received incoming enemy artillery, mortars, and rockets; many of the rounds were on target. In fact, just about everything above ground was hit. Tents were destroyed; helicopters caught fire; both a fuel storage area and the largest ammunition dump went up in flames. As if to add insult to injury, an enemy shell landed amidst a cache of tear gas cannisters; the resulting fumes and vapors spread throughout the base.

Like their fellows on the hilltops, Marines in the valley showed grace under pressure. Even though the First Battalion's trenchline ran within 30 meters of the burning ammunition dump, Marines remained at their posts. Duds nearly fell into their pockets; scalding particles of metal from antipersonnel grenades burned unprotected flesh. Support troops within the perimeter were equally ready to court danger. Truck drivers rushed to their vehicles and drove them to protective cover; artillerymen operated their guns, supplying protective fires for the hills and hitting suspected enemy gun emplacements with counterbattery fire. As duds landed among artillery pieces, Marines in volunteer parties of two lifted the hot rounds and carried them to a disposal pit some 50 meters away.

After sunrise, Khe Sanh village was attacked by a battalion-size force of North Vietnamese Regulars. A combination of artillery fire from Khe Sanh Base (conducted as hot rounds continued to drop among the guns) and close air support helped to stop over 100 enemy before they penetrated the defensive wire. Colonel Lownds then decided to evacuate Khe Sanh village. South Vietnamese troops were reassigned responsibilities at the base perimeter and civilians were flown to the safety of Dong Ha and Da Nang. While the civilians were forcibly removed, the alternative to displacement was not very attractive. An enemy probe after sunset confirmed the decision to fully clear all fields of fire. (But, compare Ed Needham's negative story on the evacuation of Khe Sanh village.)

The Marines of RLT-26 had been tested. The tactically important hilltops had been protected from enemy assault. While an embarrassing amount of material had been wasted in the valley, the defensive positions at Khe Sanh Base were undamaged. With the civilians of Khe Sanh village evacuated, there were no restrictions on fire missions. News reports, however, did not reflect these developments. Television stories focused on the evacuation of body bags and wounded rather than on the active events of the day. The high morale should not have been difficult to explain. After all, Marines had repelled the first attempts to wrest Khe Sanh and had inflicted significant casualties on the enemy. Confidence was bolstered further when more troops were flown in on January 26. Thus, it is not surprising that the Marines interviewed were reluctant to grouse before cameras. Rather than seeing themselves as victims of a powerful enemy, members of RLT-26 thought of themselves as successful marksmen who had just completed preliminary calibrations.

Hill 861 Again.   At three in the morning, preparatory fires began to hit Hill 861 followed by an enemy penetration of Echo Company's perimeter. Captain Earl Breeding led the bloody counterattack (Shore, 1968, p. 65):

> Because the darkness and ground fog drastically reduced visibility, hand-to-hand combat was a necessity. Using their knives, bayonets,

rifle butts, and fists, the men of the 1st Platoon ripped into the hapless North Vietnamese with a vengeance. Captain Breeding, a veteran of the Korean conflict who had worked his way up through the ranks, admitted that, at first, he was concerned over how his younger inexperienced Marines would react in their first fight. As it turned out, they were magnificent. . . . Since the fighting was at such close quarters, both sides used hand grenades at extremely close range. The Marines had the advantage because of their armored vests, and they would throw a grenade, then turn away from the blast, hunch up, and absorb the fragments in their flak jackets and the backs of their legs. On several occasions, Captain Breeding's men used this technique. . . at less than ten meters.

The North Vietnamese made more attempts to take Hill 861 at sunrise, and again at noon. With fire support from Khe Sanh Base, Echo Company was capable of repelling each attack. As the enemy withdrew during the afternoon, Marines from adjacent hilltops provided withering fire. After 12 hours of fighting, the Marines had lost seven troops while the North Vietnamese left over 100 bodies on the slopes of Hill 861. Marines still held the tactically vital high ground around the Khe Sanh valley. However, little information reached the American public about the courageous and victorious confrontation.

A Bad Day for Company B (In Color). On the morning of February 25, a fledgling second lieutenant was asked to take a reconnaissance patrol just outside the base perimeter. The maps issued to ground troops in Vietnam were on a 1/50,000 scale and the lack of detail made them hard to read; the inexperienced officer strayed from his designated route and the patrol stumbled into a North Vietnamese bunker complex. Twenty-six Marines were not only killed, but left behind in the ambush zone; although a member of the patrol dragged the Lieutenant back to base, the young officer bled to death along the way.

A free-lance photographer, Robert Ellison, was on the scene as the patrol stumbled back into the perimeter. He captured images of reality that would be used by *Newsweek* as microcosms. In a special story entitled "The Agony of Khe Sanh," *Newsweek* printed the final moments in living color (March 18, 1968). Against the rich eel grass, we see the wan face of the Lieutenant; a caption under an adjacent photo reads: "men had to make it back to the base as best they could." Marines have always been very sensitive about the recovery of bodies and their ability to fight as units. The ignominious implication of the story was that those few Marines venturesome enough to leave the perimeter were unable to fight cohesively. The photo essay seemed to indicate that life at Khe Sanh Base was hardly better organized. Selecting images to suit the issue's emphasis on passive suffering, *Newsweek* did not show a single marine firing back at the enemy. Even the continuously busy guns went unphotographed.

A Good Day for Company B (Unreported).   For a major raid a few weeks later, Company B left Khe Sanh under cover of darkness and silently assumed assault positions near an opposing bunker complex. A protective fog concealed the company's movement across a road south of the base; intense artillery support kept the North Vietnamese in their holes as attackers climbed the hills: "by noon, the trenchworks had become a smoking time bomb for one hundred fifteen North Vietnamese" (Shore, 1968, p. 129). With the enemy killed or captured, Company B returned to base. Success of this raid could be attributed to careful planning and flawless coordination between Marine infantry and supporting arms.

As a microcosm, the raid of Company B might have conveyed a number of messages about the Marines at Khe Sanh, perhaps even about the professionalism of US troops in Vietnam. Certainly, reports of the raid could have counterbalanced the earlier unfortunate blunder that had been so widely reported. More significantly, the raid could have represented the new posture of Marines as skies cleared over Khe Sanh, and General Westmoreland began to approve airmobile operations. But this was not the emphasis chosen. Instead, television told the story of the "relief" of Khe Sanh by focusing on the arrival of air cavalry troops at the main gate. In their "stand-uppers," some reporters stressed Marine embarrassment about being relieved by Army units; other reporters reiterated the initial doubts about why this piece of territory had been defended in the first place. The heroism and *esprit* of the morning raid went unnoticed and unreported.[4]

CONCLUSION

At least since the publication of Don Oberdorfer's *Tet* (1971), it has been public record that the Lunar New Year offensive was not a major victory for the insurgent forces: some 65,000 of the best Communist

---

[4] Jim Wilkinson was a battalion commander responsible for part of the Khe Sanh perimeter. In an April 1980 interview, Wilkinson reflected on the Khe Sanh report of one war photographer:

> David Douglas Duncan did arrive at Khe Sanh with his camera at the height of the battle... and became intrigued with my command post. He said he liked the lighting. He toured the perimeter with me, and took quite a few shots, and was very congenial and likeable. . . . He left and I thought we had had a friendly visit. . . . but low and behold if ol' Mr. Duncan didn't race out and publish a soft-cover book about Khe Sanh with some tremendous photographs in it. But, he also had an essay in which he took the approach of others in the media—not only condemning the war in Vietnam, but questioning the heroism of the Marines at Khe Sanh. . . . I don't recall seeing one smile or cheerful face in all of his photographs. And yet, he met a lot of cheerful people and saw a lot of smiles and listened to a lot of laughter, and yet not one of those smiles and laughs was portrayed in his photographs. My conclusion is that David D. Duncan was looking for a "downer" and he got it.

troops were killed in a period of two months, and none of the military objectives of the Tet attacks were achieved. The United States, however, became moved by misleading visual dramas.

Compelling images were presented, leaving the following impressions: the American Embassy, a traditional symbol of our nation, was violated by invaders who were evicted only after considerable effort; individual rights were not respected by our puppet allies like General Loan; at Khe Sanh, our toughest troops were encircled, besieged, and on the run. How could these dramatic images be contradicted by officials who had been selling invincibility for the previous year? In late 1967, government officials were manufacturing glowing reports about the war's progress; when the same officials attempted to be more realistic during Tet, they were not believed.

The Viet Cong's capability to wage war was largely destroyed at Tet. Thereafter, North Vietnam army units were essential. Soon after the event, Oberdorfer was keenly aware of the essential paradox of Tet: "The North Vietnamese and Viet Cong lost a battle. The United States government lost something more important—the confidence of its people at home" (1971, p. 329).

Prior to Tet, the Johnson administration was guilty of promoting unwarranted optimism. Legitimate doubts about government credibility were generated in early 1968 by the obvious gap between official statements and media reports. How could US officials claim that Tet was a victory when nightly news reports showed very slow progress along the streets of Saigon and Hue? Why were the North Vietnamese being allowed to destroy ammunition dumps? If the Marines at Khe Sanh were really Marines, why were they continuously running for their bunkers? Why were they not firing back? Where was the promised "light at the end of the tunnel?"

Conflicting information was plentiful. Khe Sanh Base seemed in imminent peril, yet the commander was almost jolly in TV interviews. If things were going so well at Khe Sanh, why were planes and reporters being shot down? And some of the dramatic developments were unplanned. Obviously, Igor Ogennessof did not plan to be wounded during his "stand-upper" at Khe Sanh; nevertheless, the interruption of his report seemed to confirm gloomy predictions about the doomed base. Every breakdown in standard program format intensified the message that American control in Vietnam was crumbling. Evidence in the form of television images weighed too heavily against official pronouncements.

Reporters did their homework before visiting the outpost, and required reading told the story of French defeat at a valley outpost surrounded by "angry hills." Khe Sanh was not overly supplied with troops, and all agreed that the base was surrounded by at least two North Vietnamese divisions. Bernard Fall's *Hell in a Very Small Place* sensitized newsmen to look for likenesses between the predicament of the French and that of the exposed Marines. Taking into account the bad flying weather of early spring, many factors pointed to a second stunning victory for North Vietnam's General Giap. Because Marine commanders appeared to be ignorant of history, they seemed sure to repeat it.

The Dien Bien Phu analogy drew attention to the worst news: a single plane shot down was translated to mean that supplies for Khe Sanh had been interdicted; a burning ammunition dump meant that "the North Vietnamese determine who lives and who dies at Khe Sanh"; ambushed patrols received special color coverage, while well-executed attacks and determined defenses were ignored. Tragedy and disaster were sought; as a result, tragedy and disaster were found. Because correspondents visited the valley base only briefly, it was not surprising that preconceptions shaped their stories. When uninjured troops proved to be too jaunty, reporters and film crews simply strolled over to the medevac area. Story theme dictated which microcosms should be gathered, and those microcosms told a misleading story of Dien Bien Phu revisited.

The battle of Khe Sanh proved not to be a North Vietnamese triumph; US and South Vietnamese forces were not overrun. But, as John Kaheny, a junior officer at Khe Sanh, said in a recent interview, the battle was treated by the media as a microcosm "only as long as we might have lost."

REFERENCES

Bailey, George A. and Lawrence W. Lichty. 1972. Rough Justice on a Saigon Street: A Gatekeeper Study of NBC's Tet Execution Film. *Journalism Quarterly* 49 (Summer 1972): 221–229, 238.

Braestrup, Peter. 1977. *Big Story: How the American Press and Television Reported and Interpreted the Crisis of Tet 1968 in Vietnam and Washington.* Boulder, Col.: Westview Press.

Culbert, David. 1978. Historians and the Visual Analysis of Television News. In William Adams and Fay Schreibman, eds., *Television Network News: Issues in Content Research.* Washington, D.C.: School of Public and International Affairs, George Washington University, pp. 139–154.

Herr, Michael. 1977. *Dispatches.* New York: Alfred A. Knopf.

Kearns, Doris. 1976. *Lyndon Johnson and the American Dream.* New York: Harper and Row.

Oberdorfer, Don. 1971. *Tet!* New York: Doubleday and Co.

Schandler, Herbert Y. 1977. *The Unmaking of a President: Lyndon Johnson and Vietnam.* Princeton, N.J.: Princeton University Press.

Shore, Moyer S. 1968. *The Battle of Khe Sanh.* Washington, D.C.: Historical Branch, G-3 Division, United States Marine Corps.

Westmoreland, William C. 1976. *A Soldier Reports.* New York: Doubleday and Co.

12

THE UNNEWSWORTHY HOLOCAUST: TV NEWS AND TERROR IN CAMBODIA

WILLIAM C. ADAMS
MICHAEL JOBLOVE

In April of 1975, Khmer Rouge forces overran Phnom Penh. Until their fall from power in the winter of 1979, the world was witness to one of the most bizarre and brutal revolutions of this century. Costs of Khmer Rouge rule were high. An estimated one to three million of Cambodia's eight million people died by starvation, disease, or execution.

No other single episode has involved a greater loss of life during the last quarter century. Yet, despite the barbarism and magnitude of the tragedy, little public attention was directed to Cambodia. It was ignored by the US media, government, and people.

The death toll was at least a thousand times greater than that of the Jonestown murders and suicides, but news coverage of Cambodia was a fraction of that given to Jonestown. Added together over the entire four year Khmer Rouge period, all three television networks devoted less than 60 minutes on weeknights to the new society and human rights in Cambodia. Nearly three hours were spent detailing the Jonestown deaths in the first week alone.

What, if anything, were Americans told about human rights and society in Cambodia from their preferred source of international news— early evening, network television news? To find out, we examined Vanderbilt University's *Television News Index and Abstracts* for weeknight news coverage from April 1975 until December 1978.[1]

---

[1] In addition to examining the *Index and Abstracts* for all weeknight stories, we included in this study those relevant stories that were carried on weekend broadcasts available from the Vanderbilt Archive. The collection at Vanderbilt does not include a few of the weekend programs during this four-year period, but, the focus of this research was on weeknight news, when the networks have their largest news audiences. It seems unlikely that a few weekend broadcasts would vary systematically from the consistent pattern found on all weeknight newscasts on all three networks; in any event, their complete inclusion could hardly change the central conclusions of this chapter. (Cf., Savitch, 1980.)

The Vanderbilt Archive loaned compiled videotapes of the stories we had identified from the abstracts. Stories selected were all those about Cambodian refugees, genocide, general Khmer Rouge policies, and the reconstruction of society. Excluded were purely military stories about border clashes, civil war, and the *Mayaguez*. Research was conducted at the television news studies facilities of George Washington University's Gelman Library. The findings were generally consistent for all three networks.

A FEW SAD SECONDS

Stories about the "new society" and death in Cambodia were so sporadic that even the most constant viewers could not be expected to grasp the gravity of the Cambodian crisis. As shown in Table 12.1, from April 1975 to December 1978, NBC aired 11 stories (17 minutes 35 seconds) on life in the "new Cambodia," compared with 13 stories on CBS (28 minutes 55 seconds), and 6 stories on ABC (11 minutes 25 seconds). This averages out to less than 30 seconds per month per network on the rule of the Khmer Rouge.

ABC offered a little over 4 minutes in 1975, and the next year carried one human rights story about Cambodia. Two years passed before ABC returned to the subject. In April 1978, ABC viewers heard anchorman Tom Jarriel say President Carter had condemned Cambodia as "the worst offender in the world" with regard to human rights. Carter had apparently not been watching ABC news.

Table 12.1
Weeknight Network Coverage of the "New Society" and Human Rights
in Cambodia, April 1975–December 1978
(See footnote 1)

		April– June 1975	July– Dec. 1975	Jan.– June 1976	July– Dec. 1976	Jan.– June 1977	July– Dec. 1977	Jan.– June 1978	July– Dec. 1978	Total
ABC										
	Time	0:20	4:10	3:10	---	---	---	0:30	3:15	11:25
	Number of stories	(1)	(2)	(1)	(0)	(0)	(0)	(1)	(1)	(6)
CBS										
	Time	1:00	---	2:30	3:40	2:30	3:40	11:40	3:55	28:55
	Number of stories	(2)	(0)	(1)	(1)	(1)	(2)	(4)	(2)	(13)
NBC										
	Time	1:00	2:20	---	---	0:40	4:00	6:40	2:55	17:35
	Number of stories	(1)	(2)	(0)	(0)	(1)	(2)	(3)	(2)	(11)

CBS focused on human rights in Cambodia for 60 seconds during 1975, for 6 minutes 10 seconds in 1976, and for the same amount of time again in 1977. CBS stepped up coverage in 1978. In April 1978, CBS ran two special reports—each over 4 minutes. Later in August, after Senator McGovern's call for armed intervention in Cambodia, CBS spent 2 minutes 20 seconds on the subject of Cambodian human rights.

NBC's nearly 18 minutes of coverage over four years almost equaled a single night's coverage of the Guyana massacre. NBC did broadcast a Segment Three (4 minutes 30 seconds) feature on human rights in Cambodia during the evening news on June 2, 1978. Once, NBC even opened its program with a lead story on Cambodian suffering (7/20/75). The 20-second story concerned an attempted escape of 300 Cambodians; only 12 people had survived. This story and its placement were quite exceptional. No other Cambodian human rights story was ever made the lead; the few stories that were aired were usually placed midway through the broadcast. Overall, in 1975–78, very little time was devoted to the steady stream of refugees who succeeded (or failed) in escaping what they called the "terror" of their homeland.

This accounting of air time on human rights in Cambodia does not measure the number of times when, in a story that was otherwise about a border clash with Vietnam, the regime might have been referred to as "harsh." However, the figures are actually generous because they include air time devoted to any discussion of the "new society" created by the Khmer Rouge, some of which dismissed or ignored reports of genocide. When this "harshness" was specifically mentioned, treatment of the subject of mass murders varied wildly—sometimes treated with skepticism, sometimes as undisputed fact, sometimes as mere rumor. The issue of genocide was explicitly addressed less than 1 minute by ABC, less than 4 minutes by CBS, and less than 4 minutes by NBC.

On August 21, 1978, Senator McGovern called for an international force to invade Cambodia in order to stop the genocide. The incongruity of George McGovern advocating military action in Southeast Asia was enough to attract some attention. ABC interviewed the Senator and included a follow-up clip of a refugee's personal story of tragedy. CBS covered the subcommittee meeting at which the plea was made. NBC gave minimum coverage with a 20-second summary.

NETWORK SILENCE DESPITE NUMEROUS REPORTS

Why was the massive loss of life in Cambodia given so little attention? It was not that the networks were uninformed about the new regime; as soon as news of the deaths reached the outside world, the networks were alerted. As early as June 24, 1975, in a speech covered by all three networks, Secretary of State Kissinger stressed that Cambodians had "suffered a terrible death toll" under the Khmer Rouge. CBS also mentioned that Freedom House had compared the Cambodian events to the Nazi annihilation of six million Jews.

On July 8, 1975, as eyewitness reports of barbarism were brought by escaping refugees, NBC ran a story with correspondent Barry Kalb. According to Kalb, "the story (the refugees) have been telling is one of horror." One witness saw "1,500 bodies, all knifed to death." One refugee said people were killed "if they didn't plant rice" and said he had recently seen 1,000 dead bodies. Kalb notes that skepticism first greeted such stories, "but now there are so many that it must be true."

Somehow, this remarkable NBC story did not generate others. The fact that thousands of people were filling up refugee camps across Thailand with accounts of mass murders and starvation in Cambodia was not deemed newsworthy.

ABC's single enterprising story in 1975 was an interview with the then head of state, Prince Sihanouk. This was the only network interview with a Cambodian government official since Kissinger's speech on the massive loss of life, since the Kalb story of atrocities, and since newspaper accounts of forced labor camps and executions. Harry Reasoner was not shown questioning Sihanouk about any of these matters. Instead, the Prince was shown talking about rice production and boosting the economy.

This prompted Mr. Reasoner's "roughest" inquiry:

Prince Sihanouk, you spoke of the necessary severe and austere government. Now I think of nothing more unlike the Cambodian people than severity and austerity. Have they changed?

To this hard-hitting question Sihanouk answered:

No, no, no, no. You know the Khmer Rouge, they are very nationalistic. Also, they want Cambodia to remain Cambodian. When I say severe or austere I mean that we have to walk much more than before. But Cambodians, they remain Cambodians. They like joking. They like laughing, they like singing. So they continue to do it. There is really a general way of life and there is still this way of life in Cambodia.

Sihanouk's depiction of the joking, laughing, singing Cambodian people was not seriously questioned by ABC news that year.

On January 26, 1976, CBS aired an account from reporter Peter Collins about forced evacuation from the cities, forced labor in the fields, and a refugee tale of five workers beaten to death with an iron pipe. Collins concluded that no one had been allowed to verify the refugee horror tales, "but their accounts of life across this frontier are so numerous and detailed, there seems little doubt that the new Communist regime is continuing its harsh reform of Cambodia, under what refugees describe as 'a reign of terror.'" But CBS did not pursue the story. Six months passed before CBS again considered this "reign of terror."

A SMALL SHIFT IN 1978

In 1978, after two years of near total neglect, the networks ran a handful of stories about human rights in Cambodia. On January 18, 1978, CBS covered Deputy Secretary of State Warren Christopher's condemnation of the "systematic terror and grinding down of the Cambodian people." "Hundreds of thousands of human beings," he said, "have perished under this regime." (Neither NBC nor ABC made any mention of the speech, although five months had passed since NBC had told its viewers about human rights "problems" in Cambodia and nearly two years had elapsed since ABC's last report on the subject.)

A two-part "Inside Cambodia" series by CBS's Bert Quint was aired April 20 and 21, 1978. Quint made references to estimates of one million people having been killed, though he cautioned that the figure "had not been confirmed by neutral observers." "Neither," he added, had "the new rulers bothered to deny them." Refugee accounts of harsh working conditions and mass killings were also mentioned.

Also on April 20, 1978, NBC ran a retrospective on Khmer Rouge rule. John Chancellor introduced the piece:

> It was three years ago this week that the city of Phnom Penh was captured by the Khmer Rouge revolutionary movement, and since then the story of Cambodia has been a horror story: The cities emptied— thousands killed or allowed to die in the countryside. There have been charges of genocide.

Thus, in the fourth year of its rule, the Khmer Rouge emerged on television as a nasty and tyrannical—though still rarely newsworthy— group that was probably implicated in the ominously empty streets of Phnom Penh. David Brinkley, having displayed little prior moral outrage on the subject, called them "iron-fisted murderous savages" in a brief 1978 commentary.

By late 1978, the occasional network stories had even begun to stop "balancing" the reports of mass execution with reports of "cleaning up the cities." Death estimates that had earlier been simple "reports of mass death" (NBC, 7/8/75) became in 1978 "stories of one million killed" (CBS, 4/20/78), "hundreds of thousands, possibly 2½ million killed" (CBS, 8/21/78), "one hundred thousand to one million" (NBC, 6/2/78), "one to three million" (NBC, 9/21/78).

WHY DID THE NETWORKS DISMISS CAMBODIA?

Nightly news cannot cover everything. The criticism that broadcast news people themselves make most frequently is that the program is too brief. In this light, they note, the omissions and compression imposed by brevity are unfortunate but also unavoidable. (The subject then shifts to affiliates who resist expansion to an hour of network news.) Nevertheless, it is difficult to understand why the tragedy of Cambodia never secured any sustained attention.

One explanation is ideological. Events in Cambodia appeared to contradict the supposed Lessons of Vietnam. The wisdom Americans were to have acquired in Southeast Asia was that leftist guerrilla insurgents were nationalistic and relatively benign, were likely improvements over the corrupt rightist regimes they replaced, and were certainly not worth any significant expenditure of US diplomatic, economic, or military power. As one telling *New York Times* headline put it: "Indochina Without Americans/For Most, a Better Life" (April 13, 1975). Unfortunately, Pol Pot's epigones of Marx-Lenin-Mao had not read this particular script. Thousands of Cambodian refugees brought stories of mass death and murder, but this "unverified" news could not be easily broadcast or printed to fit the Lessons of Vietnam.

There are other possible reasons for the lack of coverage. However, some of the usual explanations are inadequate.

When television news downplays a story that would otherwise appear to merit more coverage, the reason is often that the story lacked "good pictures," lacked drama and controversy, or lacked human interest. Television news, students of the medium repeatedly note, places a premium on stories that can be made visually interesting and that create emotional involvement by showing continuing sagas of conflict, danger, irony, humor, tragedy.

Cambodia under Khmer Rouge rule should have qualified superbly for the dramaturgy of television news. Only one barrier hampered coverage: camera crews were not invited inside the borders to beam home pictures of death, executions, and the forced march into the countryside. Poignant and striking footage was available without end, however, in refugee camps all across eastern Thailand. The horrible tales of death told movingly by escaped Cambodians made Kalb's July 1975 story strong and vivid. With continuous daring escape attempts, the uprooted and terrorized families, and the vandalizing of an historic culture, human interest stories were scarcely in short supply. The fact that television ignored the upheaval in Cambodia simply cannot be attributed to a dull story with poor pictures.

An even less convincing argument for the lack of coverage is that the outside world did not really know precisely what was going on within the jungle borders. Pol Pot did not issue a press release confirming the number of deaths as three million or merely three hundred thousand. Nor was it announced how many of the deaths should be attributed to starvation, the forced march, disease, bullets, or being clubbed to death. Not knowing exactly, the line goes, the media prudently overlooked the subject entirely.

When presented with the network record on Cambodia, one producer at ABC News responded, incredibly enough, by repeating the "no pictures" and "no certitude" arguments. Mary Fifield (1980) wrote that the "elemental explanation" for ABC's "difficulty" in covering the "devastation in Cambodia" was that "we could not get into the country." She said candidly:

> Since we were not able to gain entrance to Cambodia, there was *no way television news could show the actual tragedy. Although there were refugees in camps along the Thai border who were willing to describe the atrocities committed by the Khmer Rouge, some reporters and editors were reluctant to use their stories because they were not always completely reliable.* (Italics added.)

So, without good inside pictures of the tragedy and with refugees who "were not always completely reliable," ABC just ignored the suspected death of thousands of Cambodians and failed to run a single weeknight story on the subject over a two-year period at the height of Khmer Rouge rule.

(Producer Fifield notes correctly that in 1979, *after* the Khmer Rouge was overthrown, the networks' coverage "improved." In 1979, with Pol Pot's terror ended, ABC's retrospectives—presumably repleat with superb pictures and the very fullest verification—must certainly have been impressive.)

The head-in-the-sand argument is a bizarre one. Even the possibility of mass murder of thousands, let alone tens of thousands (at a time when Americans were watching "Holocaust" in prime time), should surely have triggered a sustained effort at intense and tough investigative reporting. That the dimensions of the chaos in Cambodia were not altogether clear should have prompted greater scrutiny, not less. From Three Mile Island to Jonestown to Skylab to DC-10s, uncertainty as to the possible scope of a misfortune is usually an incentive, not a deterrent, to additional coverage.

In the case of Cambodia, from the earliest days of the Khmer Rouge, there were repeated and consistent reports from refugees in camps hundreds of miles apart telling similar stories of death and murder (e.g., see Barron & Paul, 1977). Only a handful of these stories found their way onto network television.

SILENCE FROM THE WHITE HOUSE,
THE *POST*, AND THE *TIMES*

In addition to ideology, another plausible explanation for the low level of television news about Cambodia was the strange silence from the White House. Scholars observed a decade ago that television, even more than the print media, is obsessed with the Presidency. The absence of presidential concern about Cambodia would thus be likely to decrease the prospects for network coverage still further.

Neither Carter nor Ford directed any sustained attention to events under the Khmer Rouge. Both administrations engaged in the ritual of an annual condemnation of the regime, but little more—no major diplomatic offensives, no continual publicity efforts, no stream of speeches, and no public debate over more overt moves. With little but token gestures from the President, at least one major factor that would promote network coverage of the subject was absent. (This is also partly circular, because greater media attention would likely have stimulated more concern with the subject at the White House.)

One other explanation for the lack of concern with Cambodia is that television caricatures the front page of the prestige press. Assignment editors rely heavily on the *New York Times, Washington Post,* and wire services to set the network agenda. Television news usually seems afraid to veer far from the pack and is unlikely to provide extensive coverage of a topic given little attention in print. While this explanation begs the question of *Post* and *Times* coverage, it does help account for television's pattern. In fact, until mid-1978, the *Times* and the *Post* gave very little space to events in Cambodia.

In the summer of 1978, both papers began to run two or three stories a month relating to human rights in Cambodia.[2] While this falls short of the attention focused on certain authoritarian regimes in the West, it exceeded the coverage given throughout 1975, 1976, and 1977 to Cambodia. In those years, only two or three news stories regarding human rights in Cambodia were run during each 12-month period. Thus, television coverage as a proportion of available time and space compares favorably to print coverage.

The problem of inattention and silence was explained in the *New York Times* editorial on July 9, 1975:

> The picture begins to emerge of a country that resembles a giant prison camp with the urban supporters of the former regime being worked to

---

[2] Jack Anderson was notable for his concern with what he called the "wholesale butchery" in Cambodia. See, for example, his *Post* columns on May 2 and 3, 1978. (Also see, Anderson & Pronzini, 1981.)

death on thin gruel and hard labor and with medical care virtually nonexistent.

The mouthing of such high-sounding objectives as "peasant revolutions" or "purification" through labor on the land cannot conceal the barbarous cruelty of the Khmer Rouge, which can be compared with Soviet extermination of Kulaks or with Gulag Archipelago.

What, if anything, can the outside world do to alter the genocidal policies of Cambodia's hard men? Silence certainly will not move them. Were Cambodia a non-Communist or non-Third World country, the outraged protests from the developing and Communist countries, not to mention Europe and the United States, would be deafening.

Members of Congress and others who rightly criticized the undemocratic nature of the Lon Nol regime have a special obligation to speak up. Few if any have been heard from. The United Nations is silent. That silence must be broken.

After this call for an end to silence, over three years passed before the *Times* again editorialized on the subject. Nor, as we have shown, was the silence broken by the great American networks. The "genocidal policies of Cambodia's hard men" were insufficiently newsworthy.

REFERENCES

Anderson, Jack and Bill Pronzini. 1981. *The Cambodia File.* New York: Doubleday.

Barron, John and Anthony Paul. 1977. *Murder of a Gentle Land.* New York: Reader's Digest Press.

Fifield, Mary. 1980. Controversy: Letters. *Policy Review* 12 (Spring 1980): 3.

Savitch, Jessica. 1980. Controversy: Letters. *Policy Review* 12 (Spring 1980): 3–4.

PART

V

AUDIENCE

13

TELEVISION AS A SOURCE OF INTERNATIONAL NEWS: WHAT GETS ACROSS AND WHAT DOESN'T

HALUK SAHIN
DENNIS K. DAVIS
JOHN P. ROBINSON

Every evening, millions of Americans watch television news programs and are provided with brief descriptions about events from around the world. Satellite links bring vivid, live reports from countries that some Americans have never heard of and cannot locate on a map. What are the consequences of these reports? How useful are they to most Americans? Are such reports likely to increase what Americans know about other societies, or are these stories likely to increase prejudices and reinforce stereotypes of foreign events? What types of reports of foreign events are likely to be passed along by news media? How will these stories be processed and edited by news professionals to make them more interesting and attractive to mass audiences?

There have been few systematic studies of what Americans learn about international events from television news. Some findings have suggested that Americans are quite selective in their use of news and tend to screen out or misunderstand foreign stories. Public knowledge of foreign events is typically found to be much lower than knowledge of domestic events. It has been argued that the news which reaches Americans is biased by professional values which result in the selection of crisis or disaster stories while news about economic development is ignored. Foreign news is "Americanized" by writing about the importance of foreign events for Americans. Stories are more likely to be reported if interesting and attractive pictures can be obtained.

The research reported here seeks to address these questions in an innovative and useful way. This chapter presents a case study of how an international story was structured to convey the event to the television audience, and how well this story was understood by typical viewers. While it is impossible to generalize about the consequences of network news based on a single story, this case study does serve to illustrate both the strengths and weaknesses of current news reporting strategies. It suggests what people are capable of learning from typical international news stories. We hope that this study can serve as a guide for future research that will explore these questions in greater depth.

AN INFORMATION-BASED RESEARCH APPROACH

Television news research in the United States has been motivated primarily by a sensitivity for political or ideological "bias," rather than a concern for how effectively information is communicated. Researchers seeking quantifiable evidence of "bias" have concentrated on news production and content characteristics. In examining news "consumption," researchers have focused on the demographic characteristics of news audiences, or the "gratifications" individual audience members reportedly derive from the experience of watching television news. Information learned by the public from television news has attracted only sporadic and superficial attention.

The paucity of information-based approaches in television news research is surprising. There is growing evidence that many people get most of their information from television news. Most people say television is their primary source of news, as well as the one they are most likely to believe (Roper, 1979). Clearly, in American society, television is not just one more information source; it is a central public information resource. If so, researchers should be more concerned about what people learn from television news. How much of any newscast do they actually understand? How much and what kinds of information do they gain? Since 1978, we have been involved in a research project designed to answer these questions. We have examined the comprehension and recall of television network news stories, and the relationships between story attributes and the level of comprehension (Robinson et al., 1980; Sahin, Davis & Robinson, 1981). In this study, we will focus on learning from one particular news story dealing with international relations; our purpose is to provide a close-up view of some of the factors involved in the comprehension of televised news.

A simple and straightforward way of studying learning from television news is to conceptualize news dissemination as an instance of information transmission. By definition, a news report is an aggregation of bits of information, processed and structured in accordance with certain professional rules and norms, to be sent to a relatively large audience. The senders and receivers of the news messages are linked together by a channel that makes transmission possible. However, transmission alone does not settle the question of information transfer. The way in which people recall and understand information in messages cannot simply be inferred from the informational content of the sent message. How much correspondence is there between the two? What do they have in common, and how do they diverge from each other? Only by comparing the information contained in news items with what viewers remember about those items can we expect to bridge the two, in order to study television as a source (and resource) for information. Providing a model for such comparative analyses is the main goal of this case study. Undoubtedly, no analysis of a single story can provide definitive conclusions about how story attributes are related to audience reports of it. This case study is intended to stimulate similar research that might eventually lead to such conclusions.

We are aware of the limitations of using a rather narrowly defined information transmission approach to guide our analysis. The information transmission approach is ultimately based upon simplistic, mechanistic assumptions about the way in which communication takes place. These assumptions have been common in American communication research for more than three decades and are now being questioned (Fisher, 1978). Yet, this approach offers certain advantages in studying information gain from news reports. Beyond its heuristic value, it is also quite consistent with the structural features of mass media news flow in the United States. By and large, the mass media serve as vehicles of a one-way flow of information from limited sources to dispersed and heterogeneous audiences. As interposed technological instruments, the media link, but at the same time separate, senders and receivers. Opportunities for audience feedback are minimal and often confined to non-media channels (letters, telephone calls, etc.). In short, a great majority of news receivers have no direct influence or control over the quality or selection of information they rely upon for knowledge of their community, nation, and world.

Our analysis of the news stories as packages of information does not mean that the story content is reducible to nothing more than bits of information. Such a presupposition would perhaps be quite consistent with the dominant notions of journalistic objectivity whereby "hard facts" are presumably "supplied to the public through a neutral medium" (Glasgow University Media Group, 1980, p. 157). The untenability of this kind of "naive empiricism" (Tuchman, 1978, p. 211) has been adequately debunked by careful studies of the newsmaking process (Tuchman, 1978; Gans, 1979).

This case study represents an attempt to assess elements of an international affairs news story that were most noticed and used by viewers as their means of understanding this story. We have mentioned the journalistic conventions that led to the creation of these story elements. Our case study necessarily calls into question those conventions and related story elements that impeded or reduced understanding of this story. Such findings, however, are necessarily tentative.

METHODOLOGY

The news story examined in this case study was broadcast on the *ABC World News Tonight* on the evening of June 6, 1979. Two of the authors were in the ABC newsroom that day and talked to the news editors about the reasons behind the choice of this story, along with other stories in the newscast. Responses of viewers were collected through interviews conducted in nine cities within three hours of the broadcast. Procedures used in the general study have been described elsewhere in greater detail (Robinson et al., 1980).

Our research design was developed and tested by Professor John P. Robinson in 1978 while working with researchers at the BBC. Robinson used nationally representative cross sections of British adults to find out how a number of stories broadcast over the period of a week were comprehended by the audience. A similar technique was used by us to study the comprehension of network television news in the United States. On three consecutive nights (one night for each network) in June 1979, interviews were conducted with randomly selected news viewers in nine cities, immediately after the newscasts; 425 interviews were completed.

The heart of the questionnaire consisted of questions about the news stories in that night's newscast. Each respondent was first asked to name the stories that he or she recalled from the newscast. Then, the respondent's recall of stories was prompted by means of descriptive labels referring to each item in the broadcast without giving away its content, such as "Nicaragua," "Airline Passengers," and, in the case of the story under examination in this case study, "German Leader." Respondents were asked if they remembered anything about each story; if they did, they were probed ("What else do you remember?") until they said they remembered nothing more. Their responses were written down verbatim by the interviewers. It is these open-ended responses that constitute the body of audience data used in this analysis.

The central point of every news story, as defined for us by news editors, was used to assess comprehension (see Sahin et al., 1981). Each central point served as a kind of midpoint on a scale. Each respondent's recalled information was rated by us on the basis of the presence or absence of the "central point" and additional details. In this case study, we also looked at the recalled information from qualitative viewpoints and examined those elements of the transmitted message that were not recalled, or that were recalled partially or erroneously by being confused with other elements in the newscast or filled in arbitrarily by a viewer. By presenting examples of various types of recalled information below, we hope to preserve some of the color and richness of the data obtained in natural settings.

ONE INTERNATIONAL NEWS STORY

The news story examined concerned West German Chancellor Helmut Schmidt's meeting with President Jimmy Carter at the White House. The full script and accompanying video ran as follows:

Video	Audio
Frank Reynolds at the ABC news desk in Washington.	The President also met today with West Germany's Chancellor Helmut Schmidt with whom he has also had some disagreement. Here is a report from White House correspondent Sam Donaldson.
Inset photo of Carter and Schmidt	
Film of Carter and Schmidt walking and smiling (LS)	DONALDSON: (Voice Over) Ever since Chancellor Schmidt publicly backed Gerald Ford in the 1976 election, he and Jimmy Carter have had their differences. But today at the White House the two seemed to get along quite well. With Schmidt in this country on a private visit, mainly to deliver the commencement address at Harvard, they held an almost two-hour meeting. Afterwards the Chancellor said he'll be speaking out frequently now about the good relations between the two countries.
Film of Schmidt talking to microphones (MS)	SCHMIDT: We are in agreement with the United States on the basic lines of our energy policies and...in particular, and our economic policies in general. Thank you very much Jimmy for your hospitality and for the frankness and friendliness of our talks.

Video	Audio
Donaldson on camera; stand-upper	DONALDSON: The display of support by Chancellor Schmidt is welcome here on the eve of the Soviet-American summit, and suggests a partnership of sorts for the upcoming economic summit to be held in Tokyo later this month. For instance, on the important topic of energy, the French complained here this week that the US is subsidizing the purchase of spot oil at Europe's expense. Did that come up today? "Oh, no," said the spokesman. "Their energy discussion was much more serious than that." Sam Donaldson, ABC News, the White House.

In the study, this story was identified by the descriptive label "German Leader." We were told by the ABC news editors that the central point of the story—the element that made it newsworthy and should be grasped by the audience—was the simple fact that Schmidt had "met with Carter." (See Table 13.1.)

This particular story was selected for the case study for a variety of reasons: it appeared to be a fairly typical network story; it was of average length, lasting 100 seconds; as an international affairs story, it contained both foreign and domestic elements; it came in the middle of the newscast beginning at 10 minutes 20 seconds into the newscast and ending at the 12-minute point. Furthermore, it was not one of the continuing stories often appearing in the news. The German leader story was a discrete item, in the news for just one day, and given little or no coverage by other media, thereby minimizing the risk of information contamination from other media sources. The story had neither emotional nor sensational attributes, and it was presented by means of both visual content and verbal narration.

The German leader story followed a brief item on President Carter's meeting with congressional leaders to discuss energy problems. ABC news editors told us that the "Energy" story was not an important piece in itself and was included in the newscast essentially as a transitional device from a story on Nicaragua to the German leader story. No visual material accompanied the Energy story other than an inset picture of oil wells to symbolize story content. These factors may accont for why it was one of the most poorly comprehended and recalled stories in the newscast. (See Table 13.2.)

Table 13.1
The Order, Labels, Central Points and Duration of Stories
in the ABC Newscast, June 6, 1979

Order in the Newscast	Story Label Bullet	Main Point	Air Time	Cumulative Time
1	DC 10 Decision	"were grounded"	:20	:40
2	DC 10 Problems	"cracks"	1:45	2:25
3	FAA	"was not remiss"	1:15	3:40
4	Airline Passengers	"confused, stranded"	1:50	5:30
5	Overseas Flights	"confusion"	1:25	6:55
	STOCKS & COMMERCIAL #1		1:10	8:05
6	Nicaragua	"state of siege"	1:50	9:55
7	Energy	"cooperation with Congress"	:25	10:20
8	German Leader	"met with Carter"	1:40	12:00
9	KKK	"arrested man not connected"	:20	12:20
10	West Point	"last all male graduation"	:20	12:40
	COMMERCIALS #2 & 3		2:00	14:50
	Transition		:25	15:15
11	Pope's Day	"getting weary"	1:45	17:20
12	Jews in Poland	"not too many left"	2:00	19:20
	COMMERCIALS #4 & 5 & Transition		2:10	21:30
13	Salt	"Baker says serious loose ends"	:30	22:00
14	Barbara Walters	"miscl."	2:40	24:40
15	Opera	"incredible sight in N. Korea"	2:20	27:00
	COMMERCIAL #6		1:00	28:00
16	Actor	"J. Haley died"	:25	28:25

Table 13.2
Comprehension Levels of the News Stories, ABC News, June 6, 1979

Order in the Newscast	Story Label Bullet	Heard the Story %	Recalls Something %	Central Point + %
1	DC 10 Decision	96.7	93.4	89.4
2	DC 10 Problems	90.1	81.6	44.1
3	FAA	73.0	62.5	9.2
4	Airline Passengers	76.3	68.4	51.7
5	Overseas Flights	63.1	46.0	9.2
	STOCKS & COMMERCIAL #1	– –	– –	– –
6	Nicaragua	50.6	48.0	26.3
7	Energy	36.2	17.1	7.9
8	German Leader	55.3	50.7	36.2
9	KKK	50.0	42.8	17.8
10	West Point	58.9	57.6	43.7
	COMMERCIALS #2 & 3 Transition	– –	– –	– –
		– –	– –	– –
11	Pope's Day	78.3	66.5	44.1
12	Jews in Poland	63.6	58.3	53.0
	COMMERCIALS #4 & 5 & Transition	– –	– –	– –
13	Salt	35.8	16.7	3.3
14	Barbara Walters	42.4	29.1	13.2
15	Opera	40.8	40.1	17.1
	COMMERCIAL #6	– –	– –	– –
16	Actor	60.0	57.9	45.4

The Energy story concluded by pointing out that Congress had killed many of Carter's previous proposals. This was followed by the introduction of the international story: "The President *also* met today with West Germany's Chancellor Helmut Schmidt with whom he has *also* had some disagreement" (our emphasis). Thus, the story was linked to the previous story on three points: it was (also) a conflict story concerning Carter's disagreements; it was (also) the story of a meeting involving the President (an event in the daily routine of the chief executive that is a regular feature of nightly newscasts); and finally, it was (also) an energy story. This introduction prepared the mental set in which the story was to be understood, and was, in fact, understood by many viewers, as we shall see shortly.

The core of the story—Carter meeting with Schmidt—was presented in accordance with the conventions of what might be termed the "visiting dignitary" genre. Examples of this genre are found in network newscasts regularly. It is quite formalized in terms of the sequence of shots and verbal descriptions, although its length varies, depending on the perceived significance of the meeting and other considerations. The dignitaries are typically shown walking side by side on the White House lawn, shaking hands and smiling to each other, moving up to the microphones to make a brief statement in diplomatic jargon, about their talks and using standard terms such as "friendly," "frank," and "productive."

This particular story was introduced by the anchor, Frank Reynolds, from the ABC news desk in Washington, D.C. Behind him were inset photos of Schmidt and Carter, side by side but not looking at each other. Then White House correspondent Sam Donaldson's backgrounder began in the symbolic setting of all White House reports with the portico of the presidential residence at the background. With Donaldson relegated to voice over, we then saw Carter and Schmidt walking side by side, smiling and talking to each other—obviously for the press and cameras. The picture was then cut to Schmidt's brief speech, with many microphones in front of him, thanking "Jimmy" for his hospitality and friendliness. The story was concluded with Donaldson's stand-upper, again with the familiar symbols of the White House at the background, and was followed by a switch to the Chicago anchor desk.

This segmentized step-by-step format (the anchor, then the correspondent on location, then scenes from the "event," the correspondent again, and finally back to the anchor desk), though quite predictable, permits a great deal of mobility and flexibility in presenting on-location stories. It allows for smooth spatial and temporal transitions, breaks the monotony of the presentation and quickens the pace of the newscast, and routinizes the coverage of complex events. By presenting documentary evidence from the scene, while at the same time allowing room for background information and interpretation, it helps construct a tightly woven net of "facticity" (Tuchman, 1978). By breaking information into smaller units, it also helps the packaging of information. It also provides, as all genres do, the viewer with cues as to what is happening and is likely to happen. For the initiated television news viewer, a glimpse at the screen suffices to signal that another important guest has paid a call to the President.

The information contained in the news story can be cataloged either by listing informational assertions one by one or by arranging them in terms of content structure. Because all pieces of information do not carry equal weight in the story, the second approach is more appropriate. Findahl and Hoijer (1981) point out that the concept of "content structure" is somewhat different from the more widely employed concept of "narrative structure." In the case of the narrative structure, the focus is on the rules of storytelling. Content structure, on the other hand, pertains to the way informational elements within the news story are related to one another in terms of causality, temporal sequence, association, contiguity, etc. This approach enables us to break the story down to its informational constituent elements while at the same time, more holistically, enabling us to see the relationship of the constituent elements, that is, its structure.

The German leader story has a rather simple, chronological structure:

1. The antecedents of the event that is featured in the story—that Carter and Schmidt have had disagreements, that Schmidt is in the United States on a private visit, and that the French have complained about US oil policies.
2. The core of the story incorporating the four W's (Who, What, Where, When) or what we might call "the event,"—that Schmidt and Carter met at the White House today.
3. The consequences of the event—how this meeting might affect future developments such as the two upcoming summits. (See Diagram I.)

Diagram I
The Content Structure of the German Leader Story

Antecedents	The Event	Consequences
Carter and Schmidt did not like each other because Schmidt supported Ford.	Who -Schmidt & Carter What -met, discussed energy & economic policies.	Carter & Schmidt like each other better. Relations will improve.
Schmidt in the United States on a private visit	When -today for 2 hrs.	
	Where-in Washington at the White House	US-USSR Summit
French complained about US oil policies	How -frank, friendly serious	Tokyo Summit

Not all television news stories follow such a neat structure. Few provide as much historical context of the event as did this story. The same story was covered by NBC and was comprised of the core elements only, noting simply that the meeting had taken place. CBS chose not to cover the story at all.

As Diagram I indicates, most informational elements in the story fit the structure quite well. There is one exception: the point made by Sam Donaldson in his stand-upper about the French complaint concerning

American oil policies. This antecedental element appears out of context and incongruent, having ramifications for its comprehensibility.

COMPREHENSION OF THE STORY

Table 13.3 makes clear that the story of Schmidt's meeting with Carter was not an unqualified success in terms of audience comprehension and memory. A full 45 percent of the respondents said they did not remember the story, even when prompted with the title "German leader." Only 55 percent said that they did remember seeing a story about a German leader, and some of those (4 percent of the total sample) could not recall any particular elements of the story. Thus, barely half of the sampled viewers (51 percent) remembered something specific about the 1 minute 40 second story to which they had been exposed in the newscast only an hour or so earlier that evening.

A portion of those who did recall something about the story neglected to mention the main point of the story, namely, that the German leader and Carter had conferred. That is, nearly 3 out of every 10 respondents who remembered something about the story missed the central point (or at least did not answer the interviewer probes by citing the basic core element of the story). These respondents represented 15 percent of the total sample.

Over one third of the total sampled audience (36 percent) did recall the central point of the story. This figure is slightly higher than the average recall of central points for the 16 stories aired on ABC that evening (the average was 32 percent; cf. Table 13.2). Among these who correctly recalled the story's main point, 30 percent offered no additional recollections, while 43, 18, and 9 percent could remember one, two, or three additional elements, respectively. Another way to summarize this point is to note that a mere 10 percent of the total sample remembered the central point of the story along with at least two additional elements of information.

The first striking observation about the comprehension and recall of this story is the range of variation in the amount of information recalled, all the way from very sketchy and hazy bits of de-contextualized information to remarkably detailed comprehensive accounts. For instance, one respondent said he had seen Schmidt "talking on TV," while the only thing another could remember was that he was "delivering the address of graduating class at Yale (sic) University." At the other end of the spectrum, one respondent said: "The West German leader backed President Ford, so never saw eye to eye to Carter. Was here for commencement speech at Harvard. Carter and he discussed energy policy."

Another respondent said: "Schmidt is here meeting with Carter. He and Carter didn't get along too well for quite a while because Schmidt

Table 13.3
Memory of the German Leader Story
(n = 152)

45%	Did not remember the story	
55%	Did remember the story	
	4%	Remembered the subject, but recalled no story elements
	51%	Remembered specific elements of the story
		15% Recalled story element(s) but not "central point"
		36% Recalled the central point of the story
		11% Recalled only the central point
		15% Recalled the central point plus one additional element
		7% Recalled the central point plus two additional elements
		3% Recalled the central point plus three or more additional elements
(100%)		

backed Ford in the presidential campaign. Schmidt is here to give a commencement address at Harvard."

As far as the content structure, it appears that much of the recalled information pertained to the event, rather than its antecedents or consequences. The respondents' recollection of the story was heavily dominated by the four W's of the event, with considerably less emphasis on the "Why" and the "How." It could be argued that this is because the recollection of the event is the basis upon which all the other elements are built. Without it, none of the other elements has any meaning. It could also be argued that this part is more memorable because of the accompanying documentary evidence. Another reason could be that American television news viewers are conditioned by the reporting conventions of American journalism and therefore tend to tune in to the lead information at the expense of other elements.

Two major antecedental elements (Carter and Schmidt were not on friendly terms, Schmidt is on a private visit) were mentioned by almost one third of those who did remember something from the story. The other antecedent element about the French complaint, on the other hand, did not register at all: not a single one of the 152 respondents mentioned it directly or indirectly. It is quite obvious that this piece of antecedent information presented toward the end of the story was out of place and superfluous: the reference to the French complaint assumed too much prior knowledge, and was inserted into a segment of the story that already contained too much information including two rather confusing references to upcoming summits (US-USSR in Vienna and the major industrial nations in Tokyo). It obviously added little to the story from the audience's point of view. Furthermore, the correspondent noted that it was not found "serious" enough for discussion by the two leaders. It could have been deleted from the story without any loss to the audience.

Consequences of the Carter-Schmidt meeting were recalled even less than the antecedent elements. Only 10 percent of those who provided information from the story mentioned the future ramifications of the event (cooperation on the eve of the two summits, better relations). Information about the two summits was presented in rapid fire fashion, presupposing substantial amounts of prior knowledge. The consequence that did gain attention was that Carter and Schmidt were going to be friends. This is a clear-cut example of the personalization of historical events and is related to the news angle in which the story was presented.

STORY ANGLE AND VISUAL INFORMATION

ABC's story about the Schmidt-Carter meeting was presented from the conflict/cooperation angle. Schmidt's unofficial visit to the White House was interpreted as an act of burying the hatchet—the transformation of an old antipathy into a blossoming friendship. This added elements of human interest to what was otherwise a routine diplomatic event. The two heads of state were made into two persons resolving a personal quarrel. While the central point of the story was that the two met, the theme of the story was the blossoming of the friendship. This was not obvious from the event itself, but resulted from the angle imposed by the ABC journalists. NBC, in covering the same occurrence, made no mention of the previous disagreements between the two heads of state. For them, it was primarily a ceremonial occasion.

ABC's angle was adopted by many ABC viewers in their account of what had taken place. It was perceived as a personal story of two individuals making up and becoming friends:

> Him and Carter are getting along pretty good. I forgot what they were doing or saying.
> He's here—kind of kissed and made up with Carter.
> Schmidt never got along with Carter. But it shows when Schmidt visited here in Washington, they get along. It showed that they had nice talks and that they're going to try to get along.

Such personalized treatment of international stories is not rare. This adds a "human" touch to stories, making them more interesting as well as more manageable. Conflicts and contradictions between nations are thus transformed into stories of personal conflicts. Such latent informational elements constitute the meta-discourse of the news story as an "absent narrative" implying a particular understanding of history and diplomacy. Personal likes and dislikes of the leaders as individuals are presented as an implicit motor of history. This approach may also explain the inclusion of the element about the French complaint regarding US oil policies at the expense of Europe. Schmidt and Giscard are both Europeans. They have, in the past, been very close friends. Now Schmidt is becoming friends with Carter. Can Schmidt and Giscard still remain friends? (Tune in tomorrow at the same time.)

In most genre stories with their conventions and rules of inclusive and exclusive elements, pictures may not add much to the verbal information. The pictures are often stock shots, predetermined down to the camera angles (Tuchman, 1979; Glasgow University Media Group, 1980). Yet, they serve other important functions. They provide documentary proof that what is said to have happened did in fact happen. They are often used to support and supplement what is being said in the sound track, although there are occasions when the two are not congruent. In the case of the German Leader story, the pictures were supportive of the theme that the two leaders were becoming friends. References to the visual content by the respondents were few and often pertained to the element of friendship. A few examples:

> Pictured him with Carter.
>
> Was talking.
>
> Schmidt was talking to the President. They were saying goodbye to each other.
>
> They posed for a lot of pictures.

ERRORS IN COMPREHENSION

Some responses suffered from errors and distortions that deviated from the factual information in the ABC text. Almost 25 percent of the responses contained one or more such errors. Some were quite insignificant such as Yale instead of Harvard, or whether the commencement address had been delivered or was going to be delivered. In one instance, Willie Brandt was cited as the German leader. These are results of confusing bits of factual information. Another type of error is what we (Robinson et al., 1980) have called meltdowns, which combine elements of different stories into the same account. We have pointed out that such meltdowns tend to occur more frequently when two or more similar stories are lumped together. Other types of errors indicate that the story has been misunderstood:

> He was friendly with Carter and Ford.
>
> He had some remarks about the oil shortage. OPEC and oil companies are creating a false crisis.
>
> He told President Carter to stop wasting all the oil because it is going to affect Europe. They'll see what is happening and they will do the same thing.

CONCLUSION

Our close examination of the German Leader story using an information transmission approach confirms that what people understand and recall from television news cannot be easily predicted from the knowledge of story content. From the point of view of a television journalist, comprehension levels may appear to be disappointingly low because many significant story elements are not recalled or well understood. Also, comprehension levels vary greatly from one individual to another. Only one third of the viewers knew the central point of the German Leader story, while almost half of the respondents remembered nothing at all from the story. The types of information recalled by viewers were also remarkably diverse. Sometimes, recalls were distorted or factually erroneous.

On the whole, however, our television news comprehension studies indicate that international affairs news does not necessarily constitute an inherently disadvantaged category in terms of audience interest and comprehension (Sahin & Robinson, 1980). For instance, on the day the German Leader story was broadcast, items dealing with foreign and international affairs (Nicaragua, Pope's visit to Poland, Jews in Poland) were comprehended just as well as the domestic items. (See Table 13.2.) This may be due to television's linear mode of presentation, which does not allow much selectivity to the viewer. The attentive viewer must monitor all aspects of the flow—even when it deals with foreign names and distant lands.

REFERENCES

Findahl, O. and B. Hoijer. 1981. Studying Media Content with Reference to Human Comprehension. In K. E. Rosengren, ed., *Scandinavian Studies in Content Analysis.* London: Sage.

Fisher, B. A. 1978. *Perspectives on Human Communication.* New York: Macmillan.

Gans, Herbert J. 1979. *Deciding What's News.* New York: Pantheon.

Glasgow University Media Group. 1980. *Bad News.* Vol. 2. London: Routledge and Kegan Paul.

Robinson, John P.; Dennis K. Davis; Haluk Sahin; and Thomas O'Toole. 1980. Comprehension of Television News: How Alert is the Audience? Paper presented at the Association for Education in Journalism conference; Boston, Mass.; August 1980.

Roper, Burns W. 1979. *Public Perceptions of Television and Other Mass Media.* New York: Television Information Office.

Sahin, Haluk; Dennis K. Davis; and John P. Robinson. 1981. Improving the TV News. *Irish Broadcasting Review* (Summer): 50–55.

Sahin, Haluk and John P. Robinson. 1980. Is There Light at the End of the Flow? Audience Comprehension of International News Stories? Paper presented at the World Communications Conference; Philadelphia, Pa.; 1980.

Tuchman, Gaye. 1978. *Making News.* New York: Free Press.

SUBJECT INDEX

AUTHOR INDEX

Page numbers in *italics* indicate where complete references are listed, and 'n' indicates footnote.

Americans have come to see the world through the video eye of network television news, and the networks have come to devote a large share of their coverage to international affairs. That coverage has been under increasing fire from Third World leaders and from various domestic groups; it has also been under increasing scrutiny from political communication researchers who want a better understanding of the versions of world news offered by the networks to their massive constituencies.

This volume brings together thirteen provocative and wide-ranging studies of television coverage of such topics as terrorism, the Third World, Vietnam, Latin America, and Presidential summits. The studies reach some surprising conclusions about TV's orientation toward certain subjects and regions of the world. The contributors have brought a wide range of experience, perspectives, and methods to the study of television news and international affairs. Scholars of international affairs and political communications should find this book to be a new and valuable source of information.